We Will Win the Day

The Civil Rights Movement, the Black Athlete, and the Quest for Equality

Louis Moore

PRAEGER™

An Imprint of ABC-CLIO, LLC

Santa Barbara, California • Denver, Colorado

Library of Congress Cataloging-in-Publication Data

Names: Moore, Louis, 1978– author.
Title: We will win the day : the Civil Rights Movement, the Black athlete, and the quest for equality / Louis Moore.
Description: Santa Barbara, California : Praeger, 2017. | Includes bibliographical references and index.
Identifiers: LCCN 2017019469 (print) | LCCN 2017023062 (ebook) | ISBN 9781440839535 (ebook) | ISBN 9781440839528 (print)
Subjects: LCSH: Racism in sports—United States—History—20th century. | Discrimination in sports—United States—History—20th century. | African American athletes—History—20th century. | African American athletes—Biography. | Civil rights movements—United States—History—20th century.
Classification: LCC GV706.32 (ebook) | LCC GV706.32 .M66 2017 (print) | DDC 306.4/83—dc23
LC record available at https://lccn.loc.gov/2017019469

ISBN: 978-1-4408-3952-8 (print)
      978-1-4408-3953-5 (ebook)

21 20 19 18 17   1 2 3 4 5

This book is also available as an eBook.

Praeger
An Imprint of ABC-CLIO, LLC

ABC-CLIO, LLC
130 Cremona Drive, P.O. Box 1911
Santa Barbara, California 93116-1911
www.abc-clio.com

This book is printed on acid-free paper (∞)

Manufactured in the United States of America

Contents

Acknowledgments

This book was a pleasure to research and write. I would like to thank Steven Riess for recommending me to Praeger for this project. Thanks for believing in my work. A special thanks goes to the Twitter world, who put up with my tweets about sports and civil rights and gave me the confidence to write this book. I also appreciate all the scholars, including Adrian Burgos, Derrick White, Matthew Klugman, and Michael Ezra, who encouraged me throughout this process. Eric Paul has been a rock since grad school. My father-in-law, Willie Jones, has treated me like a son since day one. To my friends since grade school, Mark, Todd, Larry, and Damion, thanks for always being there. A special thanks to my brother, Lance, who taught me to love sports, and my sisters, Zenobia and Zoey, who brag about me to their friends. My mom, Mary, gave us everything when we had nothing. Most important, my wife, Ciciley, made this all possible with her endless support and love. And finally to Amaya, Grant, and Isla—you are the greatest gifts and kids in the world. Thanks for your patience while Daddy got his work done. I love you.

Introduction

James "Mudcat" Grant would not sing the right words. He knew they were a lie. Home of the Brave. Land of the Free. For who? Not black Americans. Not in 1960. Grant remembered vividly growing up in poverty in Lacooche, Florida, in a shack that had no hot water, electric lights, or an indoor toilet, while his widowed mother supported her family on her menial wages working as a domestic in white people's home and then trying to supplement her meager wages at the local citrus plant. He remembered the white kids who would bully the black kids and call them racist names, the white cop who pointed a gun at him while his partner kicked him in the rear, and the unequal school system where black kids received old school supplies deemed unfit for white kids, where he studied in a school that was really a house with blankets dividing the classrooms. There were the segregated spring training games in Florida, his Cleveland Indians teammates who yelled racist remarks at black fans, and his pitching coach, Ted Wilks, who in 1947 as a member of the St. Louis Cardinals tried to organize a boycott to avoid playing Jackie Robinson and the Brooklyn Dodgers, and as a pitcher regularly threw at the heads of black batters.

And that was just Grant's individual reality. He knew his people were starving, were segregated, and had to live under the daily indignities of Jim Crow. And he knew they were fighting for their equality. He would not sing the words of the national anthem that day. He was fed up. When he got to the end of the song, he changed the lyrics to reflect his reality, what black Americans had to live with. He added, "This Land Ain't so Free. I Can't Even go to Mississippi." That remix set his freedom-loving racist pitching coach off. The Texan, Wilks, told Grant, "If you don't like it here, why don't you get [out of here] Nigger." To which Grant replied, "Texas was no better than Russia." With that, Wilks threatened his pitcher and told the black man that "he'd better not catch his black ass in Texas." Grant, a fiercely proud black man, refused to deal with these insults, so he packed his bags and left the stadium. For leaving, the Indians suspended him for two weeks, the rest of the season. The racist pitching coach, Wilks? Nothing happened to him. Wilks represented another hypocritical white man, just like the white players who sang the national anthem, or as one black player put it, "when they sing about the land of the free all of 'em gotta have their tongues in their cheeks when they do it."[1]

While the incident barely made a ripple in the white daily press, black writers were all over the ordeal. They were waiting for another black athlete like a Jackie Robinson, Elgin Baylor, or a Bill Russell, who publicly fought back against American racism, who battled against the narrative that black athletes should just shut up and play. It was time for the black athlete to give back to the movement. Black writers praised Grant for his stance and suggested he was a "member of the new school of Americans," who "refuses to bend his principles for a price," and many denounced his teammate, pitcher Don Newcombe—a favorite among the black community since he broke in with the Dodgers in 1948—who witnessed the incident but did not challenge his racist coach. Newcombe represented the "old" black athlete who whites expected to keep quiet and remain in their place. As L. I. Brockenbury of the *Los Angeles Sentinel* put it, "Don, like Roy Campanella, and unlike Jackie Robinson, feels that a Negro should feel so honored to be with a white team that he should take just about anything."[2] The new black athlete had arrived. Or as the black writer Bob Hunter put it, "This is 1960 and the entire picture has changed."[3] Grant's protest occurred a month after black Olympian decathlete Rafer Johnson carried the American flag at the opening ceremonies of the 1960 Olympics, in the midst of the sit-in movements as black students from across the country risked their lives and reputations in order to fight for a better day, and during a time when a group of City Council women from England had arranged an airlift of baby food in order to feed starving black children in New Orleans whom the state had purged from state welfare programs. Connecting the starving children with Grant's protest, the black revolutionary activist James Boggs applauded Grant's stance, noting: "The rhyme was not so good but the sentiment was undisputable." As Boggs argued, "In a country the size of the United States incidents like these may be shrugged off as minor. Certainly, the politicians who are making the spectacular speeches wish they would go away. But they are not minor and they will not go away. All the talk about American greatness and all the talk at the UN about American readiness to help underdeveloped nations are only encouraging Negroes to fight to make this country truly the land of the free and the home of the brave."[4] In one defiant moment, James "Mudcat" Grant, the star pitcher raised in Jim Crow poverty, articulated the plight black Americans faced in sports and society.

Although Grant's defiance was just one incident, and Grant apologized profusely for leaving the stadium, Grant's protest and the support he received from the black press encapsulated the relationship between the black athlete and the black community during the civil rights movement. The moment and support indicate that during the civil rights movement, African American activists and athletes fought together to break down the barriers of Jim Crow in sports and society. Though sports might seem trivial during a time when black protesters were being arrested, beaten, and even killed for fighting for equal rights, as black sportswriter Claude Harrison Jr. of the *Philadelphia Tribune* acknowledged in 1964 when discussing the lack of black quarterbacks in professional football, "While this is no secret and no burning issue with the Negro fans, now, that there are more important issues such as the Freedom fight, riots and the drive to defeat Barry Goldwater, it does bother me."[5] For the black community, sports represented tangible proof that democracy would triumph over discrimination, and equally as important, sports offered proof that whites would accept black people. Jim Hall, of the *Louisiana Weekly*, reflected this very sentiment, when a week after Congress passed the Voting Rights Act of 1965, he celebrated, "For years, all Negroes in America, were placed in the same boat, by our brothers on the other side of the fence. However, standouts like Marian Anderson, Thurgood Marshall, Jackie Robinson, Jesse Owens, Joe Louis, Bill Russell, Sammy Davis, Althea Gibson, Willie Mays, and countless others have changed the picture." "To us," he added, "it will be the better informed and fair-minded citizens here and there, that will continue to aid in the changing of the Negro image."[6] Hall believed that the success of black athletes helped defeat negative stereotypes of black people and thus proved blacks were individuals worthy of equal rights.

The black community, in other words, heaped a lot of attention on the successful black barrier breakers, because blacks believed that whites who found a way to celebrate a black athlete like Willie Mays would eventually see the good in all black Americans. Hence, the black investment in black athletic success, or what some scholars call "muscular assimilation," relied on the hope that well-meaning whites would eventually come around, truly uphold the ideas of the Constitution and democracy, and accept black Americans as full and equal citizens.

Grounded in the hope that success in sports would help defeat Jim Crow, for most black Americans, sports became the main measuring stick to calculate American progress. At their most basic foundation, sports represented a platform for fairness and equality; the best athlete or team won, and color did not determine triumph. Thus, after each athletic breakthrough, or major victory, the black press rejoiced and then continued its fight for more athletic opportunities. "No longer isolated from the great family of nations around us," an *Ebony* editor noted in 1948, "the America which pioneered in democracy has a great obligation to the rest of the earth to keep alive the ideals emblazoned on the Freedom Train documents. Those who stand in the way of making these principles a reality in the sports arena are sabotaging the bold leadership which the U.S. is attempting to furnish to the world."[7] In other words, blacks used the rhetoric of democracy and equality to hold America to the flames of freedom. But the black press did not stand alone in its adulation. Well-meaning whites also used the inclusion of the black athlete to extol equality.

After World War II, progressive white Americans supported the integration of the black athlete, because after a war fought to defeat racism, for them, athletics proved that democracy existed. The Four Freedoms they fought for in the war—from want and fear, and for religion and speech—were meaningless if the most talented in society could not get a fair chance simply because they happened to have black skin. In other words, America was morally bankrupt and hypocritical, if whites stood by and allowed segregation to continue in sports. To be sure, sports, for supposed well-meaning whites, represented the easiest institution to integrate. The integration of the black athlete allowed many whites to perform a moral evasion of American racism. As long as a few black athletes received their opportunity, whites did not have to deal with the reality of structural racism or government intervention to combat racism. On this note, white writer Gordon Cobbledick, of the *Cleveland Plain Dealer*, writing about the selection of running back Levi Jackson as Yale's football captain, concluded, "The fact that the story was considered so important suggests that we still have a long way to go toward the goal of judging men by what they are and what they can do rather than by the color of the skin," but noted, "The fact that it could happen at all is proof that progress has been made." Cobbledick concluded that Jackson's white teammates selected him not because he was a Negro but because "he displayed qualities of leadership, sportsmanship and ability transcending those to be found in any available white contemporary." Cobbledick further opined that while politicians fought over legislation like the Fair Employment

Practice Committee, sports leaders helped solve the "race problem by demonstrating that it is possible for whites and Negroes to work together in complete harmony."[8] Blacks in Cleveland, however, remained segregated and unequal in housing, education, and employment.

Despite a desire to celebrate black athletes, sports also reinforced painful reminders about racism black Americans knew from everyday living. As great as Willie Mays was, whites in San Francisco still refused to sell him a home when the Giants moved there from New York, and no matter how many awards Mays won, whites in Birmingham still bombed black homes and churches of civil rights leaders trying to integrate his hometown. Everywhere the black athlete lived, despite the success on the playing field, whites refused to see black athletes as equal. After centerfielder Larry Doby, the first black player in the American League, helped the Cleveland Indians win the 1948 World Series, whites in Paterson, New Jersey, would not sell him a home, and white neighbors in St. Louis killed St. Louis Hawks guard Lenny Wilkins's dog, New York neighbors ran heavyweight champion Floyd Patterson out of his neighborhood, and Boston fans defecated in Bill Russell's bed.

And while black Americans celebrated sports as proof of democracy, it took 12 years between the signing of Jackie Robinson for the Brooklyn Dodgers (1947) and the signing of infielder Pumpsie Green for the Boston Red Sox (1959) before major league baseball completely integrated. And even then, spring training in the South remained segregated until Southern cities enacted civil rights laws, or teams, refusing to wait any longer for desegregation, integrated their own hotels. The Detroit Tigers, for example, did not integrate their spring training in Florida until the 1963 season. When the governor of Michigan, John Swainson, heard the news, he congratulated, "This action of the Tiger management is most welcome as an important step in making the American past time truly American." Detroit Tiger centerfielder Bill Bruton, one of the leading spokespersons for black baseball players, replied, "This, of course, is what we've been seeking ever since we came into organized ball. There was absolutely no justification for a situation of that type to exist."[9] As Bruton's statement attested to, black baseball players had been fighting for full integration since Jackie Robinson played his first spring training game in 1946, but white owners and Southern lawmakers refused to treat them as full citizens.

Although sports struggled to always display democracy, the good eventually outweighed the bad. Even Martin Luther King Jr., after the momentous 1963 March on Washington, stated, "I wish that I had a lot more time for sports. You people in sports have done a great job in giving the

Negro equal rights, and you have achieved that without bloodshed. . . . I hope you sportswriters will remember us and help our cause."[10] Of course, King uttered those words to a white sportswriter. He would never have to say that to a black sportswriter. Whether it was Maggie Hathaway, Doc Young, Jim Hall, L. I. Brockenbury, Rick Hurt, Bill Matney, Lloyd C. Wells, Sam Lacy, or a number of others across the nation, black sports-writers knew that their fight for fairness in sports helped push for democracy outside of sports. The black sportswriter made integration possible, and it was black sportswriters who challenged black athletes to get involved in the movement.

With a push from the black press, throughout the 1960s, more black athletes found ways to become activists. In 1967, for example, several stalwart athletes joined the National Association for the Advancement of Colored People (NAACP) and formed the National Sports Committee under the wing of the Legal Defense Fund (LDF). Although the LDF represented more than 400 cases at the time, it was not clear what role the athletes would play. It appears, however, in an era when the NAACP was becoming increasing obsolete and unpopular among black youth, when compared to civil rights groups like the Black Panther Party, Student Nonviolent Coordinating Committee, and Congress of Racial Equality, the athletes gave the old civil rights group a positive punch of popularity to compete with other organizations. The group included current and former stars like Bill Russell, St. Louis cardinal Bill White, Chicago Bear Gale Sayers, ex-NFL (National Football League) great Buddy Young, ex-New York Giant baseball star Monte Irvin, and current star for the Pittsburgh Pirates, speedster Maury Wells. The days of the isolated athlete contributing to the civil rights organization were gone. Now they formed a powerful block of professionals searching for a way to make a difference. Gale Sayers, the star running back of the Chicago Bears, explained his involvement, noting, "This is a fine opportunity. You see, the Negro athlete who may feel strongly about civil rights is in a pretty tough situation. If he goes out and demonstrates and gets arrested and put in jail, it hurts the sport and the league." Instead of protesting, Sayers wanted to lift as he climbed, stating, "I've gained my success. Now, through this committee, I hope to bring some others up the ladder with me." Sayers saw his commitment with the NAACP as an opportunity to get involved, but without getting "dirty," so to speak. He had already been arrested in 1964, while at Kansas trying to integrate a campus restaurant, and the likable halfback wanted no part of the instigator angry-black-man tag that came with continuous participation in the movement. As he admitted, "Maybe Stokely Carmichael won't like our methods, but we hope to achieve something with this committee." On his involvement, Buddy Young, the Hall of Fame halfback, noted that black athletes had a special role to play because they were natural leaders and added, "Those days when the gifted Negro athlete was looked on as an athlete, nothing more, are gone. It's no longer a tavern or coaching when he retires. They are going to a host of careers—stock brokers, teachers, dentists, lawyers, professional men."[11] But Young, who had a job in the NFL offices as an assistant to Commissioner Pete Rozelle, might have had his blinders on. Most athletes did not get an opportunity when their playing days were done.

After their careers, most black athletes were relegated back to the ghetto or rural area they came from. That had always been the case, but now, the black athlete had been radicalized by the civil rights movement and demanded a change. In 1966, black professional football players, John Henry Johnson and John Nisby of the Steelers and Redskins, respectively, tried to organize black football players to fight against the off-the-field discrimination in endorsement deals and after retirement where black men received no opportunities in football once their bodies were broken. Black baseball players harbored the same complaints. As Larry Doby once said, "It's like being thrown on the scrap heap, just at a time when you feel you can make a real contribution. The Negro's participation in baseball is only in terms of production, what he can do on the field. But what can he do on the sidelines, or in the dugout or in the front office, with his intelligence and experience?"[12] Sharing a similar sentiment about a lack of opportunities for black athletes, the retired pitcher Joe Black bemoaned, "[Whitney] Young says that every Negro is a revolutionary, but some are builders and others are burners. I am hoping that there will be a constructive revolution in Baseball. This is the sport that opened the door for the Negro athlete. Now it's time for baseball to take another giant step further."[13] The only thing that could change this status quo was a revolt of the system.

We Will Win the Day is a book that explores the relationship between black athletes and the black community in the fight for fairness in sports during the civil rights movement. At the book's core is the basic, yet loaded, term, "sports matter." As the black sportswriter Sam Lacy once said, "Sports has always been important in the black community. During the 1930s and 1940s (and since), talented black athletes helped spearhead the drive for equal opportunity through their successes as competitors." He continued, "Sports is a merit-focused competition through which individuals and teams seem to have, as a result of their highs and lows, an emotional impact on people that enhances respect and tempers certain prejudices."[14] To be clear, to examine this topic one most deal in, and deal with, a bit of hyperbole, because certainly nobody wants to argue that Jackie Robinson hitting a baseball is more important than Rosa Parks risking her life by refusing to budge on a bus in Montgomery, Alabama. But one must also understand that for the black community, Robinson's feats, and his public strength to withstand Jim Crow and racial vitriol, provided hope that one day ordinary citizens would not have to deal with the same atrocities. As Martin Luther King Jr. once said of Robinson, "He was a sit-inner before the sit-ins, a freedom rider before the freedom rides."[15] The breakthrough the black athletes made provided hope to a community that needed visual victories in their battle for equality.

For the sake of clarity, this book places the civil rights movement between 1945 and 1968. While seemingly arbitrary dates, and one can certainly argue for an approach for a long civil rights movement that precedes 1945 and extends beyond 1968, for the scope, organization, and clarity of this book, these are the most logical dates. The year 1945 marks the time when black veterans returned from World War II in mass fighting for their second half of their double victory—war at home and abroad against racism and fascism. It is no coincidence that right after the war Branch Rickey signed World War II veteran Jackie Robinson to play for his Brooklyn Dodgers. This book ends with 1968, because this is the year that a racist assassin murdered civil rights leader Martin Luther King Jr., and it also marks the year that black athlete activism, highlighted by the "revolt of the black athlete," made its most infamous mark in the civil rights movement, capped off by the famed Black Power salute of sprinters Tommie Smith and John Carlos at the 1968 Olympics. In between these years, in every sport, from baseball to bowling, black writers, activists, and athletes battled together to fulfill the promise of American democracy.

To provide the most authentic narrative, *We Will Win the Day* heavily relies on black newspapers. After all, the papers, and the sportswriters, represented the voices of the black community, the marginalized folks most vested in the civil rights movement. To provide the best detail as possible, I researched papers in every region of the country. Most black newspapers had a black sports editor whose job it was to provide local sporting information that the white dailies ignored, and also provide the pulse for the national scene. These writers could quickly switch from providing a take on a local "phenom" to urging the community to boycott a stadium or to providing an opinion on a major moment in black sporting history. While black writers openly rooted for "tan talent" and "Sepia sensations"—these were terms used by the black press to celebrate black athletic success—and could often be accused of hyperbole, they also never wavered and refused to mince words. Black writers would equally have harsh words for a racist sports owner as they would for a black athlete who did not live up to his or her supposed commitment to the black community. While this book also uses white dailies and magazines, they are used as a way to either capture white thought about a particular event or athlete or fill in the blank for missing biographic information. But black thought is always centered.

To be sure, this book does not just piece together editorial pieces from black sports pages. I am indebted to the tremendous scholarship that has already been produced about black athletes. By fusing a heavy dose of the black press with these publications, *We Will Win the Day* offers a unique synthesis of the black athlete and the black community during the civil rights movement.

CHAPTER ONE

Democracy in Action: Sports and the American Dream

At the close of World War II, Joe Louis, heavyweight champion of the world, a man born in the Jim Crow South, and raised in a Detroit ghetto, stood as the symbol of American democracy. During the war, Louis donated more than a million dollars to Uncle Sam's military, donned the khaki uniforms, and famously said, "We're going to win, because we're on God's side." His willingness to sacrifice his career and earnings and spout the rhetoric of freedom and democracy in a nation that legally sanctioned racism made Louis a symbol of racial hope for America. As one black writer claimed in 1942, "Joe Louis hasn't only proven to be the greatest fighting champion to ever don the abbreviated fight trunks, but he has done more to promote inter-racial good will than any other Negro individual in history."[1] Or as Margery Miller reflected in her 1946 book aptly titled *Joe Louis: American*, "Joe's accomplishments in causing good feeling between the white and Negro races are established facts."[2] How could one black man cause such feelings?

After the war, Americans looking to push a narrative of democracy and equality in a Jim Crow society looked to the black athlete to bring that story to fruition. On this belief, a black writer from New York opined, "The careers of Joe Louis and other great Negro athletes teach us that, given an equal opportunity to show their merit, there is no question whatever that the Negro people in all other areas of our national life will demonstrate their essential equality with all white men."[3] Similarly, in 1947, the year Jackie Robinson integrated baseball, black writer A. S.

"Doc" Young gleaned, "Sports are powerful factors for democracy and downright good in these United States. It may not be as intended or as it should be; but the righteous truth is that the doings of a Joe Louis or a Jackie Robinson have more gripping and moving effects on the thinking of the majority of the people than all of the long-studied and wise words of W. E. B. Du Bois, a Walter White or an A. Philip Randolph."[4] In short, because of the opportunities to succeed and publicity black athletes received in comparison to the rest of the black population, and the jubilation over their triumphs, most black Americans celebrated black athletes as their best hope to achieve and prove equality in a racist America.

Thus, as a civil rights strategy, blacks hoped that by persistently fighting for opportunities to participate in sports and proving themselves with their play, athletic acclaim would win the day and bring about equality in society. As black sports historian Edwin Bancroft Henderson noted during Robinson's rookie year, "Today our athletes are our racial emissaries. What Jackie Robinson does on the bench, on the train, at the hotel affects our relationship as a race more than what many of our professional race relations protagonists say or do."[5] By looking at the national celebration of Jackie Robinson, the tennis triumphs of Althea Gibson, and the adulation of the African American athlete during the centennial celebration of the Emancipation Proclamation, this chapter will demonstrate the powerful pull that sports had on America and the idea of meritocracy and democracy.

Baseball Has Done It

Without a doubt, during the civil rights movement Jackie Robinson stood as the most important sporting figure. The reason is simple. After America fought a war for democracy with a segregated army, Robinson broke the color barrier in baseball, a sport deemed "America's pastime," which supposedly upheld the foundation of fairness that the nation rested on. In short, Robinson's presence proved to Americans they could live up to the ideas of equality. According to white sportswriter David Halberstam, "To most citizens of the country, particularly younger Americans, anxious that their country be as fair and just as it claimed it was, Robinson's debut was more than an athletic performance; rather it was like a political work in progress, an ongoing exercise in the possibilities of American democracy."[6] And in 1960, white writer Jack Orr, in his article "Jackie Robinson: Symbol of the Revolution," wrote, "And what do we tell ourselves about his contribution to America? He pulled us a little closer together. He gave pride to a tenth of a nation."[7] While progressive whites celebrated Robinson and viewed Robinson's play as a harbinger for a more democratic America, for this portion of the book, however, I think it is important to center black thought and discuss Robinson's meaning in black America. After all, America denied them the fruits of freedom. The signing of Robinson on October 23, 1945, his first Dodgers game on April 15, 1947, and his stellar Dodgers career demonstrated the ability of a black man to succeed in a white space, and the potential to push prejudiced whites to treat black men as equal, especially white men from the South. Robinson's presence in baseball signaled to black Americans that democracy, for the first time in history, and true integration, could be a reality.

Understanding the importance that baseball played in American society, the black press used the fight for integration in America's pastime as part of a larger battle for democracy and equality. Black sportswriters, including Sam Lacy, Joe Bostic, Bob Williams, and Wendell Smith, saw baseball's integration as a double-victory strategy. "Double victory," a term coined by the *Pittsburgh Courier*, meant that black Americans would close ranks, fight in the war for victory abroad, and come home fighting with the same intensity to defeat Jim Crow. They also hoped for immediate dividends during the war, including seeing black players in professional baseball. Many black writers believed that during a war fought for Four Freedoms, in which President Roosevelt insisted that baseball continue play as a way to raise America's morale, baseball would integrate as a sign of American democratic spirit. But as the war dragged on, and the quality of play in professional baseball continued to decline with many star white players in the military, baseball owners showed no signs or willingness to integrate. In 1944, seeing the chances of integration declining, Bob Williams, the sports editor for the *Cleveland Call*, complained, "The Industry of Baseball would rather close down than become Americanized, and democratic. And they stand for fair play! If industry had taken the same un-American attitude we'd be losing the war. Baseball is certainly putting in a good bid for us to lose the peace after we win the war." Williams then challenged black fans that if baseball did not integrate they should boycott the games. "Of course," he noted, "it is too much to expect white people to blackball baseball as un-American, but there is no reason why Negroes should patronize the game when they are excluded from participation simply because of race."[8] With an increase in economic opportunities during the war, black fans, as Williams knew, had buying power. Their love of baseball had supported a number of black teams during the war, and Williams believed that their dollars could make the white owners pause on their prejudice. Of course, the irony was—and all black sportswriters knew this—the integration of baseball would destroy black ball. But at that moment, they deemed democracy more important than the death of a black institution and continued to fight for their rightful place in professional ball.

In 1945, the fight for fairness finally moved off the editorial page, past the protest phase, and directly into the direct-action stage when black sportswriters forced teams to give black players tryouts. In April, Joe Bostic of the *People's Voice* forced the Dodgers to give pitcher Terris McDuffie and outfielder David "Showboat" Thomas a tryout when Bostic brought the players unannounced to the Dodgers' spring training camp. For Bostic this bold gesture came at the perfect time, as New York state politicians had recently stated that they would pass a Federal Employment Practice Committee (FEPC) bill—they signed the Quinn-Ives law in the summer—that would forbid discrimination by employers with more than six employees based on race, religion, color. After the law passed in February, Bostic needled, "While it's a pretty sad commentary on American sport that fair play has to be legislated, it's a good thing that the bigot-minded people who run our national pastime be forced to quit desecrating the good name of sport by their actions."[9] Before taking McDuffie and Thomas to training camp, however, Bostic searched for other ideas to end segregation, including urging black players to take action for themselves. In one column entitled, "Players Must Act Now to Erase the Baseball Ban," he closed by prompting, "C'mon fellows, the next move is up to you. If necessary call this newspaper and we'll advise you of the steps to take. BUT GET MOV-IN. TIME'S A WASTIN!!!"[10] But, in truth, Bostic had no plans to wait for black players to make a move; he led the charge. On April 7, he took McDuffie and Thomas with him to West Point, where the Dodgers held their spring training that year, and according to Bostic, "The turning point in a great battle was reached—the battle to open the doors of the great American game of baseball to all American citizens—including Negroes,"[11] when McDuffie and Thomas, while wearing Dodgers uniforms, received a tryout in front of an irritated Branch Rickey. Rickey, as people would later learn, felt bombarded by Bostic because Rickey wanted all the credit for integration.

While Bostic made the first move to strikeout Jim Crow, a number of black writers felt he made the wrong move. They complained that he put Rickey in a bad spot and added that because of the players' advanced ages, Rickey would have an easy way out from this stunt. Bostic, the fierce fighter, countered his naysayers by writing, "The grandstand managers always know how someone else should blaze a trail AFTER it has been blazed," and noted that Rickey had been reluctant to sign black talent and needed to be pushed. Besides, why should black people have to worry about Rickey's feelings? As Bostic argued, "Negroes have been humiliated, sneered at and antagonized for all these years that bars have been set up against them and them alone, while people of all races and national origins have been accepted. We've tried conferences, 'surveys' and mock hearings." Anyone calling for calmness, in Bostic's words, was asking for an Uncle Tom, but Uncle Tom had no place in the baseball business.[12] A week after McDuffie and Thomas tried out, Sam Jethroe, Jackie Robinson, and Marvin Williams, with the help of writer Wendell Smith, received a tryout from the Boston Red Sox.

Even though the tryouts in Boston and for Brooklyn did not pay immediate dividends, and teams spent the 1945 season avoiding the "Negro question," those pushing for integration knew that in a matter of time baseball would have to desegregate, especially as the war came to an end and black soldiers came home. On October 20, Rick Hurt, of the *People's Voice*, demanded, "It is now, to put it plainly, a case of who triumphs. Either the jimcro [Jim Crow] owners remain unmolested on their traditional lily-white ball clubs, or jimcro goes out of the window."[13] Like Hurt, most onlookers believed that a New York team would be the first to fall. They had three teams in the state, an FEPC bill that outlawed discrimination, local politicians like Ben Davis (black) who pushed legislation to outlaw Jim Crow in baseball, Mayor LaGuardia who had started his "Committee to Investigate Jim Crow in Baseball," and local politicians and advocates who had started a "Committee to End Jim Crow in Baseball." And then the moment came. After three years of scouting the best black players in baseball, and deliberately stalling the advocate groups for baseball's integration, so he could gain all the glory, on October 23, 1945, Branch Rickey announced that the Dodgers minor league affiliate, the Montreal Royals, had signed Jackie Robinson.

When Montreal signed Robinson, the move gave black America their first post–World War II victory. After risking their lives for world democracy, black men came home expecting fair treatment and equal opportunity, but too many white Americans quickly reminded their fellow black soldiers that the fight for freedom ended at home. The Four Freedoms, in other words, had nothing to do with Jim Crow, and to keep black men in their place, lynchings and police brutality increased, and housing remained horrible and deliberately segregated. But Jackie Robinson gave black people hope, hope that if baseball could come to its senses, so too could the rest of white America. Sydney R. Williams, a black writer from Cleveland, captured this sentiment when he wrote, "In spite of the momentary set-backs, the trying and dismaying situations, yes even the brutal lynchings, the wheels of progress in our America grind on relentlessly. (Yes, our America—and never stop believing that.) The last big mud hole to be overcome by the wheels of progress was the long, sticky opposition to Negro players in organized ball." Williams, moreover, saw the bigger picture to Robinson's signing and used this moment to motivate his people to keep pushing for justice, urging "Let us keep the people's might behind the wheels of social progress so that they will keep on grinding away at the mud and much which yet clog the road to democracy in America."[14]

The praise did not stop. Adam Clayton Powell, a Democratic congressman from New York, heralded Robinson's signing as "a step that will bring cheer to all real Americans, and a move toward the winning of peace."[15] Ben Davis, the black New York City councilman who had worked for a decade to end Jim Crow in baseball and who recently introduced legislation calling for New York teams to integrate, called the signing "a milestone on the road toward full and unconditional citizenship for all Americans irrespective of race, creed, color, or national origin," and linked this signing to a larger battle for black labor rights when he posited, "There are a great number of Jackie Robinsons among the Negro people. . . . Let us keep up the fight of labor and the American people until the stand taken by the Dodgers is not the exception but the rule."[16] Ludlow Werner of the *New York Age* argued, "To 15,000,0000 Negroes he will symbolize not only their prowess in baseball, but their ability to rise to an opportunity," while Wendell Smith of the *Pittsburgh Courier* concluded, "The signing of Jackie Robinson is the most American and democratic step baseball has made."[17] But at this time, despite all the superlatives, Robinson had merely signed a contract. The black man still had to earn his spot.

Thus, when Robinson played his first game with Montreal in April 1946, after he had survived segregated spring training in Florida, the black press heralded his performance as another point of progress. If white fans cheered Robinson, black writers hoped, whites would willingly accept blacks in other facets of life. To be sure, this line of reasoning remained one of the great paradoxes in sports and race; whites would cheer black athletes on the field but would not welcome their presence off the field. Robinson dominated in his first appearance, highlighted by a historical home run. On cue, fans cheered him loudly. The *Michigan Chronicle* celebrated, "The cheers which Jackie received from white fans showed that there is a fundamental decency among Americans which will rise above the popular prejudices if they are given the opportunity. This streak of decency," the writer claimed, "is the foundation upon which democracy is built and it represents the hope of the world today."[18]

But to be clear, black jubilation went beyond fawning over white fans; black joy in this moment constituted an open celebration of black excellence. In short, Robinson made people with black skin feel special. In his writing, Rick Hurt, of the *People's Voice*, captured the spirit when he implored his readers to "remember the great round of applause that broke out from the stands" after Robinson made his first plate appearance. He asked, "Smile as you experience again the sheer joy and relief as inning after inning you saw Robinson completely cover himself with glory." Hurt triumphantly concluded, "It's a great day for all those people in the world who are trampling in the slow relentless march toward 'freedom in our time.' They're having a great day too."[19] Opening Day represented a microcosm of the season. Although Robinson had a few minor slumps, he dominated the league. After a stellar first year with the Royals, and a strong spring training with the Dodgers—this time they trained in Havana, Cuba, and Panama to avoid American Jim Crow—in April 1947, Rickey finally announced that Robinson would play at first base for the Dodgers.

Robinson's Brooklyn debut is the single most important moment in sport history. An editorial in the *Cleveland Call* claimed the adulation Robinson received that day, "told one of the most dramatic stories of American democracy," and noted the battle to "secure the admission of Negroes into major league baseball is one of the longest, hardest, and most sustained struggles in the history of American social and economic life."[20] And this adulation went beyond baseball. As a writer from the *Kansas City Plain Dealer* surmised, the social impact on a race that had been physically abused and economically exploited pointed to a brighter day. "The acceptance of this color [sic] man on a white baseball team is an act of liberalism which points the way for America," he gleaned. The Kansas City writer continued, "The average American is not concerned about racial prejudice and the color of a man's skin. Racial prejudice, segregation, racial hatred and all of the feelings that bring about riots, lynchings and misunderstanding come with the reach of social control and can be prevented, they are motivated by organized methods of sentiment building and public opinion." With Jackie at bat, he argued, "sentiment and public opinion can be turned in another direction."[21]

For some black people, Robinson's Dodgers debut denoted a simple message: give black people a chance. Detroit reverend F. B. Guthria stated, "Negroes can and will succeed in any other sport or any other phase of American life when given the same opportunities as are granted other races and nationality groups."[22] Sharing a similar sentiment, Roy Wilkins, the future leader of the National Association for the Advancement of

Colored People, concluded, "Well, our boy, Jackie Robinson made it. If you give our folks a fair chance some of them will always make it. All they ask is a fair chance. The no-gooders will flop out and the good ones will make the grade."[23] As the story is well told, Jackie made the grade.

That season, moreover, black America received a double dose of democracy when the Cleveland Indians signed the Newark Eagles' Larry Doby, to a major league contract. Unlike Robinson, Doby, who converted from an infielder to play centerfield, did not have to cut his teeth in the minor leagues; he went straight to the Indians. "For Larry Doby," Cleveland Jackson of the *Cleveland Call and Post* wrote, "it took but a few short minutes to walk up to that plate. But for 13 million American Negroes that simple action was the successful climax of a long uphill fight whose annals are like the saga of the race."[24] In Detroit, an editorial in the *Michigan Chronicle*, claimed, "America is still a land of promise and no colored boy need hang his head in despair at what the future may bring." Breaking the color barrier in baseball, he believed, "is but a symptom, we believe, of a profound change which is occurring in American life. It is a change for the better too." He also told his readers, "It must be remembered that the Negroes who are going into major league baseball are getting in only because they are darn good ballplayers and not because they are colored. This is the way it should be. If a Negro gets an opportunity and then muffs it, he is responsible for what happens, not society."[25] In the *People's Voice*, Rick Hurt heralded: "But his appearance in the Cleveland Indians line-up has a far deeper meaning to the Negro people and to all America. It proves that the Jimcro walls that have hitherto excluded Negroes from the money and fame of big-league employment are tumbling down."[26] Unfortunately, Doby, who went on to have a hall-of-fame career, played terribly in his first months as a professional. Luckily, however, Robinson's rookie year made up for both of them. His success, in other words, drew attention away from Doby's struggles.

When Robinson received his Rookie of the Year award from the *Sporting News*, a paper that was at first reluctant about praising Robinson's signing, once again, Robinson's success proved to the black press the need for fair play in society. An editorial in the *People's Voice*, praised, "A Negro has been given a chance and he has made good. Jackie is a symbol of the present Negro generation. During the past war, they fought valiantly in every branch of the armed service. During this post-war period, they can make good in every type of civilian job if freed from the shackles of prejudice."[27] And the *Philadelphia Tribune* trumpeted, "Robinson's success has several lessons for Americans. His presence on the baseball field with a team all of whose members are white is not taken for granted. The field of sports, always in the vanguard in race relations, is better for Robinson's achievements. He is a source of inspiration to other talented negro youth who may want to achieve fame and fortune on the baseball diamond. They know that from here on scouts will not pass them up solely because of the color of their skin."[28] Alvin Moses, who had been writing about the black athlete since World War I, boldly claimed, "This is, of course, as it should be. The Negro merely asks for equal opportunity, the chance to be trained for positions heretofore denied him. He sues for nothing on the basis of his color, previous injustices and inequalities."[29]

Beyond a demonstration of democracy, the Dodgers' noble experiment represented a test to the Southern man. Would he accept integration? Robinson and the Dodgers, especially his minor league coach, Clay Hopper, and his Southern teammates, including Dixie Walker and Pee Wee Reese, were the subjects. After all, many predicted that integration would not work because Southerners would not acquiesce. As Jack Horner, a white sportswriter from Durham, North Carolina, claimed, "I believe it will be a long time before the Negro will be accepted in the southern leagues." The day the Royals signed Robinson, Branch Rickey Jr. shot off a warning when he said that Southerners would "steer away" from an integrated team, but if they did "they'll be back in baseball after a year or two in the cotton mills." Of course, many Southerners acted appalled at Rickey Jr.'s remarks at the very notion that they would not accept a black man. For a number of white Southerners, at least in print, Robinson's signing gave them an opportunity to continue the same old masquerade about integration; if a black man deserved a chance, they claimed, the fair-minded Southern man would give it to him. On this notion of Southern fairness, Frank Spencer of *Winston-Salem* retorted, "If he is qualified, then give him an opportunity."[30] But, in reality, the question of "if he is qualified" represented a Southern man's way of arguing that no black man had been qualified for the job, or any important job.

Southerners did not want white Northerners meddling in their affairs. On this note, W. G. Bramham, president of the National Association (the minor leagues), argued, "It is my opinion that if the Negro is left alone and aided by his unselfish friends of the white race, he will work out his own salvation in all lines of endeavor." He continued, "It is those of the carpet-bagger stripe of the white race under the guise of helping, but in truth using the Negro for their own selfish interests, who retard the race."[31] But Robinson's signing meant that for the first time Southerners had to show and prove that they would truly give a qualified black man a chance. They could not run from the reality of Jackie Robinson. They had to deal with a black man on equal terms.

To be sure, most Southerners were slow to accept Robinson. As the story is well told, during his first spring training in 1946, Robinson, who with his wife Rachel rode in Jim Crow buses and experienced Southern racism at a New Orleans airport when they got bumped from a plane, also had to board with a black family, instead of staying with his white teammates, because segregation laws forbade him from staying with white people. And most cities tried to bar Robinson from playing in integrated games. Even the following year, when the team held their spring training in Havana, Cuba, and Panama so the Dodgers would not have to fight Jim Crow racism, Jackie and his black teammates had to stay at a segregated hotel in Havana—all of the black players got sick from the inferior food— and in Panama, Southern players, including star, Dixie Walker, started a petition to remove Robinson from the team. Rickey, however, got word of the mutiny against meritocracy and told each player they had no choice. As his son said the previous year, the cotton mills were always waiting for them. Surprisingly, that act of defiance came on the heels of Robinson winning over his first Southern opponent, his minor league coach, Clay Hopper. During his first exhibition game in 1946 when Rickey told Hopper, a Mississippian who ran a plantation in the offseason, that a play Robinson just performed was "super human," the Royals coach responded, "Do you really think a nigger's a human being?"[32] But after the 1946 season, a season in which Robinson experienced vile racism from fans in Baltimore, Louisville, and even in Syracuse, New York, and a season in which Robinson dominated the league and led his team to the championship, Hopper told his star player, "You're a great ball player and a fine gentleman. It's been wonderful having you on the team."[33]

As the Robinson story teaches us, part of the mythmaking process of democracy and meritocracy in sports is celebrating the redemption of white men, especially Southern white men. And in this case, Robinson's own words propel this story. As a civil rights leader, Robinson understood he had a responsibility to highlight Southern men in his life, like Clay Hopper, who overcame their past racism because of their interaction with black men. In his book *Baseball Has Done It*, published in 1963, Robinson took special care to mention the redemption of the Southern man in baseball and sought out his white Southern teammates to contribute to the book. In regard to Dixie Walker, a teammate who originally did not want to play with Robinson, Robinson urged, "Those who believe that the unreconstructed rebels of the South can never be brought to accept the Fourteenth and Fifteenth Amendments may learn the contrary from Dixie Walker. Soon after the '47 season began, Dixie's innate fairness and love of baseball made him cross the color line and come to me." In his letter for

Robinson's book, Walker claimed black players saved baseball.[34] Another teammate who tried to mutiny against Robinson, Birmingham-born Bobby Bragan, also contributed to the book and admitted, "At the time Jackie joined the Dodgers, I am sure that I wouldn't have invited him to sit with him in the dining car. . . . But before the season was over I was often in the same group with him at tables, in dining cars, hotel rooms, and later in card games." For Bragan his redemption happened only because of his association, based on equality, with a black man. "I think it's just a matter of becoming acclimated to the thing by association," he claimed. "I was exposed to integration daily under the shower, in the dressing room, in the next locker, on the bus, in the hotel and in many conversations." His family, however, who still lived in Birmingham, had not been "exposed" to black people. "The exposure of my seven brothers and sisters in the South has been limited. They can't feel the same tolerance that I feel today."[35] For Robinson, Bragan and baseball proved that "baseball has handled the integration question the right way. Baseball has accepted Negroes. No resentment stems from Southerners in baseball any more. When a Negro puts a run on the scoreboard no one questions the color of the run."[36] Indeed, Robinson and baseball helped clear the racially congested paths toward a better America.

Althea Gibson

The same year that Robinson made his Dodgers debut, Althea Gibson established herself as the top black women's tennis player, starting her 10-year winning streak of the American Tennis Association (ATA) championship. She capped off this decade of domination with her ground-breaking Wimbledon win in 1957 and followed that with another astonishing victory the following year. Gibson's tennis play, especially against her white foes at major tournaments like Wimbledon, galvanized the black community and stood as another symbol of hope and democracy. But unlike the celebrated moments of Robinson, Gibson, who came from a working-class background, accomplished her athletic heroics in an elite sport most African Americans did not play, unless they belonged to a small elite group of professionals—doctors, dentists, lawyers, and entertainers—who had access to country clubs and could afford the costs of the expensive game. By the time she won her first ATA tournament at 20 years old, these professionals believed that Gibson, the girl from the ghetto, could represent their middle-class interests and be their Jackie Robinson. Born to sharecroppers in Silver, South Carolina, raised in the ghettoes of Harlem, and groomed to be a polished player and person among the black elite in the North and the South, Gibson was, as scholar Jennifer Lansbury concludes, "a community project" and became the "lone representative of the race," in an elite white space becoming the first black athlete to represent the aspirations of the black middle class.[37]

Gibson's story is the most unlikely tale in sports history. Most black athletes came from poverty, but Gibson was poor, black, and a woman, and poor black women were not supposed to have access to the tennis courts. Gibson, who hated school and often played hooky, grew up in poverty in the house of an abusive father who moved his family to Harlem to avoid the meager life of a sharecropper, and was discovered by Buddy Walker, a musician and youth worker, who organized sports for kids in Harlem. There, in the streets of Harlem, he found Gibson dominating the local kids, boys and girls, in paddle tennis, a game organized much like tennis, but required the use of the street—a street blocked off by the local police to allow Harlem kids to have a chance to play sports. Walker was so enamored with her raw talent; he bought her a couple of used tennis rackets and taught her how to hit balls. Impressed by her natural ability, he brought her to the Harlem River Courts, where the black middle class played. There, a school teacher and tennis enthusiast, Juan Serrell, took interest in her skills and brought her to the elite African American Cosmopolitan Tennis Club hoping that they too saw her potential and would sponsor a membership so she could continue to play. Led by Dr. Fred Johnson, the local pro at the club, members sponsored a membership for the teenager from the Harlem ghetto.

To be clear, at this point in the teenager's early career, 1942–1945, the members' interest in Gibson seemed more charitable than an investment in a black barrier breaker. But after her first women's ATA singles tournament in 1946, a second-place finish, Dr. Robert W. Johnson, of Lynchburg, Virginia, and Dr. Hubert A. Eaton of Wilmington, North Carolina, decided she had the potential to win the tournament and also earn a college scholarship, so they invited her to stay with them—she lived with Dr. Eaton during the school year and Johnson during the summer—so she could receive tennis lessons and remove herself from the ghetto. Gibson, at first, worried about moving South and facing Jim Crow racism, but also understood that blacks living in Northern ghettoes with the "plaster falling down and the plumbing stopped up and the kids getting killed in the streets" had it rough too. She took her chances with the doctors.[38]

Very quickly, however, Gibson understood that this move was more than just the benevolence of the black elite; they saw her as a barrier breaker and, thus, an intermediate between two segregated worlds that rarely met on equal terms. She had to be at her best. The doctors believed, however, that before Gibson could beat Jim Crow they had to refine more than her game; they had to refine her attitude. Eaton reflected, "Knowing that the Jim Crow signs on the tennis courts of the world had to come down sooner or later and that a strong black contender should be waiting in the wings, Dr. Johnson and I began to plan Althea's future."[39] By her own admission, however, Gibson was crude and crass. On and off the court, she played like her personality. She learned how to survive on her own in Harlem and was, in short, nobody's fool. Rounding her attitude and play into proper shape would take years of training. She also lacked a formal education. In New York, Gibson played hooky as much as she played tennis and had not moved past the eighth grade. The school system in Wilmington put the 19-year-old in the 10th grade. Slowly, however, Gibson rounded off into a good student and an excellent tennis player, and by 1950, after she had won three ATA tournaments in a row, and the segregated walls in other sports were under attack, the doctors decided their tennis protégé was ready to serve Jim Crow tennis its first blow.

Prior to 1950, Gibson had played in minor integrated tournaments but had never played in a United States Lawn Tennis Association (USLTA) championship. To do so, she would need a white ally to break through the lily-white association. Although the USLTA clearly had a Jim Crow policy, like baseball its discriminatory rules remained unwritten, and thus it claimed it did not discriminate. Officials argued that athletes had to prove themselves in local tournaments before they received invites to major tournaments, but the racist local organizations did not invite blacks as members or players in their tournaments. Fed up with this hypocrisy, white tennis legend, Alice Marble, hit back. In an open letter to the *American Lawn Tennis* magazine, Marble urged, "If tennis is a game for ladies and gentlemen, it's also time we acted a little more like gentlepeople and less like sanctimonious hypocrites." She continued, "The entrance of Negroes into national tennis is as inevitable as it has proved to be in baseball, in football and in boxing: there is no denying so much talent." Reflecting on Marble's brave stance, Doc Young wrote, "There has seldom, if ever, been a more eloquent plea for fair-play in sports, delivered by a Caucasian on behalf of a Negro, or of Negroes, than Miss Marble's beautiful words." Noting the significance of having a white ally, Malcolm Poindexter, a white writer from Philadelphia, claimed, "If history were able to repeat itself and the tennis world could have seen fit to drop its racial barriers 40 years ago, Philadelphia would probably have the distinction of honoring Miss Ora Washington as the holder of the national women's singles title and the women who held it longer than any other in

American history."[40] Washington, as many believed in the mid-1920s and 1930s, was the best tennis player in America, regardless of race, but tennis champions like the famed Helen Wills refused to play her. Washington also did not have a white ally supporting her.[41]

Marble's words shamed the white tennis world, and Gibson soon received invites to their tournaments. She played well enough in these showcases that she received her invite to the most prestigious tournament in the country, Forest Hills. Despite losing in the second round to defending Wimbledon champion, Louise Brough, Gibson played an exhilarating match—with Gibson leading, the game was suspended due to weather, and some claimed the time off gave her too much time to overthink and allowed the anxiety of the moment to create doubt in her abilities; the tennis community was put on notice.[42] The long lanky woman, born in the segregated South and raised on the streets of Harlem, was here to stay.

Gibson's performance at Forest Hills, moreover, fostered hope in the black community for greater things to come. A writer for the *Amsterdam News* noted that like Joe Louis and Jackie Robinson, "she was a symbol of hope and a race group's faith in the unpredictable future."[43] With her performance at Forest Hills, her handlers in the ATA believed that now was the time for Gibson to break an even bigger barrier, play in Wimbledon. But these tournaments cost money, and most women in those days did not play professionally or receive endorsements; thus, if Gibson wanted to go to Wimbledon, she needed an influx of money, money she did not have. Understanding the hope she brought the black community, blacks across the country stepped up. In Detroit, Bill Matney of the *Michigan Chronicle* implored local black Detroiters to raise funds and arranged a dinner in her honor for the occasion. The great Joe Louis contributed first. At a benefit dinner for Gibson, Louis urged, "Every sports minded person who has read of Althea's tennis playing and feels pride in what she has done should be more than willing to contribute to this campaign." In leading the cause, Louis bought her a round-trip ticket, and the rest of black Detroiters chipped in $700, the bulk of that money coming from the Detroit Duffer's Golf Association, a local black golf club. With the help of the black community, Gibson went to Wimbledon.[44]

Unfortunately for Gibson, who lost in her initial trip to London, the next five years did not match the hype and hopes placed on her. While her game improved, and few could match her athleticism, the pressure of being the lone representative, the one who had to carry the barrier-breaker bags on her back, impeded her game. In addition, the lack of competition she faced in the ATA—a number of white tournaments still refused to invite her to play—did not help her game. But then in 1955, the black tennis star received a break. Her government came calling and asked Gibson to represent her nation on a goodwill mission tour across the globe. Calling black athletes like Gibson "globe trotters," historian Damion Thomas argues that America sent black athletes across the globe as part of a cold war strategy to prove that American racism had improved and that newly independent nations could count on America for fairness and democracy.[45] Thus, the American government trotted an athlete like Gibson, who had been Jim Crowed her whole life, around as proof of American democracy. These acts reeked of hypocrisy, but for Gibson, free from American Jim Crow, the tour allowed her to practice and play against top competition. The time paid off. She started the 1956 season on a remarkable winning streak, including a victory at the French Open, and when she went back to Wimbledon, many believed she would win. Although she did not win that year—she claimed that she might have been "overtennised"—she did take home the doubles championship, and her play had noticeably improved.[46] Everybody knew she would be back. Her next major move on the court would change history.

In 1957, a decade after Robinson made baseball history, Gibson finally won Wimbledon. To be clear, no moment can eclipse Robinson's entry into baseball, but this does not discount how special and meaningful it was to see a black woman rise from poverty to conquer the white elite of the world. This moment constituted a celebration of her dogged determination, the black spirit triumphing against all odds, and another sign that blacks belonged. The *Michigan Chronicle* summed up this feeling perfectly when an editorialist noted that while Southern politicians were "committed to no action on the Civil Rights front, spend a great deal of time talking about the inability of Negroes to measure up," in England, Gibson stood "at the pinnacle of achievement in her chosen sport." As the writer argued, "She did not arrive at this point overnight. It took years and years of practice and additional years of fighting her way through the racial barriers which for so long existed in amateur sports." In other words, she had the black fighting spirit. Gibson, according to the editorialist, represented "just one of many who have had the courage, foresight and ability to overcome both the obstacles of competition and the formidable obstacle of color." "People like her," the editorial continued, "prove error to the proposition that the nation or any section of the nation can impose restrictions on any group of Americans as a group without regard for the worth of individual members of that group."[47]

Some black writers, moreover, believed Gibson's victory held global symbolism for America abroad. A writer for the *Chicago Defender* noted, "Her victory is a victory for Uncle Sam, for democracy." The writer also

Althea Gibson in 1956. (Library of Congress)

added the victory would "do much to enhance the cause of the free world in areas where America's racial bias formed the basis of hostility toward Uncle Sam."[48] The following year, when Gibson repeated as champion, the *Louisiana Weekly* registered a similar statement about the global impact of Gibson and argued that Gibson and other black athletes, like track stars Rafer Johnson and Margaret Matthews, "do more good for the cause of democracy and promote goodwill with the people of the world than the petty, cheap race hate hustlings that were recently witnessed in the state legislature."⁴⁹ The victory placed Gibson, the globe trotter, in the middle of a debate about U.S. exceptionalism, democracy, and civil rights, but Gibson just wanted to play tennis.

While the black press hoped that Gibson's victory would propel the civil rights movement and help break Jim Crow and that Gibson would use her platform to get involved in the civil rights movement, Gibson wanted no part of this movement. Like most black athletes of her time, she believed her outstanding play would help blacks earn equality. In an article in the *Saturday Evening Post*, after she won her second straight Wimbledon, Gibson pleaded, "I am not a racially conscious person. I'm a tennis player, nor a Negro tennis player. I have never set myself up as a champion of the Negro race." She continued, "I feel strongly that I can do more good my way than I could be crusading." By "my way" she meant playing tennis, winning, and representing herself properly, just as Drs. Eaton and Johnson had hoped. She concluded her thoughts on the "colored question," adding, "I hope that the way I have conducted myself in tennis has met sufficient approval and good will to assure that the way will not close behind me."⁵⁰ Although Gibson's proclamation upset the black press, at the moment, she could get away with such a statement. Most in the black community concluded that athletes' performances were enough to win the day. In fact, most black writers believed that athletics offered the best proof of black advancement. But those days, to be sure, were quickly coming to an end.

In 1959, the black press attacked Gibson for her lack of so-called race awareness. The criticism started after the Westside Tennis Club at Forest Hills denied Nobel Peace Prize winner and leading international black political figure Ralph J. Bunche and his 15-year-old son membership to its segregated club. While the black press called for a boycott of the club, Gibson, the most popular black athlete in America at the time and the one most associated with the club, maintained her willingness to play at the segregated club. "As long as they treat me as a person and guest, I'll play," she stated. Hearing this, James Hicks of the *New York Amsterdam News* fired back: "I'm so mad at Althea Gibson I could break one of her best tennis rackets over hear head." Hicks, who was clearly in the wrong to threaten her with violence, asserted that he and other black citizens were upset with Gibson because they invested so much in her career. Black people like himself, Hicks urged, made it possible for her to play in exclusive clubs, and earn the fame she had, because, as he stated, "I, like millions of other negroes, took a personal pride in what she was doing and wanted to help her in what ever way I could." All that African Americans asked Althea in return was "that Althea be proud of herself. Be proud of being a Negro! Be proud of other Negroes!" When she seemingly failed that so-called race loyalty test, Hicks concluded, "Althea is not proud enough of Ralph Bunche to spit in the face of some bigots who have spat in Bunche's face by barring him from their tennis club—and who would spit in Althea's own mother's face simply because she is Negro." Moreover, after the incident, a black resident from New York wrote to the *Amsterdam News* to complain, "I respect Althea Gibson's ability as a champion in tennis and a credit to her race and country, but when asked racial questions from now on, she should say, 'no comment.'"[51] In other words, he wanted her to "shut up and play" and make the race proud. That, however, was exactly what Gibson thought she was doing. Despite this dustup, it is undeniable that Gibson's tennis victories, and later her golf success, had a large impact on the black communities' mind-set in the fight for civil rights and racial equality.

100 Years after Emancipation

Robinson's and Gibson's success, along with countless other black athletes since the end of World War II, gave black Americans their first national taste of true equality. And by 1963, in the centennial year of the Emancipation Proclamation, as America was caught up in a fierce struggle for civil rights, collectively black athletes took on a greater symbolic importance than they ever had. Black publications throughout the country reflected on the gains made in sports and optimistically hoped that they could be projected in society. Black writers knew that the black athlete offered proof that whites had the capacity to integrate black people into mainstream America and that blacks would make the most of their opportunities. Just days after the March on Washington, for example, an editorial in the *Michigan Chronicle*, which was accompanied by a political cartoon supporting the claims, celebrated the achievements black athletes made in sports. Understanding that the March on Washington was for "Jobs and Freedom," the Michigan writer argued: "A regular commentary on how the law of equal employment opportunities works is found on the sports pages of newspapers across the country." He further opinioned that most people by now knew the story of black athletic success; thus, he did not need to focus on those stories; the writer, however, wanted to emphasize "the fact that when the Negro is given an equal chance to show his worth and compete in the job market, he will do exceptionally well." And he added, "Equal opportunity in all facets of American life is the crux of the present civil rights revolution."[52] To be sure, the athletic arena had given black America a taste of the sweetness of democracy, but other black Americans still needed a seat at the table.

During the centennial celebration, Doc Young stood out as the leading cheerleader tying sports to civil rights advancement. By 1963, Young was one of the most well-known names in the black sporting community. He had worked for major black newspapers, including the *Cleveland Call and Post* and the *Chicago Defender*, and had national columns in *Negro Digest*, *Jet*, and *Ebony*. He also had three popular books in print, *The Champ Nobody Wanted* (1963), *Great Negro Baseball Stars* (1953), and *Negro Firsts in Sports*, his latest to celebrate the centennial of the Emancipation Proclamation. Writing in his book *Negro Firsts in Sports*, Young claimed, "It seems fitting, natural and normal that sports today provide for American Negroes the closest approach to the great goal they dream about, talk about, sing about, pray and work for, every moment of every living day that comes and piles into weeks, month and years. . . . It is like saying that sports are an important part of the beginning of total freedom."[53] And in *Ebony*, in an article entitled "How Sports Helped Break the Color Line," Young offered, "What Dr. Martin Luther King and other Civil Rights leaders are now fervently attempting to accomplish in the vital areas of education, employment and housing already has been achieved in most mass-appeal sports." Young continued, "In many instances, the break-through gains in the cited areas of Dr. King's concentration often are made more easily because sports have previously proven the human practicality of integration."[54]

Of course, Young had to admit that sports were not a "cure-all for America's Racial ills," but he also argued, "It would be equally unrealistic to discount the role of integrated sports." For proof, Young offered break-through moments of integrated sports, including the white adulation over Joe Louis, Branch Rickey signing Jackie Robinson, and Alice Marble fighting for Althea Gibson. On the latter point, Young pointed out, "In all cases where sports have broken the color line, integration has been the result of cooperation between the races—plus the ability of the Negro to produce when given a chance to compete on equal terms." For Young's money, the Marble–Gibson crusade represented the "American-Democratic ideal" that few moments in history could surpass.[55] To be sure, Young, like a number of black Americans in the centennial of the Emancipation Proclamation still waiting for their true freedom, looked for any sign of progress, and sports provided that relief. The success of athletes like Robinson and Gibson to break down the walls of lily-white establishments, and do it with the help of white allies, made the moments that more special. Sports offered positive proof that blacks could succeed, and equally as important, willing whites existed to uphold fairness, which is why black writers loudly cheered athletic breakthroughs and openly celebrated white allies. Both sides, black and white, showed the possibilities of true democracy.

CHAPTER TWO

White Allies

In 1948, no episode of racial democracy eclipsed the story of the "Ebony Express," Levi Jackson. On November 22, the white Yale football players, many of them Southerners, elected Jackson, the grandson of a slave and son of a butler who worked at the school, the captain of the football team. According to most outside the South, this was American democracy at its finest. Joe Louis, the greatest American of the "greatest generation," called it the "American dream." But this moment of jubilation did not come out of nowhere.

For the past two years Levi had been on white media's radar. In 1947, for example, the *Christian Science Monitor* gladly told its readers that Jackson's character was buoyed by his "refusal to become bitter at unfair treatment received, on the field and off, because of his race; and his remarkable modesty have made Levi Jackson's name the most respected in all of sports."[1] At Yale, Levi had a successful freshman season (1946) and was hurt his sophomore season (1947), but by his junior year (1948) it was clear he was one of the best backs in the nation. And then the moment came. His white teammates elected him captain. The hyperbole of white hopes kicked into overdrive. Democracy and meritocracy worked. Patience would trump prejudice. White men gave a black man a chance at leadership, based on merit and not race.

Immediately, Jackson's captaincy became a celebration of white tolerance and racial democracy. George Trevor of *Sport* claimed, "Breaking into the Yale football picture was a cinch for Levi compared to the indignities that Robinson faced when he broke into major-league baseball with the Dodgers last spring." In other words, while Robinson went through the fire, Jackson found friends on the football field. He found white allies.

Trevor ended his preview of Jackson observing, "The quickening spirit of democracy is loose in a broken field. Even the prefix 'Old Eli' (a name derived as a homage to Elihu Yale who gifted money and books to the institution in the early 1700s) has been amended. It's 'Old Levi' now!"[2] The *Chicago Tribune* writer Roscoe Simmons said, "Jackson's election by the Yale players and cheers for him by Yale alumni and students are vivid illustrations of the progress of freedom in the United States," and concluded that this moment was a march "toward freedom."[3] In *Life*, the editorialist argued that Jackson's teammates "did not vote for Lopin' Levi in the spirit of a group of self-consciously 'tolerant' do-gooders passing a resolution to endorse a Fair Employment Practices Bill." For this writer, Jackson, most importantly, stood apart from past football icon and black political leader Paul Robeson, who agitated America to give blacks full equality. Levi's success, according to *Life*, made Robeson, who had praised Russia, communism, and its supposed lack of racism, "look foolish." "One can sympathize with Mr. Robeson's hatred for Jim Crow laws and customs," the writer claimed, but argued, "The action taken by a few Yale students in 10 minutes' time has hit Joe [Stalin] a blow that will some day make him screech."[4] In other words, if blacks remained patient, white people would solve the race problem. Tom Cohane of *Look* said, "His teammates did not elect Jackson because they felt they had to prove democracy. They elected him because they felt sure he deserved it."[5] Bill Corum of the *New York Journal American* added, "The fact that he was a Negro should have no bearing, as I'm sure it didn't." And Yale proved that in sports, they judged "men for what they have done and what they are in the sports in which they participate, and on no other basis."[6] Red Smith, one of the leading sportswriters of his time, agreed. Smith argued, "Look, what the Yale kids did wasn't anything wonderful. They did only what you expect of gentlemen, and if they weren't gentlemen, what would they be doing in a gentleman's game?"[7] Levi had the talent and humility, and his white teammates and coaches did what any good citizens would do. They were beacons of American democracy.

Key to this tale of triumphant tolerance also revolved around telling the story of his white teammates, especially the Southern ones. As one reporter emphatically stated, "Levi encountered no racial prejudice when he reported for Yale football."[8] In this celebration of white Southern redemption, the story of Levi, the Northern Negro, and Southern teammate Bill Schuler worked as essential cogs in the meritocracy mythmaking machine. In 1947, after his freshman season, Jackson told the *Afro-American* that Schuler invited him to his home in Birmingham. In his feature story on Jackson in *Sport*, writer George Trevor claimed that

Schuler, who was from a "wealthy and socially prominent" family, "went out of his way to make Levi feel at ease." "Southern prejudiced?" Trevor asked, only to answer his own question, "It wasn't Schuler's make up." The Southerner picked up Levi in his Cadillac, and the two drove to town to get milkshakes. With his white teammates, moreover, Jackson fit right in. Even in the shower. "Levi jokes with his mates on the field, and sings in the shower room. This lack of self-consciousness has made it easy for him to fit into the team routine. He belongs," Trevor added.[9] Given the history of race and segregation, this was an impressive statement about interracial bonding.

Moreover, Jackson's teammates stood as symbols of so-called post-racial beacons of light. In retelling the moment, in fact, they claimed they did not see race. Teammate Stuart Tisdale confirmed, "All of us gave it a lot of thought. . . . I kept thinking about the election and Levi. That night I dreamed about it. I woke up four or five times." Tisdale asked himself if he wanted to vote for Levi "subconsciously even, just to prove I'm demo-cratic?" "I wrestled with it," he said. But he "worked it out. Levi deserved the captaincy, so I was going to vote for him."[10] According to *Varsity*, "These men knew Jackson for a man—the best man among them in more ways than one—and it was the most natural thing in the world, to them, to name him Yale's seventy-sixth football captain."[11] The tolerant white youth represented America's future.

Following white sportswriters, the black press also placed its hopes in the white youth. They knew they needed white allies to defeat Jim Crow. In the *New York Age*, its editorialist reasoned, "This unanimous vote by the young men of Yale is another clear indication of the increasing liberal-ism of American youth." The writer continued, "The youth of America is apparently ready for full democracy. The young people are today ham-pered in large measure by their elders who timorously cling to the old traditions of discriminations and inequality. A sharp break with those traditions is foreshadowed by the actions of young men and women in the South as well as in the North. Captain Jackson of Yale is a symbol of that break."[12] In the *Philadelphia Tribune*, in an article entitled "Defeat for Dis-crimination," the black sportswriter suggested, "The practical idealism of youth and also youth's willingness to deal directly with problems some-times ducked by older, more resigned people, have had some heart-warm-ing demonstrations recently in some of our eastern colleges." After noting the election of Jackson and Frank S. Jones as manager of Harvard's foot-ball team, the writer observed, "Both are colored, in universities not only predominantly white, but with reputations for occasional snobbishness. If that's snobbishness, there ought to be more of it." In these cases, he continued, "colored students were honored because of their personal qualifications, a far better standard than skin pigmentation." No black writer spoke more glowingly about this incident than civil rights activist Joseph D. Bibb. "When news of this action was flashed over the land," Bibb boasted, "the hopes of the colored American were lifted. Eyes were fixed on the horizons. New vistas were envisioned and souls of fifteen million under-privileged people were electrified." He also charged, "The change is revolutionary," "the doors are swinging ajar for us," "democracy is finding remarkable expression in this realm of athletics," and "a new day dawns over the intellectual skies. New hopes surge up, but humility and contriteness should be controlling impulses." He closed his article gleefully writing, "We are most humbly grateful."[13]

What can we learn about this celebration of democracy and white allies? The Jackson jubilation was part of the mythmaking process of white manhood and meritocracy and constituted a coronation of white self-congratulation. In other words, key moments in sports that we do celebrate and heap attention on white allies served as a reminder in a Jim Crow society that white people could do the right thing and move past race and racism. As Doc Young argued in his seminal work *Negro Firsts in Sports*, although black athletes had to "fight for the mere right to play" and "carry the burden of race on their shoulders when they first entered the fray," Young acknowledged, "It must be noted in fairness, in every case where Negroes successfully hurdled racial barriers . . . liberal Caucasians were on hand to help them."[14] To be sure, the amount of "help" whites provided black athletes is debatable, but we do know that the stories we sometimes tell about integration, or the muscular assimilation of the black athlete, are overshadowed by the need to highlight white allies. By examining the push to integrate bowling, baseball, football, and college sports, this chapter celebrates the work of white allies in tandem with black athletes and the black press for fairness in sports.

Allies and Alleys: The Fight for Fair Play in Bowling

Betty Hicks knew the score. As a white woman, Hicks had been heralded as one of the best in women's golf, but for Hicks, those honors were hollow because her success on the links came against white women. Hicks had never competed against a black golfer. In post–World War II America, where fairness in sports became part of the American dialogue on democracy, Hicks understood that her lack of competition was not due to the fact that black women did not play golf—in fact golf was one of the most popular sports among black women—but because white golf courses did not let black women compete in integrated competition. Hicks also believed that to end discrimination in sports, although a narrow white-centric thought, white athletes had to lead the fight on integration.

Along with fighting for fairness on the fairways, Hicks helped lead the battle for integration in bowling, the fastest growing sport in America at the time. In 1948, Hicks, the cochairman of the National Committee for Fair Play in Bowling (NCFPB), told a mostly white audience at their annual meeting that athletes had to be activists. In her estimation, athletes were "conscious of the full meaning of sportsmanship. But they have to be shocked into action." The NCFPB, according to Hicks, needed to mold white bowlers and white bowling alley owners into allies in the fight for integration and to destroy the un-American, "white male-only" policy of the American Bowling Congress (ABC). Hicks urged, "Our fight is also directed against practically all of the other existing organizations, most of which contain restrictive rules based upon segregation and discrimination of color, or some other un-American 'reason.'"[15] The racist ABC sanctioned every major tournament and bowling alley; thus, if blacks wanted to compete in tournaments, they had to use their own facilities or get special permission from whites. To integrate the ABC, Hicks argued the NCFPB had three options: "Public education designed to awaken Americans to the problem of free and open competition in sports, legal action pointing toward a change in restrictive rules, and the establishment of rival organizations, operating on the basis of real democratic equality." As a white woman, Hicks and the majority white leadership of the NCFPB were part of a growing cohort of white activists fighting alongside black activists and athletes for fair play.

The rise of the black bowler is a remarkable testament to African American agency in controlling their leisure time in a segregated sport. Because the ABC sanctioned most alleys across America, those lanes fell under the ABC's racist regulations and excluded black bowlers. Prior to 1939, "Negroes in search of places to bowl had to use makeshift alleys under discouraging conditions," reflected black writer Al Sweeney. If they did not have black-owned options, they had to pay a premium to sneak onto white lanes and bowl after the establishment closed.[16] By 1939, however, with America becoming the arsenal of democracy in World War II, black Southerners, as part of the Second Great Migration, a mass movement that witnessed nearly two million black people leave the South and migrate to cities in the North and West in search of factory jobs, changed the landscape of the black sporting experience in the North. Although white factory owners and workers worked in tandem to keep blacks out of the factory, those who obtained work had money to spend in their leisure time. The bowling alley became a popular destination, for men and women, because the sport was cheap, lanes were open late, and the establishments were community havens for camaraderie. In 1939, seeing the growing numbers of black bowlers in Detroit, leading black bowling entrepreneurs, including Joe Louis, formed the National Negro Bowling Association (NNBA)—they dropped "Negro" in 1946—to foster national competition among black bowlers. The NBA regulated the rules of the lanes and quickly grew the brand of black bowling. The organization also helped promote the women's game. In 1945, Jack Robinson, president of the NNBA, argued bowling was "definitely here to stay," because women participation continued to increase, and he argued bowling was "no longer frowned upon by the religious fathers because it has been taken from the billiard parlor and cleaned up as a wholesome recreation."[17] In 1947, at a time when seemingly all of the black community had been enamored with Jackie Robinson and Joe Louis, *Ebony* called bowling the top sport in the black community. By that time, 15,000 black men and women participated in the game, black businessmen had built top-notch bowling lanes around the Midwest in cities like Cleveland, Chicago, Columbus, and Detroit, and the black press had special sections in its sports pages on men and women's bowling.[18]

The game had also started to produce black bowling stars like Jack Marshall, who won the NBA championship in 1946 and had his own endorsement deal, and George Bennett, the 1947 champion, who managed Detroit's Paradise Valley, a bowling business built by Joe Louis. According to Bill Matney, of the *Michigan Chronicle*, black champions like Marshall and Bennett had a special duty to represent the race and prepare black bowlers for integration. "Winning the national title is quite a bit more than the word implies," Matney mentioned. He added, "With the rise of Negroes in other fields, bowling, too, has progressed. Today, the representative of the Negro race is in a highly responsible position as a number one bowler in the nation. And he must conduct himself as a true champion every inch of the way."[19] Matney, writing in the language of the politics of respectability, hoped that the black bowler's behavior would break down the barriers of the ABC's bigotry.

More than just a place to celebrate the accomplishments of local bowlers, the black press used its platform and pens to protest racism in the sport. For the black press, defeating the ABC's racist clause was part of the double-victory campaign. As early as 1943, for example, when Cleveland's mayor and the ABC refused to integrate local lanes, Bob Williams, the black sportswriter for the *Cleveland Call*, complained: "All he is interested in is that whites bar Negroes. And we're trying to fight a war to protect groups of people like that, who talk about Democracy!"[20] In 1948, after the ABC refused to strike down its "Caucasian clause" at its national meeting, black writers spared no ink in knocking down ABC's racist policy. While cartoonists drew powerful political cartoons to lament their frustration, black editorialists used their space to shame the lack of democracy. As one black writer complained, "Through its action, the ABC is announcing to the world that it is not interested in the fight for fair play or in making democracy work. They are treating with an inexcusable callousness the very freedom which Americans feel is being challenged throughout the world today. . . . They refuse to learn the lessons of other groups who have allowed the seeds of fascism and oppression to spring up unhampered among them. They don't believe that it can happen."[21] Black writers, however, were not alone in this fight.

In the spirit of double victory, in 1946, in Buffalo, New York, black bowlers mounted their first major challenge to the ABC's color line. To be clear, black bowlers had always protested Jim Crow in some fashion: even the act of bowling was a form a protest; but the Buffalo pickets were the first organized protest to hit the ABC's color line. In March, as the ABC held its annual tournament—its first tournament since the end of the war—black bowlers stood outside in the cold temperatures picketing the tournament with signs that read "End Jimcro in Sports" and "Jimcro Must Go."[22] A spokesman for the group argued, "We have our regular schedule in the American Legion League, yet, because we happen to be Negroes, we are prohibited from participation in this national sports event. If we can bowl in the American Legion League throughout the year, I see no reason why we should be barred from the ABC." As black bowlers picketed the ABC, a white ally stepped up. New York senator James M. Mead (D) had been on his way into the tournament to give a scheduled speech, but when he noticed the pickets, he turned around and joined the protest. Mead claimed, "I have never crossed a Jim Crow picket line." Appalled that the event took place in a state-operated building—New York had an antidiscrimination law—Mead noted, "I am hopeful that the ABC leadership will amend its rules without delay to open the contests to all qualified players. . . . I think action should be taken at once."[23] The ABC, however, took no action. At its annual meeting the following month, leadership decided to table the discussion for another year. While a clear indication that the ABC had no plans to integrate its leagues, this stall tactic also gave protesters another year to prepare for battle. To fight the ABC, white allies formed the NCFPB.

Formed in 1947, the NCFPB constituted a collaborative effort by organized groups who had previously been fighting for integrated bowling on their own accord to come together as one powerful unit. These groups included the United Auto Workers—Congress of Industrial Organization, the Catholic Youth Organization, and B'nai B'rith. As early as 1943, in Cleveland, for example, the Industrial Union Council complained to the mayor that local lanes barred integrated bowling teams and blacks from using its lanes, only to get a dismissive reply from Cleveland's mayor and the vice president of the ABC, John Ackerman, who incorrectly noted that since black bowling leagues barred whites, the ABC would continue its whites-only policy.[24] The following year, in 1944, both the Catholic Youth Organization and the United Auto Workers-Congress of Industrial Organizations adopted official policies protesting the ABC's bigoted bylaws, and by 1947 the UAW-CIO gave the ABC an ultimatum: end racism or end your relationship with the union. Nearly a week after Jackie Robinson made his major league debut, the ABC, however, refused to heed their demand. Finally, in 1947, the leading advocates for integrated bowling, including leadership from the UAW-CIO, the CYO, and B'nai B'rith, met in Chicago and formed the NCFPB. The group tabbed Minneapolis mayor Hubert Humphrey, who had a national reputation as being progressive and pro-labor, as the president, and passed a resolution declaring the ABC's racist practices violated the Fourteenth Amendment. After securing prominent leadership like Humphrey and Walter Reuther of the UAW-CIO, the group set out to battle bowling's bigotry on three fronts. They exerted public pressure on the ABC to integrate, they sponsored a competing bowling league, and they sued the racist ABC for violating the Fourteenth Amendment. Although the NCFPB had support from the black press, the Urban League, and sought legal collaboration from the National Association for the Advancement of Colored People (NAACP), at its core the NCFPB was a white organization.[25]

To fight the ABC, the NCFPB first tried to economically compete with the racist ABC and established its own inclusive bowling tournaments. This, however, was easier said than done. Bowling lanes and leagues had had to have ABC sponsorship, thus giving the racist organization an illegal and state-sanctioned monopoly on the sport. Owners who hosted inclusive tournaments felt immediate retribution from the ABC; thus, for an owner to have a successful inclusive tournament, he or she had to have open-minded patrons, on the one hand, and deep pockets to fight off the ABC's retribution, on the other. One such racially inclusive owner, Herman A. Fenton, operated the successful Dexter Recreation in Detroit and hosted the first international and interracial bowling tournament in 1948. When the ABC attacked Fenton for his fair play—they sent him a letter warning him against running unsanctioned events—he boldly stated, "I'm a member of the B'nai Brith, a national organization that refuses to tolerate any kind of discrimination. I am also a member of ABC. My alleys are sanctioned and there are 14 ABC sanctioned teams rolling in leagues here. But I cannot go along with the discriminatory clause in the ABC constitution. The tournament may be held here."[26] Fenton also predicted that if the ABC did not drop its prejudiced policies, then members of the B'nai B'rith would withdraw from the ABC. The UAW-CIO counseled its members to do the same. The ABC did not budge.

The following month, after Fenton's inclusive tournament, the ABC held its annual meeting, and once again members and leadership refused to strike down segregation. After the ABC's meeting, Walter Reuther, head of the UAW-CIO, argued, "There can be no Joe Louis in bowling. There can be no Jackie Robinson or Jim Thorpe. Every bowling match is 'fixed' in the sense that every ABC bowler is 'protected' against free competition from all comers." Reuther concluded, "ABC is recklessly spending the fund of goodwill it has built up over the years because it stubbornly insists on overstepping the foul line in its approach to non-white bowlers." Reuther also told members of his union and the NCFPB that the organizations had to "conduct a fight to the finish."[27] The following year, in 1949, at the 46th Annual ABC Convention, pleas for prejudice free play, once again, fell on deaf ears. That year, Rev. Charles T. Carow of the Brooklyn CYO argued at the ABC convention that "racial discrimination is not only a violation of the principles of democracy, but it is conflict with the accepted practice of racial equality in law, politics, industry, religion, society, education, and all fields of sport except bowling."[28] Member delegates, however, quickly shot down any chance at fair play when white bowler Frank Gebler, from Chicago, urged, "Bowling today is a good clean sport, so let's go ahead and defeat this proposition."[29] Members followed his lead. To finish the fight for fairness, whites needed more than rhetoric and economic competition; they had to use the law.

In 1949, the NCFPB and its members took their fight to the courts and pushed members to appeal to politicians to end the ABC's legalized racism. The NCFPB's legal counsel understood that every Northern state had antidiscrimination clauses that should have made the ABC's policies illegal. If states allowed the ABC to operate with a "whites-only" clause, then these same states sanctioned segregation. The tactic to get states to fight the ABC worked. By 1950, New York, Wisconsin, Michigan, Ohio, and Illinois—these states had some of the highest memberships—had sued the ABC for violating antidiscrimination laws. Illinois, in fact, had successfully won its legal case and fined the ABC $2,500 for violating the state's antidiscrimination law. Other states also made the same case. The racial barriers were coming down.

At their 1950 annual meeting in May, facing the realization of losing their license in a number of states, ABC leaders and members revoked their whites-only clause. Upon hearing this news, a black writer for the *Los Angeles Sentinel* praised, "The American Bowling Congress has done under fire what it should have done voluntarily a decade ago: it has erased the color ban from its constitution. Here again is a situation in which men of goodwill have been forced to spend much in time and effort that might have been put to more constructive use had not a few die hards clung to a Jim Crow rule that serves no useful purpose."[30] The fight was finally over. The only question remaining was, after years of playing on inferior lanes, could the black bowling compete with whites?

Very quickly, the bowling community found out that black bowlers had the talent to compete. In an article celebrating the centennial of the Emancipation Proclamation, Ormond Curl, the black bowling writer for the *Michigan Chronicle*, proclaimed, "Since the racial barrier has been dropped, many Negro bowlers have gone on to achieve great fame."[31] In 1951, the first year that blacks were allowed to play in the new integrated ABC, a black team from Detroit, bowling for Allen and Son's Supermarket, competed in annual ABC tournaments. After a first round of jitters, the team featuring local luminaries Maurice Kilgore, Bill Rhodman, Clarence Williams, and George Williams played their game and finished in the money winning $750. Rhodman, the most celebrated black bowler in the early 1950s, was the first to place in the money as an individual in an ABC tournament.[32]

The next question that needed answering revolved around television. When would bowling programs on television show black bowlers? For blacks, this moment did not come until 1958, when Detroit bowler Maurice Kilgore, who learned how to roll on Joe Louis's Paradise Valley Lanes, was featured in a competition in Chicago. Although he did not win, his prowess, and coolness, marked a major step for black bowlers. According to Curl, Kilgore's showing "was an accomplishment for our race due to the fact that this was the first of its kind in the nation, and again because Kilgore performed with grace of a champion in showing those who were able to see this video show that we also are ready for big time bowling."[33]

Although the fight for fairness is not as well documented, black women also had to battle to bowl. Unfortunately, most of the legal and moral battles to end discrimination in bowling were aimed at men's bowling, and although women joined the fight, they did not get the same commitment in return. By the mid-1940s, the sport was black women's favorite and amassed the most participation. In fact, in 1948, a team of black women won the first integrated bowling tournament in Buffalo that the NCFPB hosted. While the NCFPB hosted an integrated tournament, the Women's International Bowling Congress had a "Caucasian-only" clause that was not lifted until 1950.[34] But once the color bar dropped, women like Louise Fulton—the first black woman to win an integrated singles tournament in Philadelphia—and Sadie Dixon, "the female Jackie Robinson of bowling," starred on the lanes. According to black sportswriter Claude Harrison Jr., Dixon had "broken down more barriers than any other women." During the 1950s, Dixon integrated the Bowling Proprietors' Association of America (BPAA), the World Invitational Tournament, and various other local tournaments in the Philadelphia area. Throughout the 1950s and 1960s, while Dixon made her living in the BPAA tournaments, she still played in the NBA tournaments. She indicated, "All of the Negro bowlers, including those yet to turn pro, owe much to the NBA. The NBA gave us something to shoot for when the BPAA classics were out of reach."[35] Despite Dixon's praise of the NBA, most black bowlers stopped paying dues to the NBA and instead joined the ABC. The lack of dues, combined with the loss of tournament players, ultimately led to the demise of the NBA.

Branch Rickey

In the field of sports, no white man gets more credit for integrating sports than Branch Rickey, who, as general manager of the Brooklyn Dodgers, signed Jackie Robinson in 1945. Although prominent black sportswriters helped integrate baseball, as part of the desire to celebrate white allies in the civil rights movement, writers assign Rickey the majority of the glory. Of course, Rickey never missed an opportunity to remind others of his essential role, as he noted on signing day, "No pressure groups had anything to do with it: in fact, I signed him in spite of such groups rather than because of them."[36] In his self-congratulatory role, Rickey noted that he spent nearly two years intensely scouting black players looking for the last untapped talent for his ball club. He even created another black baseball league, the United States League, to maintain his cover so white owners would not grow suspicious of his search for untapped tan talent. For if they did, Rickey believed, his plans would no doubt backfire, as it did for Bill Veeck when he informed Commissioner Kenesaw Mountain Landis of his plans to buy the Philadelphia Phillies and stock the team with black players, only to have Landis orchestrate another deal so an alternative white buyer could buy the team and keep the Phillies lily white. Rickey stayed silent and made history.

Besides the practical reasons for improving his ball club, Rickey also noted that moral reasons swayed him to sign Robinson. He claimed he did so because "I cannot face my God much longer knowing that His black creatures are held separate and distinct from His white creatures in the game that has given me all that I can call my own."[37] "The Mahatma" as sportswriters dubbed him because of his religious convictions, also told the story of Charles Thomas, a black player whom he had coached at Ohio Wesleyan in 1904 who could not stay with his teammates in a Jim Crow Indiana hotel. According to Rickey, he protested the decision until the hotel let Thomas share a room with him. That night, however, Thomas cried throughout the night and openly wished he could change his skin color. Moved by Thomas's tears, Rickey promised himself he would use his power so that other blacks would not have to face the indignities of prejudice. Forty-one years later, signing Robinson constituted a culmination of that self-promise. As Roger Treat, of the *Daily News* (Washington, D.C.), said, Rickey "slapped Jim Crow in the face, broke an un-written law which has endured since the beginning of organized baseball, and opened a new road for several million Americans who have waited long for baseball to start following the creed of America."[38]

Because of the way Rickey positioned himself as a self-congratulatory savior, and because of the importance baseball played in America, a number of writers, both white and black, likened Rickey to Abraham Lincoln, a point that could be congratulatory or criticism depending on who wielded the pen. One of his toughest public critics, W. G. Bramham, president of the minor leagues, mockingly mused, "[African American spiritual leader] Father Divine will have to look to his laurels, for we can expect Rickey Temple to be in the course of construction in Harlem soon." Unsatisfied with this satire, the Southerner, Bramham, also complained, "It is those of the carpet-bagger stripe of the white race under the guise of helping, but in truth using the Negro for their own selfish interests who retard the race."[39]

While resisters ridiculed Rickey as a carpetbagger and mocked his Lincoln-like pretensions, others truly believed that his decision to sign Robinson put him on an even plane with Lincoln. *Look* compared his vow to remedy the race problem to a "young Lincoln" who made the same promise when confronted with slavery.[40] And Jackie Robinson biographer, Arnold Rampersad, offered that for Rickey the Charles Thomas incident "begged comparison to another, lodged in American lore, about Abe Lincoln going down the Mississippi and seeing slavery, and vowing to see it end one day," and that when signing Robinson, "Rickey saw a chance to intervene in the moral history of the nation as Lincoln had done."[41] In the *Montreal Gazette*, the hometown paper for Robinson's new team, appeared a cartoon of Rickey holding the Emancipation Proclamation while looking at Lincoln lauding, "Wonder how I'd look in a stovepipe hat."[42] In 1948, Dan Parker of the *Sporting News* noted, "Any resemblance between Branch Rickey and Abraham Lincoln is purely coincidental. . . . True [Rickey] is given to making addresses, but he modestly disclaims credit for having topped Honest Abe's Gettysburg effort, at least to date."[43] Ten

The first page of a *Look* magazine article titled "A Branch Grows in Brooklyn," 1946. The article includes a photo of Brooklyn Dodgers president Wesley Branch Rickey and a small inset photo of Jackie Robinson. (Library of Congress)

years after Rickey signed Robinson, with the Dodgers and Yankees playing in the 1955 World Series, Ed Rumill, of the *Christian Science Monitor*, reflected, "Abraham Lincoln would have enjoyed this World Series between the Dodgers and the Yankees. . . . It was Branch Rickey, a great admirer of Lincoln, who beat down the discriminatory barrier back in the spring of 1947 and introduced Jackie Robinson to the National League."[44]

Black America heralded Rickey as a hero too. Rickey represented their hope for the future, an open-minded white man in a position of power. After Rickey signed Robinson, Sam Lacy, of the *Baltimore Afro-American*, wired a letter to Rickey, thanking: "Your action is the first time in the long history of organized baseball that the sport has proved it deserves to be classed the 'national pastime.'"[45] While in Arkansas, an editorialist observed the great paradox of the moment: Jackie Robinson had to make the team while living in Jim Crow conditions in Florida, but, still, Rickey gave Robinson a chance to play an integrated game: "It is unfortunate that Robinson, an officer of World War II will not be allowed to enjoy privileges of first class accommodations that he so bravely fought for, as his other teammates when to go in training in the deep sought, but this is just one of the enigmas of American democracy. But, we have to take our hats off to Branch Rickey."[46] In 1946, after Robinson played his first game for Montreal, an editorialist for the *Michigan Chronicle* wrote, "We believe that Branch Rickey deserves some sort of Congressional Medal of Honor also. . . . Jackie and his democratic boss have demonstrated that the time is always ripe for fair play."[47]

After Robinson made his Dodger debut in 1947, the cheers from the black press got louder. One writer applauded, "If ever there was a white man who merited the gratitude of the Negro, Branch Rickey is one."[48] The *St. Louis Argus* applauded, "America owes to you, one of her brilliant sons, a debt of gratitude for the part you are playing in helping make democracy work. In thinking this matter over, we feel like crying from the depths of our soul for more men and women in strategic places, like Branch Rickey, to pen the gate and give every other man and woman an equal opportunity to measure up to their full possibilities."[49] And an editorialist in the *New York Age* cheered, "All honor to Branch Rickey and the Dodgers. All luck to Jackie and more power to those who intend unswervingly to perpetuate the fight for the Negro, in the main stream of American life in sports, politics, social activities and education."[50] David Bethe, of the *Arkansas State Press*, praised, "Rickey's name will be read along with such names as the Rev. Henry Ward Beecher, William Lloyd Garrison, Wendell Phillips and Abe Lincoln."[51] Nearly ten years later—Rickey was working as the general manager for the Pittsburgh Pirates—the

Birmingham World compared him to both Lincoln and Booker T. Washington, and favorably suggested that Booker T. Washington "ventured a great prophesy that has been daily unfolding in visible racial progress. Branch Rickey now comes to another generation to unfold a vision of equality and opportunity."[52] That same year, after hearing Rickey speak at a banquet for black sports fans in Atlanta, Marion E. Jackson wrote: "With Churchillian eloquence Branch Rickey, the Abe Lincoln of Baseball gave the 'Sports sermon on the Mount,' . . . His moving, stirring and dramatic pronouncements, anchored in historic fact, and provocative in context, probed the deeply entrenched stereotypes and myths of our times and dynamited them with unshakable fact."[53] And nobody appreciated Rickey more than Robinson, who claimed in 1961 that "for the people of my race, this was a heroic saga, and I was the hero. For years it was my name that was in the headlines, but the real hero of the story was Branch Rickey. . . . He did more for the Negroes than any other white man since Abraham Lincoln. He helped bring about a new national outlook on race relations."[54] Rickey, the great emancipator, broke the first chain of the gentleman's agreement.

Bill Veeck

When Jackie Robinson made his Dodgers debut in April 1947, black Clevelanders turned their attention to Indians' owner Bill Veeck. Veeck, who had previously tried to buy the Philadelphia Phillies and stock them with black talent, was seemingly the perfect man to integrate baseball in Cleveland. As the Indians' owner, he even hired a black press release man, promoter Louis Jones, to prep black Clevelanders for a potential black player. He also promised Cleveland fans a winning team and claimed he would sign the best talent available. For black fans, this meant scouting the Negro Leagues and signing young talented players like Sam Jethroe, Monte Irvin, or Doby. But as of April 1947, Veeck still had not integrated his club. Taking Veeck to task for his unwillingness to sign a black player, Cleveland Jackson, of the *Cleveland Call*, lamented, "A number of Negro sports figures including your scribe had heard Veeck say that he has no objections to hiring a Negro Player. Usually he qualifies such statements with the remark that such a player would have to be the finest possible type."[55]

What did the "finest type" mean? In a broader context of economic integration, it meant that the black man who would potentially take a white man's job had to be clearly better than that white man, whether he worked in the factory or the infield. He also had to have proper character.

But the prevailing feeling among white fans, owners, and players, including famed Indian pitcher Bob Feller, was that no such black man existed. Feller, like a number of white players and writers, never hesitated to belittle black ball players. Jackson complained, "When top flight players like Feller make such foolish remarks spontaneously, it is easy to see why so many high baseball figures carry distinct attitudes about Negro players." He urged, "The petty jealousies of little men have no place in the analogs of big jobs well done." Instead of listening to white naysayers, Jackson implored Veeck "to show 125,000 greater Cleveland Negroes and 13,000,000 American Negroes (most of whom are in American league cities) that he has the right sort of sporting blood when the blue chips are down."[56] But a month later, Veeck made matters worse when he chastised Robinson's play and claimed he was not ready for the big leagues. "It would be better for interracial relations," Veeck assured, "were he either to fail miserably or to be an outstandingly brilliant performer." But Veeck had not witnessed Robinson play; he had only heard complaints from Cleveland's white sportswriters. If Veeck harbored these sentiments based on white media accounts, then so would other whites, derailing the process of integration. "It appears therefore," the black writer C. L. Peoples argued, "that Veeck is doing the Negro lad a grave injustice when he makes such remarks without giving the lad a fair chance to prove his true ability."[57] After hearing Veeck's vitriol, Cleveland Jackson sent Veeck a letter imploring him to scout Doby, a good, respectable black player.

On July 3, Veeck made history and signed Doby, making him the first black player in the American League. In language characteristic of post–World War II American democracy that tried to wipe away a racist past and instead focus on character and not color, Veeck told the press, "I don't think any man who has the ability should be barred from major league baseball on account of color." In similar sentiments, Indians player/manager Lou Boudreau wrote, "Creed, race or color are not factors in baseball success, whether it be in the major or minor leagues. Ability and character are the only factors."[58] These democratic feelings were not lost on local legislators. After wrapping up a meeting about future Fair Employment Practice Committee legislation in the city, Cleveland's City Council "moved that the body send a letter to Bill Veeck for his recent acquisition of Larry Doby."[59] An editorial in the *Cleveland Call* read, "Bill Veeck is both a real American and a good businessman. We owe him much for his forthright action in the Doby transaction."[60] But, equally as important, Veeck's commitment to integration went beyond the ball field.

Although some saw Doby's signing as a publicity stunt—the sports editor for the *California Eagle* ridiculed Veeck for the month of July—most black writers continued to treat Veeck as a hero in the community, because not only was Veeck the first owner in the American Leagues to sign a black player, but he continued to integrate his team with more black talent, like the legendary Satchel Paige, and the Indians remained a favorite team in the black community. Most important, Veeck used his position in baseball, and the clout he earned from being an integrationist, to champion civil rights.[61] Bill Matney of the *Michigan Chronicle* once wrote, "I found him to be a man who will not hedge when discussing the question of Negro baseball players in the major leagues—and for that matter—Negroes and the entire problem of equal rights and first class citizenship. Bill Veeck impressed me as a believing a man's a man, regardless of all else."[62] In 1948, for example, after a white fan complained in the local press that too many black fans were attending Indian games, Veeck published an open letter in the *Plain Dealer* about the importance of merit and being colorblind. He told the naysayer, and others who had a problem with Doby, that "the pigment of one's skin or the method in which one worshipped had nothing to do with his ability as a player" and that Doby had a chance to be an excellent baseball player and "neither you nor anyone else has a right to deprive him of his opportunity." He closed his letter suggesting: "I don't believe this lecture will convince you of anything, for intolerance is in some cases, almost a disease. Just ponder for a minute, however that it was none of your choosing that you are whatever color you may be."[63] Every team he owned, Veeck carried this attitude with him and always signed black players.

Throughout his career, whether he was with the Indians, the St. Louis Browns, or the Chicago White Sox, the black press continuously celebrated Veeck for his persistent stance against baseball's prejudice. When he was with the Browns, for example, the *Argus* applauded: "Mr. Veeck may or may not know it, but the stand he has taken in hiring ball players on merit, has had a tremendous effect upon human relations here. It has been a favorable effect as evidence in the interracial harmony that was seen Monday night, when white and black sang the 'Star Spangled Banner,' cheered and applauded that symbol that was Satchel Paige." First and foremost, Veeck brought in black talent to win ball games, but he also believed his black players could change racial relations. That night in July 1952, the community of St. Louis, led by the Browns and the city's Interracial Committee, celebrated the legendary Satchel Paige and the goodwill he brought to the city. In short, Paige was the celebrated black figure in a city notorious for segregation. He won games and stood as a race symbol of progress, but he did not rock the boat. For that, Walter Wagner, the executive director of the Metropolitan Church Federation, gave Paige a letter that read, "Your noble example of sportsmanship and good citizenship are giving the world an example of the best way to build democracy. In so doing, you are giving the best gift of all. God bless you."[64] The city had Veeck to thank for bringing a black man to help create a bridge of goodwill in the segregated Gateway City.

Moreover, whether writing for *Ebony* or *Negro Digest*, Veeck pushed the boundaries of what was deemed acceptable for many white people in sports, and he challenged Americans about race. In an article in *Negro Digest* about so-called black domination in sports, in 1966, he observed:

> The white players are aware, if only subconsciously, that what is really bugging [t]he Negro are the conditions that have been imposed upon him as a Negro. Human nature being what it is, their reaction is to turn the situation completely around. Since his moodiness arises out of the fact of his being a Negro, then it becomes a simple matter for the white player to tell himself that is the natural result of his being a Negro. Sure, he thinks to himself, all of them are like that. It is far more comforting, we can all agree to blame him and his race than to blame us and our race.[65]

In the end, although Veeck did not receive the Lincoln-like lauding reserved for Rickey, black Americans still recognized his proper place in the realm of sports and civil rights.

Paul Brown

To be sure, in Cleveland, Veeck followed the lead of another ally, Paul Brown, who integrated the newly formed All-American Football Conference in 1946 when he signed "Sepia" stalwarts Bill Willis and Marion Motley to the Cleveland Browns. As the white sportswriter Hy Turkin put it in 1948, the "hero," who gave Jim Crow the boot, was a "'Brown' man who is a white man," who also was a "rabid foe of racial discrimination."[66] Gordon Cobbledick, the local sportswriter for the *Cleveland Plain Dealer*, argued that Veeck and Brown did "more to break down the ancient racial barriers than any of the social groups that pay lip service to tolerance but do nothing about it."[67] Or as one black writer urged, "The Cleveland Browns are not only the all-time champions in the victory column but qualify as a hall of fame choice in professional football's democracy league."[68] While other teams in the new football conference had no plans on breaking the color bar, Brown, who had coached black players as a high school coach in Massillon, Ohio, at Ohio State, and coached the integrated football team at the Great Lakes Navy Academy during World War II, professed to having no prejudices—he famously said he would field a team of 11 black players if they would help him win the most games.[69]

When Brown agreed to coach the newly formed Browns in 1946—many speculated he left Ohio State because he disagreed with the Big Ten's racial quota system that allowed only one black player on a squad—he informed other teams that he planned to give black players a chance and warned that if teams or other players did not like it, they could go to the National Football League (NFL). Before the season, Brown called Willis, whom he coached at Ohio State, and Motley, whom he coached at Great Lakes, and asked them to try out for the team. The two standouts easily made the squad. During the season, Brown said, "The color of a player means nothing to me. It never has and never will. Motley and Willis are two players who are part of my team, a team whose greatest asset is its team spirit. They're good ball players, both gentlemen, and fit perfectly into the organization. That they are colored is something that doesn't enter into the picture."[70] Beyond just making the team, writers selected Willis and Motley to the all-league squad. Most important, the Browns won the championship, prompting six of the seven teams in the league to sign black players. The following year, Brown signed another black player, Horace Gilliam, the extraordinary fullback and punter. In 1947, all but one team in the All American Football Conference (AAFC) had a black player.

Brown's success, both in the AAFC and the NFL, after the Browns joined the league in 1950, made him a hero of democracy and proof that integration could work in the workforce. In 1956, black writer William "Sheep" Jackson recalled, "In the many office conferences I have had with Coach Brown the one statement that always sticks in my mind: 'I'm interested in football talent, not the pigmentation of a player's skin.'" His star quarterback Otto Graham argued, "The Browns will always be champions because they are not interested in a players' nationality, but only as a player."[71] Looking back at Brown's career, in 1963—the Browns had just fired Brown—black writer Al Dunmore called Brown a "Grid Abolitionist" and reasoned "Brown abolished the color line because he knew Negro players could handle assignments better than any white player he knew. . . . Remember him also as the man who did more to abolish the color line in football at the collegiate, service and professional level than any other individual in the history of the game."[72] An editorialist for the *Cleveland Call* concluded, "The Browns and their superb coach, Paul Brown, have done much more than provide thrilling football for the fans of the cities included in the youth All-America conference. It has set an example in fair employment practices that should give some of our deaf-and-dumb legislators cause for reflection."[73] Rick Hurt, of the *People's Voice* wrote, "Brown is a quiet, determined individual not to be influenced by the pressure of the bigots."[74] To be sure, the idea that Brown just wanted to win with the best players gave the black community hope of a brighter economic future.

While Brown is celebrated as a white ally, an equivalent does not exist in the NFL, despite the fact that in 1946 the Los Angeles Rams signed Kenny Washington, four months before Brown signed Motley and Willis. In the case of the NFL, the black community had to put political pressure on the Los Angeles Rams' owner, Daniel F. Reeves, and general manager, Charles F. Walsh, to sign their black players. In fact, when the NFL originally opened in 1920, the league did not have a color bar, and great black stars like All-Americans Fritz Pollard and Paul Robeson starred. But in the 1930s, league owners followed the path of baseball and decided on a "Gentleman's Agreement" to bar black players. Hypocritically, however, NFL owners allowed their teams to play league-sanctioned integrated games against college all-star teams. Prior to a game between the Cleveland Rams and an integrated college all-star team in 1941, the black writer Al Sweeney complained, "Somehow we can't get worked up over this grid battle, which usually heralds the beginning of the season for our favorite sport—football. Why we can't effervesce over with unbounded enthusiasm is because of the vicious Jim Crow that is practiced by the Pro League." Sweeney suggested that the best way to break the color line was to "drum up a 'March on Washington' and have the president issue a proclamation on the situation."[75] That protest, however, never materialized, and the NFL remained lily white until 1946 when the Rams moved to Los Angeles to avoid economic competition with the Browns.

When the Rams arrived, the local Los Angeles black community, led by the *Los Angeles Tribune*'s Halley Harding, sprang into action. The Rams wanted to play home games at the famed Coliseum, a public stadium controlled by public officials of the Coliseum Commission, but black leaders protested that if the Rams maintained a color bar then they should not be allowed to use the public facility. If the Rams wanted to use the stadium, Harding argued, they had to prove in good faith they were giving black players a fair tryout. In order to use the stadium, in January 1946, the Rams allowed ex-UCLA star Kenny Washington, who was playing semi-pro ball for the Hollywood Bears, to tryout. In April, the Rams signed Washington and ex-UCLA teammate Woody Strode.[76] The local black community showed up in droves to celebrate their players, but a year later, the joy in the black community had left. The Rams rarely used Washington and Strode, and despite the fact that other teams followed their lead—the local Los Angeles Dons of the AAFC signed four black players after the black community boycotted their games the previous year—the Rams did not sign another black star, prompting A. O. Prince of the *California Eagle* to charge that the Rams signed the two black players to attract black fans and complained, "The Cleveland Browns, unlike their [football] counterparts, are more like the Brooklyn Dodgers since they placed Motley and Willis on their squad with the idea that it would better the team."[77] Emphasizing Brown and his desire to place merit over race helps align the story of the Browns, and professional football, with the American myths we like to tell about merit and democracy.

College Sports

As professional baseball and football slowly shifted toward a more democratic sporting space, so too did college athletics. In his sports review for 1946, Joel W. Smith, of the *Atlanta Daily World*, celebrated, "The 'jim crow' in sports was given a staggering blow in 1946. . . . To make a long story short, it seems that at long last, the athletic officials and players of Northern institutions are getting 'fed up' with the out-moded Southern traditions."[78] As historian Charles H. Martin notes, "The Second World War represented the turning point in this revolution in northern athletic policy. The democratic values that the United States repeatedly stressed in its wartime appeals, the contributions made by minorities to the war effort, and the shocking disclosure of the depths of the Holocaust exerted a powerful impact on racial attitudes in the North, especially on college campuses."[79] More specifically, white administrators, coaches, and players started a slow battle against the Gentleman's Agreement, a corrupt bargain in which Northern schools agreed to withhold their black players from competition in the South and if necessary—it was usually the case that the Southern team requested this—they would keep their Sepia stars from playing in their Northern home games. But as white GI's entered college to play sports, many of the white Northern veterans brought the democratic ideas of the war with them and took a stand against the Gentleman's Agreement. As Cleveland Jackson of the *Cleveland Call and Post* noted, "For Negro athletes the backing of the armed forces has been a springboard for heretofore impossible opportunities. With GI backing, sepia athletes, for the first time in the history of the race, have been able to pick their college and follow their hearts in their own line of endeavor."[80] If Southern teams wanted to play Northern teams, and reap the financial profits from these games, they would have to play integrated competitions or not play at all. Of course, some Northern schools still acquiesced to the South, but by 1950, most Northern schools had integrated and refused to segregate their black stars. While looking at every sporting battle against segregation is beyond the scope of this book, it is important to view the first few years after the war as a watershed moment of both white tolerance and black resistance to racism that would foreshadow the civil rights movement.

With more black players integrating teams, the black press recognized the importance of having white allies in college sporting spaces. White players could protect their black teammates from physical harm, and equally as important, by their actions, white allies proved that the American youth would push for great equality. After the 1947 Rose Bowl that featured star black player Buddy Young of Illinois, an editorial for the *People's Voice* proclaimed, "So it can be—and will be—in the broader struggle for a free and secure America. The progressive white and Negro masses, fighting together in firm unity, can achieve, here in America, the greatest victory for democracy our world has ever known."[81] The message was clear: if white schools accepted black athletes on their teams, then they also had to accept the responsibility of democracy, and soon, the black press hoped, democracy would be extended beyond sports.

In college sports, 1946 was a watershed moment for rejecting racism. One of the most celebrated blocks occurred on the basketball court. On December 23, 1946, "Chick" Davies, the white head basketball coach of Duquesne, joined the short list of celebrated white coaches when he refused to concede to the Gentleman's Agreement. On that night, his team, led by their star black player, Charles "Chuck" Cooper, a World War II Veteran, was scheduled to take on the Tennessee Volunteers, but the Tennessee coach, John Mauer, wanted assurance that Cooper would not play, for Mauer, hiding behind his Southern pride, argued that since all of his players resided in the South, playing against Cooper would become an embarrassment for them when they had to go back home. At first, Coach Davies tried to negotiate and offered that Cooper would not start, and only play if the team needed him, but that concession still was not enough for the opposing coach. Angered, Davies told the coach to play an integrated game and get paid, or forfeit the game, take the loss, and go home without payment for a game. The Tennessee coach chose the latter. After the cancellation, a Duquesne official publicly rejected prejudice and told the press that the school would not allow discrimination and that "principle of the entire matter means more to us than a mere basketball game." Summarizing the meaning of the moment as it resonated with black America, Cleveland Jackson wrote, "To 15,000,000 American Negroes, the Dukes proved their right to the sports hall of fame early in the season," and that the team "combining excellent natural ability with a fine sense of team loyalty, they presented that rare sports accomplishment, a really great team."[82] The moment gave black writer Bill Matney hope for the time when Southern teams would "go ahead and play basketball like clean, college boys should." Matney also applauded Davies and Duquesne and determined "the blow struck by 'Chick' Davies and Duquesne University resounded throughout the sports world, and notorious Mr. Jim Crow is pulling himself to his feet after being floored by this unexpected blow to the solar plexus."[83] In the *St. Louis Argus*, its editorialist complained: "It looks to us that there are still in this country people so blind, so foolish, so ignorant as to allow a thing like that to rob them of all the real blessings and genuine pleasure this life affords." The writer also noted that it was the "Southern boys" and not Cooper who were "hurt" by this incident. He added the incident "shows very plainly that only those who are free from race prejudice are free indeed."[84] But, to be clear, if freedom meant to be free from race prejudice, there were still plenty of white men, even at Northern schools, who were not truly free. Race prejudice continued to blind them.

Duquesne's demonstration that day mirrored that of another school in Pennsylvania, Penn State. In one of the first major moves of solidarity against segregation, in November 1946, Penn State canceled a scheduled football game against the University of Miami. The two teams had scheduled to play each other for their final game of the season in Miami, but Miami insisted that Penn State's two black players, Wallace Triplett and Dennis Hoggard, could not play because their participation would violate the local Jim Crow laws. When word of this prejudice got back to the white Penn State players and students, they protested this action and demanded that their school avoid acquiescing to Jim Crow. One student wrote, "We at Penn State realize that there is only one way to play football—the democratic way. Either all of our players should participate—or none." He continued, "The ideals of Democracy are more important than any football game."[85] But the democratic spirit did not stop in Penn State; it traveled down to Miami where a student writing for the school newspaper and several faculty members protested the action. Two white professors turned in their season tickets and refused to attend any more games, while English professor James W. Hoffman resigned. Hoffman, the managing editor of *The Week*, a popular weekly paper in Miami, wrote a scathing editorial about Miami's Jim Crow policies. Unfortunately for Hoffman, his newspaper, after receiving pressure from the school, refused to publish his editorial. Hoffman rejected this censorship and resigned. He told a *Pittsburgh Courier* representative, "Those who want to halt this process of equalization hide behind the convenient verbal fence of tradition. But traditions change, and so do people, and the ones who don't or won't realize this are ostriches with their heads in the Miami sands." Likewise, in a less publicized rejection of Southern prejudice, Syracuse University, whose team did not even have a black player, rejected Miami's offer to replace Penn State. An editorial in its school newspaper, the *Syracuse Daily Orange*, critiqued, "Unless Miami changes its athletic policy it would be better for all concerned if they dropped from the realm of college athletes."[86] But not all Northern teams had the necessary fortitude to defeat discrimination.

As long as Northern teams willingly accepted Miami's prejudice, Miami could maintain its intolerant traditions. While Penn State and Syracuse took a stand against segregation in Miami, other teams obliged. That year, Paul Brown, the great white ally of the Cleveland Browns, left his two star black players, Motley and Willis, home when the team traveled to play Miami in a December game. And after Penn State and Syracuse scorned segregation, another Northern school, the University of Detroit, willingly accepted. Detroit, a team that started out the season with a black player, Guy Brown, did not have to worry about their black player when they played Miami, because the school expelled Brown after he was charged with rape in August. Furthermore, Detroit's athletic director argued that playing Southern teams improved race relations, because it allowed Northern teams to teach the Southerners a lesson about fair play. Reportedly, after Detroit became a last-minute replacement, only two students complained, and the student newspaper did not write about the venture into the Jim Crow South. Surprisingly, Detroit's loudest critics came from students at the University of Michigan who protested in their paper and also traveled to Detroit to protest the administrators. In Michigan's school newspaper, an editorial denounced Detroit and discrimination, declaring, "America football and southern tradition do not mix."[87]

Because white administrators acquiesced to Miami's Jim Crow, black athletes and activists had to blow down the racial barriers in Miami. In 1956, for example, local golfers successfully forced the city to integrate the municipal course, and when the city tried to renege on their rights, the golfers took the city to court. In 1957, a state judge ordered the golf clubs to desegregate. In 1961, in his championship match with Ingermar Johansson in Miami, heavyweight champion Floyd Patterson forced the local promoters to sign a $10,000 bond guaranteeing integrated seats stipulating that if the company segregated black fans, or Patterson sensed a hint of prejudice, the fight would be off and the $10,000 would go the NAACP.[88] Of Patterson's civil rights victory with the stadium and his move to donate his fight money to the NAACP, L.I. Brockenbury of the *Los Angeles Sentinel* commented, "when it was announced Tuesday that Floyd is sending his personal check to the NAACP for $10,000 I had to put him down even ahead of my favorite—Jackie Robinson—for his doings on behalf of the race."[89] Black fans had no problems finding seats, and after the first round—Johansson knocked down the champion twice in the first—Patterson's fists found no resistance either, and he stopped the challenger in the sixth round. By the following year, 1962, according to Jackie Robinson, Jim Crow in Miami sporting events had been stopped. That year, in one of his weekly columns, Robinson touted the improved race relations in the city. In his article entitled "New Respect for the Negro," Robinson told his readership about how fair the city treated him and other black celebrities, including Althea Gibson and Ralph Metcalfe, at their annual black celebrity golf tournament. According to Robinson, city leaders realized that if they wanted black tourist dollars, they had to treat blacks better. And in a 1965 article entitled "Its Changing Racial Attitude May Make Miami 'Your Ami' Too!" Robinson again celebrated the city's change in race relations and noted "It's a good feeling to know you are being accepted, not because of awards and trophies and membership in the Hall of Fame, but in spite of these things; accepted because some folks who didn't know it before are beginning to realize that the Declaration of Independence was not written to be mocked, the Constitution not framed to be ripped apart and the Golden Rule not created to be scorned."[90] Of course, blacks living in segregated sections of Miami and still facing the daily indignities of racism would have disagreed with Robinson.

In the North, moreover, black activists also had to push whites into being allies against discrimination in sports. Back in 1946, ironically, while the University of Michigan students protested the University of Detroit's decision to play in Miami, they did not publicly complain when their in-state rival, Michigan State, sat their star halfback, Horace Smith, in a home game against Mississippi State. In fact, white students, coaches, administrators, and the white press remained silent toward segregation in Lansing. Without any resistance to racism in the Mississippi game, the school also forced Smith to stay home while the team traveled to Lexington for a game against Kentucky. Bill Matney, of the *Michigan Chronicle*, complained, "Such action must certainly have destroyed a great deal of Smith's trust and confidence in his coach and school. . . . For rather than cancel the game or even lodge a protest against the existing southern custom, Bachman and his boys took the easier and most obvious way out by claiming that Smith was suffering from a recurrence of an old injury." Smith was not hurt. He was sidelined by segregation.[91]

The following year, once again, Michigan State punted on racism rather than tackle intolerance and sat Smith again against Mississippi State. When questioned by the *Michigan Chronicle* about the football team's actions, athletic director Ralph H. Young claimed, "Horace is a good boy and we are very proud of him. But whether he plays or not will be determined by the coach."[92] If Michigan State was going to change its ways, Michigan's black community would have to teach the school a lesson. Led by the *Michigan Chronicle*, the black press, black business leaders, and Detroit's NAACP branch petitioned the school and protested to the governor about MSU's (Michigan State University's) racial bias, forcing the state senate to investigate the matter. For the *Chronicle*, the fight for integration was "waged on the highest principles of sportsmanship and democratic democracy."[93] An editorial in the *Chronicle* noted that other college teams had refused to surrender to Southern segregation, but not so with MSU. "Time and again," he said, "we have railed against the ugly practice, and yet our tax-supported State College persists in flouting in the face of Negroes this example of outright discrimination. . . . Michigan State is not only paying deference to the 'white supremacy' myth, it is also out of step with colleges of similar rank and importance."[94] Black sportswriter Russ Cowans contested, "No longer are the school heads willing to make a courageous stand against the racial prejudices of southern institutions of learning. Instead, they're taking the line of least resistance—bowing to the southern gentleman." For Cowans, "what hurt the most," he claimed, was the lack of white students' support for Smith who matriculated to Michigan State because "[Smith] believed the spirit of democracy prevailed there." But Smith "discovered that the tentacles of racial bigotry can clutch him in East Lansing just as tightly as they can in Mississippi."[95]

In the end, shaming State for their role in upholding segregation worked. That season, in a home game against Kentucky, Smith played. "Yes, Smith played against University of Kentucky—and nothing happened. The stadium didn't shake and quake. . . . Kentucky players didn't walk off the field—everyone played football, and forgot about a Negro playing against a southern team."[96] After MSU reversed its policy, the *Chronicle* celebrated that State "joined the ranks of the great colleges of the land which practice the democracy which students in the classrooms are taught."[97] In fact, from that moment on, Michigan State coaches made a concerted effort to recruit black players. The team had so many black players by the 1960s, in fact, that the *Michigan Chronicle* claimed their coach, Duffy, should have won an NAACP award.

In 1947, other schools and their white students joined Michigan State in their refusal to bow to Jim Crow. At the University of Nebraska white students voted to withdraw from the Big Six Conference until Oklahoma and Missouri abolished their Jim Crow teams, and Ohio Wesleyan—Branch Rickey put public pressure on them—cancelled a game against Rollins College of Florida because they could not play their black player. In the most celebrated moment of democracy, Penn State made a decision that would have a lasting impact on Jim Crow in sports. At the end of the season, the board of the Cotton Bowl game in Dallas, Texas, invited Penn State to play in the annual tilt on New Year's Day, 1948, against Southern Methodist University (SMU). Penn State, however, refused to play in the game if their two star players, Triplett and Hoggard, could not play with the team and stay with the team. Without Penn State, the Cotton Bowl would miss an opportunity to pit two of the nation's best teams, one Southern and one Northern, against each other. Placing revenue over racism, the Cotton Bowl made sure the two men played. The largest crowd in Cotton Bowl history to that point witnessed a wonderfully played 13–13 tie between Penn State and SMU. In encapsulating the meaning of this game, a black writer applauded the white Cotton Bowl officials, school administrators, and white players, reflecting, "This was more than another intersectional game, more than another splendid instance of bi-racial patter of sports activities in the South . . . it was a heartening demonstration of the ability of the deeply entrenched South to recognize and, even if dictated only by expediency, to abide by the finest tenets of American sportsmanship."[98] Indeed, this game changed the trajectory of sports and discrimination in Dallas.

Because of the success of the Penn State–SMU Cotton Bowl game, Dallas was the first major Southern city to fully integrate sports, making the city a model of the potential hope for white support of integration in the South. In 1952, the city integrated its golf course and allowed blacks to compete in a tournament for the first time, fans cheered the integration of its minor league baseball team that featured stalwart prospect pitcher Dave Hoskins, and crowds celebrated the settlement of their new profession football team, the Dallas Texans, who moved from New York with three black stars—Buddy Young, George Taliaferro, and Sherman Howard. When the Yankees football team—unaffiliated with the more famous baseball team—moved from New York, naturally outside onlookers worried that Jim Crow would become a nuisance, but ownership quickly shut down that notion. As one owner told the press, "I foresee no difficulties in using Negro players."[99] Head Coach Jimmy Phelan, who previously coached Taliaferro on the Los Angeles Dons of the AAFC, noted, "Trade the colored boys and you'll have no offense." Coach Phelan, whom the black press portrayed as a white ally, also reassured, "I don't give a damn whether they're black or white. I'm interested a hellova [*sic*] lot in the way they play football."[100] Although the team could not enforce integrated seating in the Cotton Bowl—state law still mandated segregated seating—owners made sure blacks fans had at least 7,800 seats available. White ownership also helped the football players find housing—albeit segregated housing. While Taliaferro decided to keep his house in Los Angeles, Young and his wife bought a home in the black section of town. Young even discussed a permanent move and potential business deals. In an article entitled "Texans Like Negro Grid Stars," *Ebony* celebrated this breakthrough by highlighting the ease with which integration occurred and the respect the two men received from white coaches, teammates, and fans.[101]

The elusive runner, Young, perhaps the best of his generation, an athletic hero in the black community since World War II, and noted by Coach Phelan as the first showman in football—a term celebrating Young's agility and jaw-dropping breakaway speed—at first held out racial reservations about the move, but understood his position as a racial pioneer for integration. As one of the first post–World War II football stars, both in college and the pros, Young was used to having the racial spotlight on him, his play on the field, and demeanor off the field, and helped pave the way for others, especially whites, to feel comfortable with integration. Born poor on the Southside of Chicago, the fleet-footed running back swerved past the issue of race like he did defenders. In an interview, he noted, "Playing in Dallas will be like playing in any other city, I imagine. . . . The fans are interested in a winning team, and I hope I can make a contribution toward helping that situation develop." He understood the impact his play and his words about race had on the black community. In another interview, he called the team owner a "prince of a fellow" and a "fair-minded, square shooter." The white fans, he urged, cared only about winning and not race, and his coach was "one of the finest men I've ever met in football." Besides, Buddy had been there before. The black writer Bill Matney reflected, "Buddy developed friendships among players on opposing teams, regardless of race or geographic origin."[102] And Young told *Ebony*, "I've had a lot of fine experiences with southern football players, especially Texans."[103] One of these incidents played a significant role in the mythmaking of meritocracy and whites. According to the legend, while Young played on the integrated Fleet City Naval Base team during World War II, his white opponents on the El Toro Marines piled on Young and tried to hurt him after he got two long touchdowns. To add extra insult, a white opponent yelled, "I'm gonna tear your head off, you little Nigger." Hearing this insult, "Bruiser" Kindard, a white teammate from Texas, told the El Toro quarterback to run the next play behind him. Bruiser knocked out the defender who called Young a "Nigger." In Dallas, Young became best friends with white teammate, Zollie Toth, a fullback from Louisiana, who became the godfather to one of Young's children.[104] But while Buddy publicly made white friends, he also understood that his role as a pioneer on the Southern gridiron was made easier by the success of ace pitcher Dave Hoskins.

By the time Young and Taliaferro toted the ball for the Texans, Hoskins hurled his way into celebrity status, already having his own "Dave Hoskins" day in Dallas, and more important, symbolized successful integration in the South. The Dallas Eagles, a Double A affiliate of the Cleveland Indians, signed Hoskins, the first black player in the Eagles 56-year history, because the millionaire owner Richard W. Burnett wanted a black player. To be sure, while seen as a white ally, Burnett wanted to make money and attract black fans more than he wanted to embrace integration. And his move paid off. In total, an estimated 94,000 fans paid to see Hoskins's first 15 outings. In fact, white fans could not get enough of Hoskins. *Jet* noted, "His story, both from the viewpoint of democratic progress and sports achievement, is one of the season's prizes." The magazine continued, "It is at once the story of a skilled athlete, of baseball's growth as a matured sport and of changing racial attitudes in the South." Hoskins dominated the league, was a unanimous selection in the all-star game, and said all the right things about racial progress in the South. In fact, he told *Jet* magazine that in Texas he received far less racial animosity than he did when he played in Michigan in 1948.[105]

But, in reality, the racial tolerance displayed by whites had its limits. Although he said he received better treatment in Texas than Michigan, Hoskins faced his share of taunts and threats. In Shreveport, Louisiana, city officials tried to bar him from playing, and when that did not work, somebody sent him a death threat. As Hoskins recalled, "I received three letters that morning, one at a time. First one said I'd be shot if a sat in the dugout. Second one said I'd be shot if I went on the field. And the third one said I'd be shot if I took the mound."[106] Hoskins risked his life and played, but at the end of the season, his white manager Dick Burnett received the recognition for being a beacon of democracy. The local YMCA gave Burnett a plaque that read, "The One Who Has Done Most to Improve Race Relations in 1952."[107] It seems it considered Burnett, a Southern man, and his white ally-ship more important than Hoskins's play and fortitude to survive Southern racism. Despite the success Hoskins had, and the white ally-ship of Dallas, there was still work to be done to fully integrate sports. And the heavy lifting would have to come from the black community.

CHAPTER THREE

The Press and the People: The Final Fight for Fairness

In the post–World War II era, in one of the most important battles for civil rights and fair play, the black press fought for equal and fair participation in youth sports. Propelled by the triumph of democracy and the spirit of "double victory," black writers and activists made sure that black youth did not grow up with the same restrictions, indignities, and bitterness the previous generation had experienced. After Jackie Robinson's debut, for example, black sportswriter Arthur Kirk, of the *St. Louis Argus*, where the black high schools did not have baseball fields to play, complained, "If the colored race is going to keep pouring players into the major leagues, then the high school is the place to train them. . . . Are we going to let them close that door in the faces of future ball players or will we train them while they are young so that door will remain open?"[1] The black press understood that if young black athletes could face a sporting world free of injustice, this justice would also transfer to their daily lives. As Charles Loeb, a black World War II journalist, said at a 1946 banquet at Cleveland's Central High, high school sports built leaders for the community. "Players," Loeb lauded, "are like policemen with a special responsibility of leadership, and they are looked upon with deference as above and apart from the general run of students."[2] Sports trained future leaders and also showed black youth they had unlimited potential to succeed in post–World War II America. Thus, creating opportunities for youth to play sports on an equal basis represented an extension of the freedom movement. And the black press would lead this fight.

To be sure, every city had a battle for equal and fair play in youth sports. Black sportswriters believed that if the school received adequate funding, and the kids received a fair chance, this brought hope to the many communities struggling with overcrowded, inadequate housing options. For most black youth across the country, regardless of where they lived, they ran up against some form of Jim Crow. Kids in Cleveland found themselves ousted from bowling leagues; in Detroit youth swimmers faced Jim Crow from segregated public and private swimming clubs—in fact most city kids had to face the unjust discrimination if they wanted to take a dip in the public pool. In the Deep South, most black kids could forget about swimming or playing on adequate fields. Well-kept pools and play areas were strictly for white kids only. When the federal government forced integration of public recreational facilities, some Southern cities closed their pools rather than follow the law.

In St. Louis, the unheralded black sportswriter Arthur Kirk led the crusade to integrate high school sports at the public-school level. In the fall of 1948, right after the London Olympics ended, encouraged by the level of celebratory democracy bestowed on black Olympians, Kirk used his editorial column to challenge the black community to battle with him in his fight with Missouri's Jim Crow athletic board. Black students in St. Louis had to attend overcrowded schools and play in outdated gymnasiums, and most lacked proper outdoor facilities to participate in football and baseball. When a black resident challenged Kirk for turning school funding and integration into a political battle, Kirk called him an "Uncle Tom" and set the letter writer straight, telling him, "The athletes in these schools do not have the opportunity to advance that the white kids have of their age. . . . I merely want to see justice done and civil rights carried out in the schools where it will do the most good."[3] Kirk, who shared the same sentiments as many black writers and activists across the country, believed that if black kids received an equal chance, they "would prove to the world that they are equal." It took some time, but Kirk's main crusade eventually paid dividends in St. Louis. By 1952, the city had integrated all of its high school sports programs and offered integrated championships in baseball and track and field, with a plan to extend integrated championships to football and basketball in the coming seasons. Moreover, the municipal league also integrated its sports, which meant that black champions in these leagues represented the city in state tournaments. Examining the progress that had been made, in 1952 Kirk concluded, "Sports has played a major role in wiping out a large part of the Jim Crow in St. Louis and is still fighting a winning battle on that front."[4] Black youth in St. Louis finally had hope for a future of integration and equality. And they had a black sportswriter to thank.

Like Kirk's battle in St. Louis to provide black youth an equal opportunity to play, black sportswriters played an essential role in breaking down the last racial barriers for black athletes in professional sports. They used their platform in the press, and their ability to tap into the black community, to put pressure on owners and other leaders who refused to integrate. To be sure, while white allies helped the cause, the black press made the complete integration of professional sports possible. As black sportswriter L. I. Brockenbury of the *Los Angeles Sentinel* said in 1959, "The present group of Negro stars are not in the majors just because they can hit a ball or run fast. . . . It's because over the years Negroes, many of whom could play no sports at all, fought and picketed and paid their money to the NAACP and the Urban League and prayed for integration." Brockenbury brilliantly continued, "Without the agitation for fair employment and equal protection of the laws, the Negro players might well still be riding the rickety buses in wet uniforms playing a double header today in Baltimore and another double-header tomorrow in Jacksonville. . . . We forget too easily, but worse than that many never even stop to think about anything except our own comfort for the moment."[5] By examining the last racial barriers to fall in baseball, football, and golf, this chapter highlights the story of black resistance in the press and the community for fair play.

Detroit, Boston, and the Battle to End Baseball's Segregation

When the St. Louis Browns, Brooklyn Dodgers, and Cleveland Indians played black players in 1947, black writers in baseball cities, and black fans around the country, figured their teams were next. Black fans had seen better black ball players than Willard Brown (Browns), Hank Thompson (Browns), Larry Doby (Indians), and Brooklyn's Jackie Robinson. Moreover, the success that Robinson had in 1947, and the skills Doby displayed in 1948, added to the seeming inevitability that teams would quickly sign black talent. But integration, as black America learned, would be a long process as teams stalled trying to avoid the inevitable. And black America swiftly sensed the stall strategies; they smelled the same racial trepidation teams displayed before Robinson broke the color barrier. Thus, when integration did not occur immediately, black writers and fans took the fight to the teams. Unfortunately, this would be a long-fought battle, especially in Detroit and Boston, teams that did not integrate until 1958 and 1959, respectively.

In Detroit, a city that saw a massive influx of black migrants during World War II, and a city that had a strong black sporting tradition, matched by a politically active black community, the push to integrate the

Tigers started the moment the Cleveland Indians signed Larry Doby. In July 1947, Russ Cowans, of the *Michigan Chronicle*, asked Tigers' general manager Billy Evans about their plans to sign black players, and although Evans said they had no plans—over the next three years Evans maintained no interest in black players—Cowans whetted black fans' appetites by telling readers that the team had scouted stalwarts, Sammy Jethroe, Piper Davis, and Goose Tatum, and predicted that once the Tigers signed black stars, attendance would quickly rise, just like it had in Brooklyn, St. Louis, and Cleveland. Cowans surmised, "Detroit is the baseball city in America. The Tigers are always among the top teams in attendance. With a Negro on the team, the Tigers will attract thousands of fans to each game played at Briggs Stadium and on the road." As predicted, when Doby played in Detroit a few weeks later, local black fans showed up in mass to support the barrier breaker. This excitement only increased the speculation for when the Tigers would sign a sepia star. Thus, the following year, after the Indians added pitcher Satchel Paige to their squad, and the Tigers had not signed tan talent, black fans and the black press became agitated. Police arrested black fans who picketed at Briggs Stadium with "placards that denounced the all white policy of the Detroit Tigers," and Cowans ripped the organization in print for their prejudice.[6]

As teams kept signing black players, especially their rivals the Cleveland Indians, the demands from Detroit's black community increased. In 1951, after the Indians' Luke Easter and Larry Doby single-handedly beat the Tigers in a series in April, the *Chronicle* openly wondered if the Tigers were bigoted or just blind to black talent. Bill Matney mused, "Whether the Tiger attitude is actually bigoted in nature or whether the management simply doesn't give a hang about acquiring the BEST available players, regardless of color or eyes, skin or texture of hair, etc., is something no one has been able to ascertain accurately." Matney added that whichever the case, "it is imperative that the Tiger organization change its present attitude, and practice democracy inherent in the game of baseball, something called the national pastime—national, that is, except for Detroit."[7] The following week, however, all speculation went out the door, after the *Chronicle* interviewed Evans on his position on integration. The GM reiterated what he had been telling the *Chronicle* for the past two years and concluded, "I think it would be unreasonable to say that the Tigers would be better if they had Negro players. The Tigers got along many years without Negro players. They won pennants and they stayed at the top. In fact, all teams in the major leagues got along without colored players." Evans also took the standard line that many organizations used when it came to ending segregation; he denied that black talent existed for the taking and asked "Are there any good Negro players now available?"[8]

The continued conversation about the integration of Detroit's baseball team, along with the Tigers' insistence they were not going to hire any black player for the sake of appeasement, curved blacks' critiques about their ultimate aims for inclusion and forced a number of protesters to claim that they wanted integration only if the player was good; they did not want tokenism. In response to this increasing line of thinking from the black community, Roy W. Stephens, an editorialist for the *Michigan Chronicle*, explained the importance of racial representation: "All well-thinking Negroes want representation and will fight for it. We want our representatives—whether they're throwing law books or horsehide—to be well-trained and able. But we also want them to be Negroes."[9] In 1952, after pressure from the black community, continuous losing by the Tigers, and the firing of Billy Evans, the team finally started to scout sepia stars. But this did not produce any professional players. The Tigers' owners, the Briggs family, were racist and refused to integrate. The reality of integration seemed unattainable until 1956, when a new owner bought the team.

When Fred Knorr, a radio executive from Dearborn, Michigan, bought the team in 1956, it renewed black hope in integration, because his new ownership removed what many blacks thought was the main barrier to integration: the Briggs family. Blacks in Detroit, especially baseball fans, knew that Briggs was a racist owner who openly complained about black fans coming to his stadium, and an owner who refused to hire black workers. In fact, when Briggs owned the team, the only black workers at the stadium served in servile positions handing out paper towels in the restrooms. Thus, when the new owner arrived, the headline in the *Chronicle* read, "Question: Will New Owners Change Tiger Policy?" But even with a new owner, Black Detroiters could not help but be wary. Bill Veeck, the man who brought integration to the Cleveland Indians, placed the highest bid to buy the team, and many speculated his liberal baseball hiring policy persuaded the Briggs family to refuse to sell the team to Veeck and instead allowed Knorr to increase his bid.[10] Knorr, who was set to take over the team after the 1956 season, had his work cut out for him, especially considering the fact that prior to the takeover in ownership, the *Michigan Chronicle* ran a five-part series detailing the history of discrimination with the Tigers.[11] In the fourth piece, entitled "Tiger Policy Has Definite Impact on Relations Here," the paper claimed that the Tigers' policy had an impact on the race relations in a city many called a "racial powder keg" waiting to explode. The *Chronicle* claimed, "In this day and age when all Americans are earnestly concerned with making democracy a reality for all, the national sport has seen its responsibility and has taken the lead in many instances." But, the paper added, "The Detroit Tigers, home town team of the Arsenal of Democracy and representative of one of the most dynamic and growing cities in the nation, still insists on a 'bush league' approach to player recruitment. They do themselves and the citizens of the Motor City a dis-service."[12] Despite the fact that the Tigers had a history of exclusion, fans held out hope that the new ownership would do the right thing and integrate. Those optimistic sentiments, however, lasted only a year.

At the beginning of the 1958 season, with Boston and Detroit left as the only two teams to refuse integration—the Phillies had integrated the year before—Black Detroiters were seemingly done with the Tigers. Black writers had been fighting for inclusion, and protesters had been picketing for a decade, and the Tigers still did not budge. The *Chronicle* continued to denounce Detroit's discriminatory policies, including noting that "the area of professional sports is vitally important since it has been through the achievements of athletic excellence that the true meaning of team-work and brotherhood has been most graphically demonstrated to the Free World," and that "the Detroit Baseball Company has not yet adopted a realistic attitude toward its responsibility to all citizens of our city."[13] Letters poured in to the *Chronicle* from black fans about how embarrassed they were to be associated with the city. Instead of simply writing about discrimination, they advocated that black fans boycott the Tigers. But the boycott never came to fruition.

In June 1958, the Tigers finally got with the times. They signed black Dominican infielder Ossie Virgil. Of this long overdue move, Bill Matney wrote, "The great spirit of fair play which has been a basic characteristic of American sports has manifested itself in a way which only American sportsmanship can do." He concluded, "We are happy and proud that one more institution in our community has demonstrated its belief in, and adherence to the principle of equality of opportunity in our democratic way of life."[14] After the team signed Virgil, the Tigers continued to sign black players, including local talent Willie Horton, who played a vital role in helping quell the flames of the 1967 riot and bring a championship the following year to a hurting city. Virgil's signing, moreover, meant that only one team remained segregated in America's pastime, the Boston Red Sox.

Like the Tigers, the racist owners of the Boston Red Sox played a vital role in maintaining a lily-white franchise.

The push to force the Red Sox to integrate America's game was a battle that spanned 24 years that included local politicians, the black and white presses, and the black community looking for racial representation. What made the long-drawn-out fight even more appalling was the fact that the Boston Celtics basketball team fielded a racially integrated team. Even worse for the Red Sox, they had a chance to be the first team to integrate. In 1945, black journalists, Sam Lacy and Wendell Smith, and a local Jewish American politician, Isadore Muchnick, who sat on the city council, forced the Red Sox to hold a tryout of black players Sam Jethroe, Marvin Williams, and Jackie Robinson.

As the initial 1945 tryouts indicated, white allies supported black writers in their quest to integrate the Red Sox. As writer Howard Bryant notes in his book *Shut Out*, Muchnick, a white ally, used his position on the city council to force the millionaire owner Tom Yawkey to give the black players a shot. In Boston, at that time, the city outlawed Sunday baseball unless the city council voted unanimously to let the teams—the Red Sox and the Braves—play on the Sabbath. Since most people did not work on that day, Sunday baseball was a lucrative affair that owners did not want to pass up. Knowing this, Muchnick maintained that he would withhold his vote, unless Yawkey showed an attempt to end segregation. To be clear, Muchnick had already been part of a local fight to democratize the great game. In 1944, for example, he wrote to the team's GM, arguing, "I cannot understand how baseball, which claims to be the national sport and which . . . receives special favors and dispensation from the Federal Government because of alleged moral value can continue a pre-Civil War attitude toward American citizens because of the color of their skin." Muchnick's sharp words mirrored those of local white writer, Dave Egan, of the *Boston Record*, who asked in a 1945 column, "Could we, by chance, spare a thought for the Negro here in the United States? Do we, by any chance, feel disgust at the thought that Negro players, solely because of their color are barred from playing baseball?"[15] But even a popular white writer and a powerful city councilman could not get the Red Sox to budge.

In reality, the Red Sox had no intentions of signing the black players. Though the three men played tremendously in the tryouts in 1945, all three players quickly realized that ownership was insincere in its quest for black talent. If they did not have to sign black players, the Red Sox had no plans on removing their color line. Racism permeated the organization. In fact, a scout refused to give Birmingham native Willie Mays an adequate evaluation, because the white Southern-born scout believed it was beneath his sensibilities to scout a black player. Racism kept the team away from having a stellar lineup with Jackie Robinson, Willie Mays, and Ted Williams. While the Dodgers and Jackie Robinson blazed a new path in baseball, the Red Sox dug in their heels along the same racist path.[16] Something had to give.

In 1959, the Red Sox made another move that showed their insincerity toward ending segregation, when, right before the season started, the team sent down black infielder Pumpsie Green to their Minnesota affiliate in the minor leagues, despite Green hitting nearly .300 and having an impressive spring training for the Red Sox. For black activists in the Boston area, and the black press across the nation, demoting Green instead of ending discrimination sparked another collective fight that would finally end segregation. Local activist organizations, including the National Association for the Advancement of Colored People (NAACP), filed discrimination charges at the Massachusetts Commission against Discrimination. Herbert E. Tucker Jr., head of Boston's NAACP, charged "that what happened to Mr. Green is purely symbolic of a history of discriminatory employment policies by the Red Sox club." As testimony from the Red Sox revealed, in the team's history, they had hired only four black men to work in their concession stands and had only two black men working for them in 1959. And yet, despite the fact that everyone knew the team had a long history of racism, a team representative used the same threadbare lie to avoid more charges of discrimination. During a hearing in front of the Discrimination Board, Richard H. O'Connell, business manager of the team, claimed, "The Boston Red Sox are entirely American. We have no discrimination against race color or creed. We think these charges have been unfair. . . . We think we have a right to manage our own ball club. People from City Hall and the State House don't hire people for us. We hire them." But in the eyes of the NAACP, its stance against the Red Sox was not merely to force them to hire Green; it wanted black men to get a fair chance. As Tucker told the Discrimination Board, "We are opposed to the hiring of any persons because they are Negro. If Pumpsie Green cannot play well enough, don't hire him. But give the Negroes a fair opportunity, the same chance that anyone else would receive."

But Green did not get a fair chance. During the Arizona spring training, the team did not even house Green with the other white players, and when they went barnstorming with the Cubs, Green traveled with black players, like Ernie Banks, from the Cubs instead of his own teammates. How was Green supposed to feel like he was a part of the ball club if he could not sleep and eat with his teammates?[17] The Discrimination Board, however, did not see things the way the NAACP did. In the end, it ruled that the Red Sox, despite never having given black players a fair chance, and only employing four black men in their entire history, did not break any discriminatory laws.

In July, however, roughly a month after the state dropped the charges, and after Green had dominated the minor leagues, collecting 112 hits, including 16 doubles, 3 triples, and 7 home runs, the Red Sox finally called Green up to the majors, ending their history-long drought of segregation.[18] With Boston finally integrated, this left one major professional sports team still segregated—the Washington Redskins.

The Washington Redskins and the Fight for Fairness in Football

That black sportswriters and activists intensified their protest over the Redskins did not come as a surprise, especially in the Washington area. A decade prior to starting their fight to integrate the Redskins, activists and writers, including Edwin B. Henderson, the dean of black sports history, and the local NAACP, led a fight to integrate the Amateur Athletic Union (AAU) boxing in the nation's capital. Although the local AAU professed to have a nondiscriminatory clause, and allowed black boxers to join if they paid their 25 cent fee, the organization persisted in hosting segregated boxing events in the capital. In 1945, during the war, the AAU announced that its annual tournament of champions, where the winners received the right to represent their area in the national Golden Gloves event, would once again bar black boxers, and the *Washington Times* and the *Washington Post* sponsored the event. A black writer, Louis Lautier, tried to get the local boxing commission to drop the color bar by highlighting the inherit discrimination in the event. He argued, "May I remind you that Staff Sergeant Joe Louis, the heavyweight champion of the World and a great credit to his country as well, was a product of boxing tournaments? Had he lived in Washington, he would have been denied an opportunity to compete."[19] This fell on deaf ears.

The next year, while black newspapers across the country were busy fighting the AAU over their segregated track meet in San Antonio, the Committee Against Segregation in Recreation (CASR) and the NAACP took the AAU to court and tried to force integration. Still nothing happened. Instead of planning for the first integrated tournament, the CASR picketed the tournament.[20] In 1947, after protests from black activists, both the *Washington Post* and the *Times-Herald* dropped their sponsorship of the segregated tournament, but, unfortunately, the boxing championships still found a host in the Washington Boy's Club. Once again, CASR picketed the event and this time also included a powerful letter about sports and fair play. Noting that the white fighters had no quarrels fighting black boxers in other cities, the committee argued, "American sport is based on fair play and good sportsmanship. What is fair or good when in city-wide contests in the nation's capital a boy must be white to enter? Such patterns followed by the AAU are leading to a third world war which the boys boxing tonight, as well as those who are barred, will have to fight." They continued to plead with the segregationists, "We hope that each of you will demand democratic sport here in the nation's capital that supposedly exemplifies what is good in a Christian country."[21] After persistent pressure, the following year, 1948, the local AAU hosted its first integrated tournament.

Although integrating the Golden Gloves signaled a step in the right direction, prejudice problems persisted. D.C. lacked integrated indoor facilities, and the AAU hosted its boxing tournament at Uline Arena, with Jim Crow seating. Instead of sitting in indignity, black spectators boycotted the event. Edwin B. Henderson, who advocated for the boycott, wrote about the continued problems in an article entitled "Democracy in Sports Beneficial to All" and argued that integrated sports would eventually bring racial barriers outside of sports. "The AAU," he claimed "has done a great deal for the improvement of race relations, the reduction of juvenile delinquency, and the motivation of our youth for better health habits and good conduct."[22] Still, despite the rhetoric of fair play and democracy surrounding sports, the professional baseball team, the Washington Senators, refused to sign black talent until 1955. That left the Redskins and their racist owner, George Preston Marshall, as the only segregated team in the area. In 1957, when President Eisenhower desegregated D.C., it left the Redskins as one of the last racist segregated bastions in the nation's capital.

Caught up in the Cold War and the civil rights movement, the black community and the press took this opportunity to end the embarrassment and the indignity in D.C. and attacked Marshall and his racist policies. They felt that in this climate, pressure from pickets and the pen would be able to push past prejudice. The local NAACP branch sent a letter to Marshall urging him to integrate for democracy's sake and patriotically protested, "As a local team carrying the name of the Nation's Capital, a policy of racial discrimination becomes a symbol before the world contrary to our avowed position of democratic leadership."[23] In *Jet*, Doc Young wrote a scathing piece about the Redskins, noting that the team played in a predominantly black neighborhood, and argued Marshall placed "the evil luxury of race prejudice above country, flag, and world opinion."[24] Young also called out other owners for remaining silent in the face of segregation.

Because owners refused to condemn Marshall, and the Redskins refused to integrate, black organizations in Washington led boycotts and pickets whenever the Redskins came to town. After a local Washington protest, an *Afro-American* editorial linked the growing civil rights movement with the move to push Marshall to integrate when he noted, "When the people of Montgomery, Ala., broke the back of discrimination and jim crow through the intelligent use of the boycott, they proved something. . . . It is natural then that the Washington Pigskin Club should hit upon this technique to try to force the diehard management of both the Washington Redskins football team and the Washington Nationals Baseball team to drop their bars against players of color." The writer continued by reasoning, "If the people of Montgomery could give up using public transportation, which was necessary to their very economic existence, to win the right to sit where they please, then surely Washingtonians can forgo patronizing an industry which merely furnishes recreation."[25] Black Washingtonians were not alone in their fight.

In pro football cities across the country, black activists protested the racist Redskins. In New York, a black organization, the Red Roosters Sports Committee, sent a letter to Giants' owner Tim Mara and warned that blacks across the country would boycott every Redskins game, including the lucrative Redskins-Giants game at Yankee stadium, if their rivals did not drop the color line. The committee also warned the NFL commissioner that blacks would picket the draft in Philadelphia if the Redskins showed no signs of desegregating. Commissioner Bert Bell, however, called the picketing a "very foolish and blundering thing," and argued that professional football was a leader in racial integration. Regardless of what the commissioner believed, black protesters picketed games in Washington and New York, holding signs, including one that read "Ike Doesn't Discriminate, Why Should Marshall."[26] In a sign of solidarity, several ticket holders, white and black, sold their tickets or ripped them up, to join the protesters. None of this, however, moved Marshall.

The most successful and largest protest occurred in Los Angeles in 1961, just months after the federal government, led by Secretary of the Interior, Stewart Udall, told Marshall he had to integrate his team or lose the use of the new public stadium taxpayers built. In Los Angeles, led by black writers L. I. Brockenbury and Brad Pye, and the local chapters of the NAACP, Congress of Racial Equality (CORE), and various integrated unions, black and white protesters—estimates suggest that whites comprised 40% of the protesters—formed a picket line around the Los Angeles Coliseum to protest the Redskins. Protesters picketed the charity event "to let Marshall know that it is the beginning of the end for his type of thinking: to inform the [Los Angeles] *Times* that charity or no charity, this is the last year Negroes are going to sit still for this game; and let the *Times* (and the other guilty Metropolitan papers) know that Negroes are not unaware of their discriminatory hiring practices."[27] Protesters, including activist Maggie Hathaway, who led the way to integrate golf in Los Angeles, held up signs that read, "No Jim Crow Charity," "We Protest Racism," and "Don't Spend Your Money Where You Can't Play." One protester had recently arrived from the Freedom Rides demonstration, integrating interstate transportation in the South, and remarked that he had to show up to this event in solidarity. For him, the move to end Jim Crow segregation in interstate transportation and segregation in the NFL was interlinked.[28] Despite a few local black leaders chastising the protesters—the naysayers wanted to give Marshall a chance to make good on his word that he would draft a black player—the protest succeeded in its mission and spread up the coast to San Francisco. In San Francisco, the local CORE chapter in San Francisco tried to get 49ers players to join the picket, but none joined. As cornerback Abe Woodson said, "This is different from situations where there are segregated audiences and things like that." But in reality, Woodson had no intention of being an activist-athlete.[29] Two years later, when asked about athletes' role as activists, Woodson told a writer, "That boycott stuff is not the answer. I think the best way to improve race relations is to be just like anyone else." He continued, "I feel that I can do more for the racial situation by signing autographs after the game and being nice to people who ask."[30]

In the end, the increased national protests from black activists and the political pressure from the federal government forced Marshall's hand. Finally, in the 1962 draft, Marshall drafted Heisman Trophy winner Ernie Davis. The Redskins, however, traded Davis away for the productive and proven Bobby Mitchell, who broke the color barrier for the racist Redskins, leaving one last major barrier in professional sports, golf.

Fight for Fairness on the Fairways

Maggie Hathaway moved to Los Angeles with dreams of becoming a famed actress. With her beautiful face and caramel-colored skin, she quickly found work as a body double for starlet Lena Horne, the leading black actress at the time. From there, Hathaway received scores of credits in the industry, mainly playing small roles in black movies, but nobody would have imaged that the actress from Louisiana would soon play an integral part in the civil rights movement. A chance meeting with Joe Louis in the early 1950s changed the course of history for black golfers in Los Angeles, especially for black women. Hanging out with the fighter one day on an LA course, Louis, who loved to gamble at golf—he lost

$7,000 to black golfer Bill Spiller in one day—bet Hathaway a new set of golf clubs if she could hit the green on her first shot. The actress, who had claimed to have never played the game, reeled back and hit a perfect shot. She got the new set of clubs and was also hooked on the sport, an activity quickly becoming a favorite pastime of the black middle class.[31]

In 1926, excluded from white golf organizations, black golfers formed the United Golf Association (UGA) to regulate play and handicaps, and host tournaments among black golfers. By the time Hathaway first teed off, blacks owned a number of clubs, including Shady Rest Club in Westfield, New Jersey, Lincoln Country Club in Atlanta, Wayside in Chicago, and the Sunset Hills in Kankakee, Illinois, but most had to rely on public courses to play.[32] In the South, most cities did not build black courses until the 1950s, and they only did so to avoid complete integration with black golfers, but outside the South, black golfers who had the time and the money played at municipal courses. As Hathaway quickly found out, however, black golfers, mainly women, were not allowed to play in tournaments outside of the UGA-sponsored competitions, because the county-sponsored clubs would not have them as members, and if they were not members of a county-sponsored club, they could not play in the Women's Public Link's tournament, the governing body that oversaw women's amateur golf. And if they could not gain membership to a county-sponsored club, then they could not play in locally integrated tournaments hosted by, and scored by, the Women's Golf Association.

In 1954, led by Maggie Hathaway, the Topflighters golf club, a group of 20 black women in Los Angeles, decided to push the local county clubs to integrate. In Los Angeles, the county-sponsored golf clubs—each course received one sponsored club—did not have any rules restricting participation based on race, just on ability, so Hathaway and the others decided to put them to the test. In 1955, Hathaway qualified for acceptance into the Western Avenue Women's Golf Club, with an average score under the prerequisite 90 score for five games of golf. Despite the fact that she had the scores to qualify for the club, and thus make her eligible to play in tournaments, the white women of the club refused her entry. At that point, Hathaway, an actor, athlete, and now activist, got the county involved. After all, Los Angeles County sponsored the segregated club and also hosted segregated golf tournaments. Led by supervisor Kenneth Hahn and the head of the city's parks and recreation department N. S. Johnson, the county gave the white women two choices: integrate or disband. They chose to disband. When Hathaway showed up to integrate the club, they locked her out of the front door. When she made her way inside the club, the white women went inside the clubroom and locked her out.

Instead of playing golf with a black woman, and integrating their county-sponsored club, the white women chose not to play at all. In their place, Hathaway and the black women in the Topflighters gained sponsorship from the county. The *Californian Eagle*, a local black newspaper, reflected, "A new day was inaugurated in the local sports world Wednesday morning when a club of Negro women golfer were officially installed as the L.A. County Western Avenue Women's Golf Club."[33]

Hathaway and her group of black women athlete-activists continued to work to bring fairness to the fairways. The following year, they sued the Women Public Links Golf Association for racial discrimination, because the regulatory group would not admit the black women into the organization. In 1957, they won the right to play in the integrated tournament. Not satisfied, and wanting more black people to experience the pleasures of golf, the selfless women continued to fight and formed the Militant Allied Golf Association (MAGA). Led by Hathaway, who also founded the Beverly Hills NAACP, MAGA protested and picketed a number of golf courses around the area that refused to let black players play. Hathaway also forced the parks department to hire their first black golf pro—he worked at Western Avenue—and she made the county put antibias clauses in its lease agreements for golf courses.[34] Hathaway, who also had a golf column in the *Los Angeles Sentinel*, later worked with and mentored the athlete turned actor Jim Brown when he became an activist, even helping him set up the Negro Economic and Industrial Union, a business initiative headed by Brown to help black people economically. In 1998, after fighting for nearly 40 years for equality and equal access to golf for everyone, the county recognized her feats and named the course after her.

Hathaway and the black women in Los Angeles did not stand alone in their fight for fairness on the fairways. As Hathaway battled in Los Angeles, black golfers in the South were inching closer to victory against segregated Southern municipalities. As part of a post–World War II double-victory strategy, black citizens in the South demanded equal access to golf courses. No longer were they going to idly sit by while their tax dollars went to build and maintain public facilities from which they were excluded. For the black community, this battle would mirror much of their previous battles to fight Jim Crow, moving from a battle of separate but equal to a fight for integration. And, as usual, whites resisted at every turn. In Louisville, in 1948, when blacks demanded integration, the Circuit judge Lawrence P. Speckman denied their right, citing "the net result would be an infringement upon the rights of white persons."[35] And that same year, when blacks in Baltimore sued for the right to use all municipal courses—they could only use one subpar course—a judge agreed that the city had to integrate courses, but left it up to the city to determine how they would integrate, even suggesting Baltimore could have a day or a slot of times for black golfers.

After the Baltimore decision, black citizens across the South pushed their cities to integrate public course, however, instead of acquiescing to their black tax-paying citizens, Southern lawmakers built substandard segregated black courses in hopes of quieting the courts. In 1952, for example, Atlanta, Jacksonville, Baltimore, Houston, New Orleans, and Fort Worth had all committed to build black public courses.[36] That same year, after a court ruled that Louisville had to let blacks play on their public courses, white citizens petitioned the city to build black courses. They refused to integrate their fairways.[37] In Nashville, in 1954, the city allowed blacks to use its courses for the first time, but blacks received only two days of segregated golf a week.[38] While the white city courses were nice and well maintained, the separate facilities were subpar. All across the South, black golfers complained about their subpar conditions. As Maggie Hathaway reflected when she visited her old hometown of Shreveport, when she saw the course for the first time, "We sat down and cried." According to Hathaway, "The course was nothing but pine trees down [and] they left a stump as tall as me and if your ball missed the tree the stump was sure to catch it. It was like playing a game of checkers and when we approached the green someone had been kind enough to place a stick with a flag on it into the ground."[39] In other words, the public separate and unequal courses stood as public daily reminders that the city did not value black taxpayers as equal citizens.

Fighting for fairness on the fairways, blacks across the South, including in Baltimore, Charlotte, Greensboro, Houston, and Atlanta, forced the issue and decided they were going to play on the white public courses. In fact, the same week in 1954 that the Supreme Court passed *Brown v. Board* the court also ruled that Houston had to let black players use its public courses. Still, like Nashville, Houston offered only set days. Black players wanted full inclusion and the ability to play whenever they wanted to play. That, however, would not come for another year. In November 1955, after hearing cases from Baltimore and Atlanta, the Supreme Court ruled that city courses could not segregate public facilities, including golf courses, parks, and swimming pools. Citing this glorious decision, which came after a Mississippi court freed the murderers of Emmett Till, the *California Eagle* celebrated that the decision "put another nail in Jim Crow's coffin" and concluded, "It is plain now that the Supreme Court has arrived at the conclusion that states and cities cannot classify citizens on the basis of race and apportion the use of public facilities on that basis."[40]

And in Atlanta where local black citizens won the case—Atlanta's mayor cited he would integrate the course rather than closing it down and keeping 70,000 white golfers from golfing—two weeks into the Montgomery Bus Boycott, the editorial from the *Atlanta Daily World* celebrated, "It is truly keeping with the spirit of goodwill so evident at this season of the year, that there emerges from the Civil Rights hopper another avenue of unmolested enjoyment for those citizens often denied on the grounds of their color use of tax supported facilities." The writer added, "It was no matter of surprise that such a decision should come from a source already on record as having placed itself on the side of justice for all men."[41]

But the mayor's reaction in Atlanta, a city trying to become a model Southern city, was not indicative of other Southern cities. Across the South, city leaders resisted integrating the fairways. Cities sold their golf courses to private groups just so they would not have to integrate. And in Greensboro, North Carolina, somebody burned down the golf course to eliminate any possibility of integrated golf.[42] The city did not finish building an integrated public course until 1962, two years after four brave black college students at local North Carolina A&T started the sit-in movements and a year after black golfer Charlie Sifford played in the first integrated PGA tournament at a private golf course in the South. Of the major moment, Sifford mused, "It had to come. I thought it might come first in Texas, because that's a pretty liberal state and they've had mixed athletic for some time. But I'm glad in a way that it's North Carolina because that's my home state."[43] Sifford finished in fifth place, an excellent finish considering the fact that he had not competed in seven weeks.

When the PGA tour moved South, and the white players packed their bags to continue to earn their living, Sifford had to stay behind. But Greensboro was just a mirage. The night before he played somebody called his room—he had to stay at a private home since there was no black hotel for him to stay—and threatened, "You'd better not bring your black ass out to no golf course tomorrow if you know what's good for you, nigger. We don't allow niggers on our golf course."[44] And all through the tournament, the white fans from the gallery spewed racial hate, making his job even more difficult. And despite Greensboro opening up to Sifford, the next tournament, the Houston Open, barred him from their grounds, prompting local black activists to picket the course.

To be sure, Althea Gibson, the first black woman in the Ladies Professional Golf Association (LPGA), also faced seemingly insurmountable racist odds as she worked her way through professional golf. Gibson, who retired from tennis to start a career in golf in the early 1960s, found that there were golf courses in the South and the North, like in Cincinnati, where she could not change in the clubhouse with other white golfers, could not stay in the same hotels, and could not play in some Northern tournaments that denied her "invites" because of the color of her skin. Some golf courses situated in exclusive housing tracts, for example, would deny her entry worrying that potential white home owners would not buy houses if the course let black people play on their greens.[45] Understanding her role as a barrier breaker, however, Gibson rolled with the punches. She played where they let her play, and she let her play do the talking. On being excluded from Southern tournaments, though agitated, she took a nonconfrontational approach to the racism. On this she reflected, "There were a lot of tournaments that wouldn't accept me. I don't know if they thought I was going to eat the grass. All I wanted to do was hit the ball off it."[46]

Despite the racial barriers, Gibson found instant success. Known for her long drives and athletic shots, by the mid-1960s she ranked as one of the top women golfers in the nation and paved the way for other black woman golfers, like Renee Powell, who joined the LPGA in 1967. On Gibson's importance, Powell asserted: "Althea is not a role model for just people of color. Althea Gibson is a role model for women, because she came along at a time when women were breaking a lot of barriers." Gibson clearly understood that just like in tennis, her presence played a bigger role in society than her white counterparts. On being a potential role model for black golfers, Gibson stated: "If my being out here and playing golf can be of some stimulation to other young ladies of my race to play golf, then I feel I've made a contribution."[47] But in reality, being the pioneer limited her ability to play at her best. Charlie Sifford knew this reality well.

Although the press labeled Sifford the "Jackie Robinson of Golf," Sifford and other black professional golfers would say Robinson had it easier compared to them. When asked about the comparisons, Sifford simply stated, "My job is harder." On Sifford's tough times, a black writer for the *Michigan Chronicle* added, "Not even Jackie Robinson, who broke baseball's rigid color line, was required to combat both race prejudice and the proverbial financial wolf."[48] As Sifford explained, he had to face the racism alone, black fans did not cheer him on the course, and the pressure of being a barrier breaker and also facing racism at the same time had an immediate impact on his livelihood. The moment a black golfer thought about racism, his whole game was off, thus inhibiting his ability to earn a living. While both the baseball player and the golfer would be equally affected by racism as they played their games, professional black golfers like Sifford did not have a set salary and had to compete against a group of guys every week for purse money, and they did not receive sponsors which would help eliminate a lot of the costs. In other words, if the golfer missed his shots, and did not place, he received no money for his work. Robinson, Sifford noted, could go 0–4 and still received a paycheck.

Moreover, as long as the South remained segregated, Sifford's game would slip because he could not play in Houston, Baton Rouge, New Orleans, and Augusta, Georgia, where the Masters was played, a course they did not let any black player on until 1975. Whereas other sports did not have clauses mandating segregation—they had gentleman's agreements—professional golf, like bowling, had a defined "Caucasian-only" clause that made it nearly impossible to integrate the sport. When Sifford played in Greensboro, the PGA still had its racist clause barring black membership.

Moreover, Sifford and black golfers were largely alone in their battle to break the barrier. They had the near-impossible task of being activists for justice, while also trying to earn a living hitting a small white ball with consistency. One player, however, despite the odds and the impact it had on his golf game, consistently and publicly fought the PGA and also tried to maintain his professional career, Bill Spiller. For that, for his persistence against prejudice, others labeled him as ornery, bitter, and even militant. And, of course, Spiller was all of these things because the persistent prejudice gnawed at him. Sifford said Spiller was "the most militant of black golfers," Hathaway recalled, "The PGA caused Bill Spiller to die with a broken heart," and his son surmised, "He was the angriest person I've ever known because he felt cheated out of an opportunity to play the game."[49] Spiller, from Tulsa, Oklahoma, and a Wiley College graduate, first picked up golf in Los Angeles while working as a Red Cap porter at the train station. Spiller's late entry into golf set him apart from most professional black golfers who learned the game while working as caddies for white golfers. And unlike the legendary black golfer Ted Rhodes—Rhodes, who was known as the best black golfer, and also had the best swing of any black golfer, found employment as Joe Louis's golf coach—Spiller had an unusual swing pieced together by studying books and the swings of top golfers, white and black. And like their swings, the two men, Rhodes and Spiller, could not be any more different when it came to fighting Jim Crow. While people tagged Spiller as the "angry black man," it was clear to see that Rhodes wanted no part of confrontations. Rhodes, himself, admitted that much, stating, "If I had my preference, I'd take the nice way, because when you get something that way, it's a lot sweeter to have." According to Hathaway, "Teddy was not a fighter. . . . He was, let's say, a compassionate peacekeeper."[50]

The different approach Rhodes took to Jim Crow compared to Spiller makes it even more remarkable that Rhodes joined Spiller in the first major crusade to integrate the PGA. In 1948, officials at the Richmond (California) Open golf course barred the two golfers and Madison Gunter, an amateur, even though they had all qualified in the previous Los Angeles tournament. Seeing this as their opportunity to end discrimination, the three black golfers sued the PGA for $315,000, arguing the Caucasian-only clause violated their civil rights. As they awaited trial, Mark Harris, writing for *Negro Digest*, remarked: "At the moment big-time golf is a white man's game, and the clique who controls it is struggling firmly against the pressure of those who want to see the grand old sport Americanized once and for all."[51] Despite what many people deemed a winnable case, the NAACP refused to give the golfers funds, which severely limited their ability to fight their case. The PGA, living up to the name black golfers gave it "Please Go Away," did not eliminate its Caucasian clause, but instead it agreed to be more open to black golfers. In reality, it had no plans of allowing black golfers in the PGA. And to avoid interracial competition, the PGA switched the designation of its tournaments from "opens" to "invitational," which meant that a white person or sponsor would have to invite a black man to a tournament.[52] This effectively ended any racial confrontations it had until 1952.

In 1952, the PGA, once again, showed its true racial colors and demanded that officials at the San Diego Open, who had invited Joe Louis, an avid golfer, and Spiller, who qualified in the previous tournament in Los Angeles, bar the two from the tournament because the PGA did not want to sanction a tournament with black golfers. The previous week in Los Angeles the PGA attempted the same segregation policy, but the Los Angeles Chamber of Commerce refused to condone racism. San Diego, however, followed the PGA's orders. When Louis, the ex-heavyweight champion and full-time American hero, heard about this, he used his platform to make waves about the racism. For all to hear, during a radio interview, he called Horton Smith "Hitler." Louis's statement signaled a call to action to black sportswriters. They knew that if this could happen to Louis in San Diego, in the integrated West, it could happen to any black person. Writers, like John Fuster of the *Cleveland Call*, noted, "The sports world is not perfect. It is just a little better in its morals, in its real-Americanism, in its honesty, than most other phases of life in these United States."[53] Embarrassed by the negative national publicity, Smith worked out a deal, where Louis, who was an amateur, could compete in the tournament, but the pro players, whom Smith said did not qualify for the tournament, could not compete. Spiller, however, could not qualify because he was restricted from playing in PGA events. The point, to most, was clear—the PGA did not want black men competing for money on its tour.

In response to the San Diego protest, the PGA also established a new rule that would allow sponsors to invite nonqualified players to play, opening the door for a limited number of black players—Louis and other golfers created a preapproved list—in some western tournaments. Louis lauded for his stance, and being the first golfer to break the PGA's color line, played his round of integrated golf. Fuster celebrated the moment, and argued, "There is no gainsaying the fact that Joe's outspokenness on the P.G.A. vs Negroes scramble has made possible advances in golfing which might otherwise have been retarded for years."[54] But while many people celebrated Louis, others saw this gesture as tokenism. They wanted full integration. A writer for the *California Eagle* opined Louis went for the "Okie Doke" and said Louis "accepted the appeasing offer." He argued that, "Their acceptance of the responsibility of screening Negro golfers for play in PGA tourneys is just like the Negro who fights for a jim crow hospital, school, or housing projects, so he can be top dog in a segregated pound." He also scolded, "A person who compromises on principle is lower than a man who has no principles."[55] And, of course, Spiller remained upset. Spiller told reporters, "I'm greatly disappointed in Joe. . . . I play for money. . . . Joe, here, he just plays for fun." Spiller, who threatened to sue the PGA again, went along with the charade but also demanded that the PGA had better strike out its Caucasian clause at the next meeting.[56] Even in the short term, of course, the black players still faced racism. The next week, at the Phoenix Open, when Louis, Rhodes, Spiller, and Sifford played, somebody defecated in their first hole. And club officials would not let the black golfers change in the locker room. Spiller, the activist of the group, pushed passed the prejudice and entered the locker room to take a shower but stopped after hearing a threat made on his life. Spiller simmered at this racism, and it required Louis to calm him down. Eventually, however, Spiller's activism paved the way to integrate golf, as his fire spread to other people, especially black writers.

By 1957, L. I. Brockenbury, of the *Los Angeles Sentinel*, was the most consistent voice in the press chipping away at the racist PGA. Brockenbury, who noticed the apathy among African Americans to this fight—he argued that too many black people saw this as a rich man's game—implored the black community to support Spiller. "Now Spiller is bucking the PGA trying again to get them to eliminate their restrictions against Negro professionals playing and WORKING. This is a fight that needs backing from all of us," he said. Brockenbury, who noted that Hathaway was the only black writer organizing in the fight to integrate, argued that the fight for fairness on the fairways was "just as important a fight as the one so gallantly waged for many years to get Negroes in professional baseball."[57] In another article that year, he asked his readers and black golfers to get together to force the PGA to ban its Caucasian clause at a local tournament. He also ordered, "What is needed is education on the part of the Negro public as to what it can do about golf. It was the Negro public opinion which actually broke down color bars in baseball and football, (aided by men like Branch Rickey and Paul Brown and there will be always be men like them)."[58] The following year he called the NAACP to take on this fight—Thurgood Marshall reportedly said that if a black person could afford to play golf he could afford to fight this in court on his own—and urged that blacks needed "united action on the part of our Negro leadership to overcome an injustice that is victimizing several fine Negro athletes."[59]

While the NAACP never picked up the fight for fairness on the fairways, black golfers got the next best ally, Jackie Robinson. In 1960, Robinson, who by then had his own column that ran in white daily papers and in the black weeklies, hit the PGA. Robinson, the leading activist-athlete at the time, argued, "Golf is the one major sport in America today in which rank and open racial prejudice is allowed to reign supreme. Though often called the sport of gentleman, all too often golf courses, clubs and tournaments apply the ungentlemanly and un-American yardstick of race and color in determining who may or may not compete." Robinson also alerted his followers to the fact that President Eisenhower had a membership at a segregated club, Augusta National, and that popular actor Bing Crosby, who had his own celebrity golf tournament, refused to invite black players. For Robinson, the overt discrimination coming from the PGA constituted a clear violation of a black player's civil rights, and Robinson ordered, "Not only should court action be considered, but I feel the issue is one for a thorough investigation by the Civil Rights Commission."[60] After Robinson's column, a PGA official told Sifford, "Robinson hit us pretty hard, didn't he?"[61] While Robinson's column raised more awareness on a national level to the plight of black golfers—his article also came on the heels of *Sport* magazine writing a feature on Sifford—black golfers also needed a white ally to bring down the barriers prohibiting blacks from playing in the PGA.

In 1959, black golfers found their white ally in the sympathetic Stanley Mosk, California's attorney general. Mosk, who played golf with leading black golfers at a Jewish-owned country club, Hillcrest in Los Angeles, used his power to put the first legal pressure on the PGA. In 1960, Mosk, who as a superior court judge in the city outlawed racially restrictive housing covenants, told the PGA that it could no longer use public courses in California as long as it had a racially restrictive clause in its membership laws. The following year, Mosk upped his stance by barring PGA events from private clubs. Mosk strongly believed that law and government could bring about the change needed for a true democracy, and claimed: "Society and the law can ultimately defeat overt bigotry."[62] Mosk's stance put tremendous pressure on the PGA, which moved its 1962 PGA tournament scheduled for Brentwood (Los Angeles) to a private course in Philadelphia, only to spark debate from the NAACP for the first time. With pressure from California, which led to legal pressure from others states, including New York, and now the NAACP chiming in the middle of a growing politically active nationwide nonviolent civil rights movement, the PGA and its membership felt compelled to act. It knew its discriminatory days were over. In 1962, at its annual conference, in a vote of 87–0, the PGA voted to drop the "Caucasian clause" from its rules, paving the way for golfers like Sifford. The move also finally ended the last legal racist hurdle in professional sports.

CHAPTER FOUR

Deep Down in Dixie: Segregated Sports in a Post-*Brown* Era

Perry Wallace thought that he had prepared for this moment. As a boy growing up in segregated Nashville, he would skip to the library to check out books about racial violence in the South, listen for the latest Emmett Till news, and watch adults navigate the strange customs of Jim Crow. He excelled at his books, he excelled in the band, and when he hit a growth spurt and got some coordination, he excelled at basketball. By his senior year in high school, 1966, Wallace was a top recruit in the nation. Most locals figured the 6-foot 6-inch Wallace, who could seemingly jump out of the gym, and slam the ball with the authority of a Bull Connor police force, would follow the footsteps of other local talented black basketball players and matriculate to the local athletic power house, Tennessee State, a black college.

But instead he chose to be a pioneer. He went to Vanderbilt and became the first black basketball player in the Southeastern Conference (SEC). As Wallace biographer Andrew Maraniss puts it, "He was attracted by the promise. The promise that the world was changing, that the playing field was being leveled, that if you worked hard and played fair and made the right decisions, you could participate in the full measure of society whether you were white or black."[1] Emotionally, he would pay dearly for that decision. He had to play games in Alabama, Florida, Louisiana, and Mississippi, and by his sophomore year, when he played on the varsity team, he was the lone isolated black man on the team. The other black recruit Vanderbilt signed, Godfrey Dillard from Detroit, did not make it in Nashville. "There were waves of tension that accompanied those trips," Wallace said. "There was a long wave that started back in the summer before the season, and this eerie note or eerie voice that would come in about what I was going to have to deal with down there, and what could happen—what's the worst that can happen."[2] He found out in Oxford, Mississippi, home of the Ole Miss Rebels, the school that rioted and fought the National Guard in 1963 because the white students, and white citizens in the area, did not want James Meredith, a black man, integrating the university. As expected, "nigger" and "coon" flowed freely from their white mouths, and so did "Go, home, nigger! We're gonna kill you, nigger! We'll lynch you, boy!" And the play on the court mirrored the vitriol in the stands, culminating in a nasty elbow to the head that left Wallace dazed. Wallace recovered and went out in the second half to prove himself to the racist crowd. He sparked the Commodores to an important road victory, and led the way with 14 points and 11 rebounds, leaving white fans wondering what happened, and how he got here.[3]

Before Wallace matriculated to Vanderbilt, most Northern schools had eliminated their racial quota system designed to limit the number of black players on their team. The quotas were intended to keep white fans, students, and alumni happy, but winning cured racial restrictions. Nobody, however, predicted what was coming in the South. While the North seemingly grew more accepting of the black athlete, the South dug in its heels and refused to budge. It saw athletic integration as an extension of Northern aggression, the tool the North would use to pry open the dam and open the flood gates for integrated education. After the 1954 *Brown* decision, although a few minor league teams had black players on their squads, states in the Deep South, like Alabama, Georgia, and Louisiana, passed more restrictive laws to eliminate all contact between whites and blacks in athletics. As a writer in *Sport* magazine observed in 1956, "Under present standards one must be honest and say it is seriously doubtful that the Negro will be integrated any further into the athletics of the South." He continued to predict, "It is reasonably safe to say that the Negro will never appear on the college athletic scene in the South on an unsegregated basis, except as a visiting performer from an outside school."[4] For Southerners, amateur athletics assumed social equality; thus, it was not far-fetched to believe the seemingly impregnable racist walls of segregation would never be broken. But just a decade later, after *Sport* predicted segregation would never fall in Southern athletics, *Sports Illustrated* published an article entitled "The Negro Athlete Is Invited

Home," to highlight athletic integration in Southern schools. What happened in that 10-year span?

It is easy to answer that question by suggesting the federal government finally forced the South to comply with integration. It is also simplistic to say Southern schools finally accepted fate and saw athletics as an easy transition to integration. With black athletes, the South could build its coffers and also sell a version of a "new South," that it was more modern and accommodating and that somehow it got past race. And all of this is true. But something else happened. The black press and black activists in the community forced integration. After *Brown v. Board of Education*, Southern legislators and citizens built a wall around their lily-white sports and refused to let black people in, but believing that sports represented the most visual proof that democracy existed and that athletic integration had its tangible benefits, the black community fought back. In short, they made Southern institutions pay for their racism.

Led by black newspapermen in Southern cities, the black community refused to pay for Jim Crow to "slap them in the face." Knowing that they held an important financial power in sports in the South, black fans used their dollars as a lever to exact change. And everywhere they protested they eventually got what they wanted. Perry Wallace matriculated to Vanderbilt because he wanted a great education and felt like he would be a positive pioneer. But deep in Dixie, the black community that fought segregation in Southern sports made it possible.

Birmingham

By 1954, with Southern minor league professional baseball leagues starting to integrate—Atlanta, Chattanooga, Jacksonville, Montgomery, and Mobile all had black players by 1954—it seemed that the South could move in the right direction and peel away racially restrictive laws. However, the *Brown* decision gave strict segregationists a needed boost to convince other Southerners that they had to maintain their racist segregated ways. In other words, pro-segregationists saw sports and education as interlinked Northern causes to infiltrate and integrate the South. Southerners supposed that if the South agreed to integrate the playing field, then their schools were soon to follow, and if the schools were soon to follow, that meant miscegenation would be next. This fear that schools and sports would be the downfall of the South first played out in Birmingham, Alabama, a city many understood as the most violently racist city in the South.

On January 26, 1954, Birmingham's City Commission repealed a portion of the city's draconian 1950 anti-integration sports law that ruled, "It shall be unlawful for a negro and a white person to play together in company with each other in any game of cards, dice, dominoes, checkers, baseball, softball, football, basketball or similar game." The city passed the original 1950 law to eliminate racial confusion over Jim Crow and blunt blacks' hopes of integration after the Washington Redskins and the Detroit Lions had scheduled to play an exhibition football game in the city, despite the fact that the Lions featured a black player, receiver Wally Triplett. Fearing the racial reaction from hardcore segregationists and also a potential press that would shame the city if Triplett, who had played in the South before in the 1948 Cotton Bowl, were not allowed to play, the teams and the city came to a "gentleman's agreement" where Triplett would warm up with his team but would not play.

To avoid future integration incidents, the city strictly forbade athletic integration. The next year, for example, when the Giants brought black players, defensive back Em Tunnell and running back Robert "Stonewall" Jackson, to play against the Redskins, the two black players had to sit in the stands. But with black players playing on Southern teams in minor league baseball, Birmingham's team, the Barons, had to be prepared to face teams with a black player. In the summer of 1953, when it looked like the Barons would make the Southern minor league World Series, and thus set up a game with a team that had already integrated, the City Commission said that it would pass an ordinance that would allow integrated baseball games. The proposal to change Southern laws led to immediate backlash, but for a brief moment the bigots did not have to worry about the law changing, because the Barons did not make the playoffs. In October 1953, when Jackie Robinson brought an integrated barnstorming all-star team to the city, he benched his three white players to avoid breaking the segregation rule.[5] That Robinson had the audacity to bench white men irritated the racist sensibilities of the racist whites in town.

The furor Robinson's move sparked, however, gave the City Commission the impression that time was ripe to integrate sports. With superstar black players on a number of pro teams—local Willie Mays played on the Giants—the city also wanted to capitalize on the economic windfall that exhibitions featuring professional teams brought. In January 1954, anticipating several professional baseball teams playing exhibitions in Birmingham—the Dodgers, Braves, Giants, Cardinals, White Sox, and Indians with a possible 26 black players in total were all scheduled to play in spring games—the City Commission passed a new law that removed baseball, football, and "similar games" from the old segregated list of banned sports. The city, however, continued to ban interracial competition in softball, basketball, card games, checkers, and dominoes.[6]

Although a limited gesture, for those interested in democratic progress and fair play, it seemed that the city was moving in the right direction. Marion E. Jackson of the *Atlanta Daily World*, wrote, "Time simply ran out on sports bigotry in Birmingham, Ala. . . . The end came suddenly but not surprisingly. The bell had toll [sic] long ago but there were some forces who grudgingly stayed the hand of the clock." The local black newspaper, the *Birmingham World*, celebrated, "The action is on the healthy side and is certain to produce good will and favorable notice. All good citizens have the civic challenge to cooperate in building our city." Nearly a month later, after the commissioners rejected a plea from racists to scrap the ordinance, the *World* editorialized, "All good citizens should applaud, commend and back up our city officials when they seek to advance our city in the spirit of democracy and civic decency."[7] In its initial editorial, the white *Birmingham News* exuded: "We now take a forward step, and the decision to do so was sound. We believe that the majority sentiment in the community will approve and that the results will be constructive." The white sportswriter for the *Birmingham News*, Zipp Newman, added: "In judging athletes, the code of sports never has recognized race nor creed but the skill of the athlete—be he white, brown or black. . . . The new law will test the spirit of fair play and good sportsmanship." Birmingham failed the test.[8]

In March, the strict segregationist faction mounted a public fight to repeal the semi-integrated bill. The outcry against the bill grew so loud and strong that the mayor and City Commission quickly tried to clarify their previous intentions. Even though they had suggested the newly passed ordinance applied only to professional baseball and football, they authored a new ordinance, declaring, "It shall be unlawful for a Negro and a white person to play together or in company with each other in any game of cards, dice, dominoes, checkers, baseball, softball, football or basketball: provided, however, that the foregoing prohibitions shall not apply to professional games of baseball or football."[9] For strict segregationists, that still was not enough.

Led by local attorney Hugh Locke, who reportedly collected 10,000 signatures, double the amount needed to place an initiative on the local ballot, segregationists demanded the old law restored. "We are not making this fight just to keep Jackie Robinson from playing in Birmingham," Locke lamented. They wanted a "permanent solution" not a "hedge"; they wanted segregation "for all time." In reply to this insistence on racism, the *Birmingham World* remarked: "Christian teachings seem to be taking another beating in Birmingham as its spokesmen retreat to timid silence. . . . That leadership could be found in Birmingham, and much of it from the protestant church, to sponsor a petition of this kind, reflects a jarring gap between Christian teachings and practices. Here again is either a faulty understanding of democracy or a lack of belief in its doctrines of equality of opportunity, free from competition, individual merit."[10]

In May, the city announced that the sports issue would be placed on the ballot of a special runoff election on June 1. Politically powerless—blacks had only 5,250 registered voters in Jefferson County, yet they were 40% of the population of nearly 600,000 people—black leaders used the only lever they had: they sued the city. In April, when integrated professional baseball teams came to town for their exhibitions—the new ordinance was still the law—the black community got a taste of integration, a step toward equality, and they refused to budge or go backward. They argued that the proposed law violated the Fourteenth Amendment, the state Constitution, and called the ordinance "repugnant to the Constitution and laws of the State of Alabama and the Constitution and laws of the United States." The lawsuit also argued that the law was "arbitrary class legislation based on race. It undertakes to deprive citizens of property without due process," and it "grants special privileges to one class of citizens." The city did not move. Black had no rights that they needed to respect.[11]

On June 1, 1954, less than two weeks after *Brown v. Board of Education* decision, which ruled separate but equal unconstitutional in public education, Birmingham voters went to the polls and overwhelmingly voted to maintain strict segregation in sports. The *Birmingham World* pleaded with its black voters, "We oppose the 'Locke Petition' because it is an attempt to drag our city backward. It is emotional negativism. It appeals to ignorance and prejudice. It is unworthy of support by those who believe in fair play. Vote AGAINST it."[12] In a 16,686 to 5,890 vote, however, voters reinstituted the 1950 sports ordinance and also prohibited blacks and whites from "mingling at swimming pools, beaches, lakes, and ponds." Assuming that all of the 5,250 registered black voters voted for integration, only 640 whites voted to maintain athletic integration. Although the *Birmingham World* derided the decision, it also seemed rather optimistic that this racist bill would allow them to fight the legislation in court and tear down the whole system of Jim Crow.[13] Unfortunately, history, and Bull Connor's racist police force, had other plans.

As expected, most whites blamed the *Brown* decision for pushing white voters to their racial limits. But to be clear, Birmingham had always operated under Jim Crow conditions; the *Brown* decision was just a red herring, so they would not have to deal with that reality; they remained stuck in the racist past. Locke ordered that although the Supreme Court ruled to integrate schools, a distinction existed between sports and education. "This new law," he suggested, "deals with a mere social privilege and not with a right. I think the passage of it is perfectly legal." Locke also added that the vote "indicated that the people of Birmingham are not going to take the breaking down of segregation lying down. And it tells that to the people of the United States." The editorialist for the *Birmingham Post-Herald* finally weighed in on the controversy and acknowledged that the vote represented "protest against the recent Supreme Court ruling outlawing segregation in the public schools." Surprisingly, and perhaps risking business, the *Post-Herald* denounced the vote: "Adoption of the ordinance is unfortunate. Although it does reflect majority sentiment toward the court it contributes nothing constructive toward amicable race relations which, we believe that same majority hopes to see maintained." The writer continued, "The problem created by the Court will be with us for a long time to come. Since we must live with it members of both races should see that every effort is made to avoid friction."[14] The majority of the voters, however, did not see things that way. In fact, most white political leaders in the South agreed. Birmingham's knee-jerk reaction to potential athletic integration in a post-*Brown* world was only just the beginning. Sports in Birmingham remained legally segregated until 1962.

Little League in South Carolina

Despite having a national clause warning teams that they would be compelled to play against teams with players from all races and nationalities, in Southern states, especially in the Deep South, Little League baseball mirrored the segregation of society. White Southerners viewed the popular and rapidly growing institution as a great paradox in their life. On the one hand, Southerners loved baseball and were proud of the imprint their white players had made on the game historically and viewed Little League as an opportunity for their kids to make a mark on the game. But on the other hand, they also worried that Little League represented a Northern invasion into their Southern ways, as the organization advocated fair play among all youth. Making matters worse for racist white Southerners, the growth of Little League happened as the South fought against the Supreme Court and the 1954 *Brown v. Board of Education* ruling. In other words, they thought that if they surrendered to integrating youth baseball, the schools were next.

For black Americans, however, playing Little League baseball represented a two-pronged approach to improving the lives of black youth.

Across the nation, unheralded members of the black community, especially mothers, worked hard to bring the program to their cities. For one, Little League gave many juveniles an opportunity to do something constructive. In an article with the byline "Juvenile delinquency program shattered," one writer in South Carolina noted that people regarded Little League as one of the "strongest forces yet conceived in the nationwide battle against juvenile delinquency."[15] Moreover, the league gave many kids hope, especially since as an organization it professed to promote fairness and equality. The all-star teams comprised the best players in their local leagues, regardless of race, and promised black players an equal shot to make the team. In the case of all-black teams, like those in the Southern states, the promises of equality meant an opportunity to test their skills against white youth on an equal level. Until the creation of Little League in the South, no sports organizations had provided young black boys a fighting chance to imagine a future free of Jim Crow. Thus, anything short of justice and fair play in Little League would be a signal that black youth's lives in the age of *Brown v. Board* would be racially restricted like their parents' lives.

Southern segregation in youth sports became a national issue in 1955 after 55 all-white Little League teams boycotted the South Carolina state tournament because they refused to play against Charleston's black team, the Cannon Street YMCA, in the state tournament. Explaining his racist decision, Daniel Jones, South Carolina's state commissioner of the Little League, announced, "I am fully convinced that it is for the best interests of the people of our state to continue our way of life and customs on a separate but equal basis, and will do everything I can to preserve that way of life." When Jones used the terms "separate but equal" they were a clear signal to Southerners as a reminder about their fight against the recent *Brown* decision. For those Northerners who might not understand, he clearly spelled it out when he noted, "The schools set the pattern for everything. Until segregation is ended in the schools, our people will resist all attempts to end segregation in recreation and in other social activities." He closed by linking Little League baseball to a Northern conspiracy to end segregation, suggesting, "There is no question in my mind that this situation is being used as an opening wedge to put all recreation facilities on a non-segregated basis."[16] To be clear, Jones's comments were not isolated remarks; rather, they fit in line with the South's staunch reaction to *Brown*, in which state and local officials, combined with white terrorist organizations, like the White Citizens Council, worked in tangent to make sure *Brown*, and by extension the North and the federal government, would not disrupt their way of life. While cities shut down whole school districts to ensure schools never integrated, in sports, Southern citizens made sure to push back against any perceived progress.

South Carolina's decision quickly spread throughout the South, giving white racist parents a chance to indoctrinate their kids to the ways of the South. In Birmingham, for example, fathers pleaded with other cities to set up a "whites-only" Southern Association of Little Leagues. On reading this racist resentment, Marcel Hopson, the local black writer for the *Birmingham World*, mockingly interpreted their racist plea as really meaning, "We will continue to deny Negro boys the opportunity to enjoy recreational facilities and continue to deny them the right to grow up to manhood with the knowledge, feeling for freedom and sense that they are citizens of this city, county and the United States, as long as their skin remain dark or black." In Florida, following South Carolina's lead, Little League and local lawmakers tried to bar a black team from competing in the state tournament, but a city attorney in Orlando overruled the action, citing no state law forbade black and white youth from playing sports together. As Hopson observed, "Several clean-minded white Florida LL directors had a change of heart and elected to (and did) permit their white-skinned boys to play against their young dark-skinned brothers on the baseball field."[17] When left up to a vote, however, the white kids in Florida voted to play in mixed games. According to the black coaches and players from the Pensacola team, the fans and opponents treated them as equals and cheered loudly for the team. Kids could not care less.[18] Looking at South Carolina and Florida's reaction to integrated play, Peter J. McGovern, the national president of Little League, who also forced Florida to play an integrated tournament, argued, "Little League must not become a political football or a racial issue. Our rules, based on fair play, do not recognize barriers of race, creed, or color. The program will withstand such storm as long as we adhere firmly to the democratic principle which made possible its phenomenal growth."[19]

These remarks about fair play and democracy, however, did not mean McGovern was off the hook; in fact, his words were inconsistent with how he treated the Cannon Street black team. Instead of letting them represent their state as champions, McGovern ruled that since they did not earn their status on the field, Cannon Street could not compete in the regional championship. After this decision, the white writer Dave Egan, of the *Boston Record*, attacked McGovern as a "mental midget" who failed to uphold the American creed. In his article attacking McGovern, Egan eloquently used the words of the "Pledge of the Allegiance" and cited America's commitment to democracy to point out that McGovern failed America's black youth. "He had the chance of a lifetime to make the words of the Pledge of

Allegiance mean what they say," Egan blasted, "but he preferred to walk the narrow road with the advocates of white supremacy." Egan also added that McGovern sold to the black youth the idea that they had no hope in America, coldly stating, "Here is baseball in its very cradle, and here is a man named McGovern telling the colored population of the South that there is no hope, no future, no freedom to dream for their little ones."[20] Egan was one of a few white writers to come to the defense of the black youth.

In its attack against Little League, the black press remained focused on fairness as it related to the hopes and potential opportunities of black youth and attacked white Southern adults as the problem. Black writers, in other words, supported the stance by Robert P. Morrison, president of Charleston's Cannon Street YMCA, who said, "We feel our children should have the same right as any others to at least attempt to go to Williamsport's for the national competition."[21] They did not want a guarantee; they just wanted a fair chance. In New Orleans, an editorialist for the *Louisiana Weekly* bravely stated, "The soft headed officials were not thinking of the kids to whom it probably made no difference who they played. They think of nothing but preserving white supremacy and segregation which is fading faster than the sun after 6:00 p.m. on a cold winter day in December." "Sooner or later," he added, "if these white kids show anything in baseball they will be playing on integrated teams. So, the sooner they learn to meet and compete with Negroes the better off they will be when they do make the grade."[22] The *Pittsburgh Courier* opined that Communists would use this against America, and the paper also argued that the discrimination hurt both the white and black players. He also added, "We believe it is dastardly for adult Americans, such as Danny Jones, to instill into boys from eight to twelve years of age, the outmoded, unchristian ideas of racial superiority." The writer further reasoned, "Every study that has ever been made has proven conclusively that children have to be TAUGHT racial prejudice. They are not born with it and they don't learn it easily. They are brain-washed by their parents, such as Danny Jones."[23] In the *Chicago Defender* a writer deduced the discrimination "proves nothing about baseball but it emphatically documents the bigotry, narrow-mindedness and prejudice of a benighted people." *The Defender* also recognized that white youth were not the problem, and observed, "The white kids would hardly have kicked up such a fuss."[24] And Doc Young, writing in *Jet*, said the white players were "'chickened' out of a baseball tournament solely because their adults didn't have the guts to grow up." Young further complained, "They talk about progress—and surely there must be some of it around. But how can you prove it by the South Carolina Little Leaguers?"[25] But all was not lost.

Despite the fact that the Cannon Street team did not get a chance to play, other black kids from across the nation competed in their local, regional, and even in the national tournament, thus making the final tournament in Williamsport an example of American democracy and hope for American youth. Sam Lacy, of the *Baltimore Afro-American*, reported on the tournament as a way to highlight the black youth involved and also to promote the contest as a democratic game that demonstrated hope for the future. He truly believed that inclusive participation in the Little League tournament would go a long way to break down the barriers that black youths would have to face—despite the fact that the Alabama team flew the Confederate Flag in their dugout.

To prove his point, Lacy interviewed coaches and parents from Alabama and Louisiana to get their views on the integrated tournament. Alabama's coach, who had twin sons on the team, said, "I'm just not ready to accept them," and told Lacy, "It's just one of those things that probably will take place when we're ready for it. I know a lot of my friends feel that we'll do a lot of things if we can do them in our own good time. . . . We don't like the idea of being told we've got to do something, that's all." But in Williamsport, the coach and his players had no choice in the matter. If they wanted a chance at the championship, they had to play black talent. They played against black kids. They played against Jewish kids. They played against Catholic kids. And the white kids did not care: "It didn't make any difference to me," claimed the twin sons, George and Frank. "As long as they know how to play ball and it wouldn't be a runaway, it was all right with me." And white Louisiana kids shared the same sentiments, despite the fact that their parents reluctantly let them play. "Colored kids," a white ball player from Louisiana reflected, "played against us at Monroe . . . it wasn't any difference. . . . I struck them out, too."[26] As Lacy's article demonstrated, if the race question was left up to fair-minded Southern white kids playing sports, the black youth stood a chance. This was a powerful reminder of what the black press fought for, especially considering the fact that the tournament in Williamsport coincided with the disappearance and death of Emmett Till, the black 14-year-old youth from Chicago whose body was found mutilated in Mississippi. Till, like most black boys his age, loved playing Little League baseball.

The Sugar Bowl

After the *Brown* ruling, white politicians in Georgia became rigid in their defiance against the legislation. In Georgia, in 1955, to maintain a strict segregation state, white voters elected Marvin Griffin, a man who promised to protect their white ways and campaigned that he would leave the state in its segregated space just as his previous predecessor, Eugene Talmadge, who was known as one of the most racist governors in post–World War II America, had done. In the realm of sports, this meant that Griffin would use his political power to ensure blacks and whites would not mix, a tough job to accomplish as the flagship city in his state, Atlanta, faced a Supreme Court decision about its segregated public golf courses, and leading football schools, like Georgia Tech, played in a sport where black and white players were more frequently expected to play against each other. By the end of 1955, Governor Griffin had his first major public bout against sporting integration on his hands when he had to deal with the reality that Georgia Tech had agreed to play in the 1956 Sugar Bowl, located in New Orleans, on New Year's Day, against a Pittsburgh football team that had a black player, Bobby Grier.[27] With little power to control the Supreme Court's decision to integrate golf courses, Griffin chose college football to make his stance on segregation.

In November 1955, after the final game of the season, Georgia Tech coach Bobby Dobbs accepted a coveted bid to play in the Sugar Bowl against Pittsburgh, knowing the Panthers had a black football player. While this was not the first time Georgia Tech played against a black player—they played an integrated Notre Dame team in 1952 in South Bend—it would be the first time they faced a black player in the South. Making this gesture more important, especially for people who believed in racial progress in the South, the Sugar Bowl had also announced that tickets would no longer have "Caucasians Only" on their face. The previous Sugar Bowl (January 1955) when Navy destroyed Ole Miss, the Midshipmen asserted their right to sell their tickets, regardless of whether the tickets had the Caucasian clause on them, to whomever they liked. Navy's bold move forced the Sugar Bowl's committee to take a more inclusive approach to both ticket sales and team invitations to the game.

Selecting Pitt to play in the game and also offering tickets to anyone regardless of race—the Sugar Bowl still had segregated seating—was seen as a proper step in the right racial direction. The move prompted Marion E. Jackson of the *Atlanta Daily World* to write, "U.S. court decisions against segregation will slowly but surely be pinpointed in Southern sports. As it stands the Sugar Bowl is crawling slowly towards democratic lines." Jackson, however, also knew the political score; the racist governor would not take this lying down. In his November 30 column, Jackson joked, "It would have been in character if Georgia Governor Marvin Griffin and Atty. General Eugene Cook had shouted defiance of Georgia Tech playing in the Sugar Bowl against Bob Grier." Jackson, an astute observer of white politicians who loved to hone in on the race questions just to gain political support, conceded, "As it is, someone is missing the boat in not raising the race issue here." Jackson believed that white Southerners would not stand for an intervention; they valued their football more than segregation, and any demonstration against the game, he hoped, "would be a good time to expose the hoax of the white supremacy banner these flag-wavers have been keeping wind-borne."[28] Jackson did not have to wait too long.

On December 2, the governor wrote to the Board of Regents to stop Tech from playing in the Sugar Bowl, arguing Georgia teams "not be permitted to engage in contests with other teams where the races are mixed or where segregation is not required amongst the spectators."[29] Invoking the *Brown* decision, Griffin warned, "There is no more difference in compromising integrity of race on the playing field than in doing so in the classroom. . . . The battle is joined. We cannot make the slightest concession to the enemy in this dark and lamentable hour of struggle. One break in the dike and the relentless seas will rush in and destroy us." The governor also cautioned, "We are in this fight 100 per cent, not 96 per cent, not 75 per cent, not 64 per cent, but a full 100 per cent."[30]

Griffin's reaction to Tech playing a game against a team with one black player sparked immediate response from an unlikely source, white college students. While some college students protested on their campus, nearly 2,000 white students made their way to the state capitol and onto the capitol lawn, shouting at Griffin and holding protest signs, like one that read "Griffin Sits on His Brains"; some climbed the statue of Confederate General John Gordon, and others hung Griffin in effigy, all because he wanted to keep Tech from playing in a football game. In a letter of apology to Pittsburgh, Georgia Tech's student body president George W. Harris pleaded, "The student body of Georgia Tech sincerely apologizes for the unwarranted action of Georgia's governor. We are looking forward to seeing your ENTIRE team and student body at the Sugar Bowl." The students' actions forced the Board of Regents to reject Griffin's racist request and allow the Yellow Jackets to play in the integrated game. After losing his fight, Griffin griped, "I will give no comfort to Negroes and white folks playing on the same field. But if other people in other states want colored folks sitting in their laps we'll have to abide by it if we go there to play."[31]

Most important, this episode that transpired during the beginning of the Montgomery Bus Boycott, a boycott that lasted nearly a year as blacks bravely refused to ride the Jim Crow city buses, gave black onlookers hope for a better future in the South. At the time, black sports fans truly believed that sports would break down Southerners' racist resilience. In the *Michigan Chronicle*, its editorialist wrote, "The American people despite their personal prejudices have passed the stage where these prejudices have [been] allowed to conflict with the more powerful force of 'good sportsmanship.'" The editorial also professed hope in Southern white youth and projected, "The younger generation in the South wants to join the United States. They are weary and disgusted with the fears and prejudices of their elders. They are the hope of the future." The editorial staff at the *Baltimore Afro-American* took a different tact in their observation and thanked the governor for exposing "the comic aspects of the Dixiecrat struggle to prop up the tottering structure of segregation." "He also laid bare," the writer claimed, "the dismaying fact that the once Solid South no longer remains solid on this issue."[32] Doc Young argued that Griffin's move made "thousands of southerners who had never seen the foolhardiness of Jim Crow began to realize that race prejudice is the most ridiculous of the luxuries." He also believed that with all the heartache from the Emmett Till case, Tech's white students protesting the governor proved "that sports is America's greatest force for grass-roots democracy. Disagree, if you must," he added, "but can't you beat this?" As proof Young offered, "When Emmett Till was lynched, nobody in Mississippi burned Hugh White in effigy."[33] An editorial in the *California Eagle* called Governor Griffin an "All-American Heel" and argued that "the fracas proved that there is far more demand for segregation among the politicians who have been making careers out of negro baiting than there is among the people who are affected by the onsweep [sic] of integration." The writer also suggested that although the move "won't sound the death knell of segregation," the fight to play the game was important, because "it alerted many Georgia Tech students, and students of other Southern schools, to the absurd lengths to which proponents of segregation must inevitably be driven if they are to uphold a way of life that has long since outlived whatever small justification it ever had."[34]

As the black press also understood, the white reaction had an immediate impact on neighboring states. The *Eagle* noted the protest alerted government officials in Mississippi who were faced with the same fight Griffin had after a junior college team, Jones College, in Ellisville, Mississippi, agreed to play in the Little Rose Bowl—a bowl game for junior colleges—against a Compton (California) Community College that featured eight black players. Just months after the murder of Emmett Till in Mississippi and the subsequent farce of a trial that let the murderers off, seeing the black players from Compton "whip" the segregated white

Mississippians was a small consolation for black fans searching for small rays of hope after the Southern atrocity.[35]

When Grier finally played in the Sugar Bowl, his presence became one of the most important stories for black America that month. Marion Jackson called Bobby Grier the "Jackie Robinson of the Sugar Bowl" and noted that Americans who watched the television saw "Tech gridders show their Stars and Stripes on the gridiron" in interracial play. Jackson, however, also wrongly claimed, "Racial tension in sports even in the South simply doesn't exist."[36] In New Orleans, the local black newspaper, the *Louisiana Weekly*, also believed, wrongly, that Grier's gritty performance was a sign of things to come. Jim Hall predicted, "Allowing Grier to play is just another step towards the American way of life." Hall continued, "It's about time we toss 'Customs, traditions and prestige,' in the muddy Mississippi river, for today, when one of these racial segregation issues explode in the face of the nation, the South looks asinine and absurd." After Grier played, Hall declared, "Democracy in action is a wonderful thing to see."[37] But, to be sure, Hall's words were as much celebratory as they were a jab at local racist sporting organizations, especially the local minor league baseball team, the Pelicans, who refused to sign black players.

New Orleans

In New Orleans, local blacks glorified Grier's gridiron grit and filled the turnstiles, because his appearance represented a rare moment when they could actually sit in integrated seating and watch an integrated sporting event. It had happened only three times before, and all those opportunities featured basketball games within the previous year. A week before Grier played in the Sugar Bowl, the San Francisco Dons basketball team featuring black players, Bill Russell, K. C. Jones, and local star Warren Baxter, played against Loyola University, where the arena had integrated seats. Of this important contest, Bill Russell told a local black banquet, "Playing against Loyola is better than twenty-five Supreme Court Decisions."[38] In an editorial the *Weekly* praised Loyola "for making it possible for democracy to work in the true manner in which it was meant, whether at home or abroad." The writer continued, "It is even sweeter when considering that at last we are practicing democracy and the Christian concept we boast to the world about, right here in the haven of racial bigots."[39]

No doubt, lauding Loyola represented a dig at the local baseball team, the New Orleans Pelicans. At the time of Russell's visit, the *Weekly* and

Bill Russell, a dominant basketball player of the 1960s, led the Boston Celtics to 11 National Basketball Association championships in 13 years of play. (Library of Congress)

local black baseball fans had just finished the first year of what would be a three-year-long economic boycott of the local white baseball team, the Pelicans. The boycott, which began eight months before the Montgomery Bus Boycott, started in April 1955 after Jim Hall learned that the team, who had planned to play five black players that season—Ramon Majias, R. C. Stevens, Herb Bush, Ben Daniels, and Roberto Sanchez—suddenly dropped the players without warning. To make matters worse, the team's brass gave a sorry excuse as to why they chose to maintain segregation rather than integrate their squad. Jake Nowak, the general manager, explained that they cut the players because Stevens, Bush, and Daniels were not good enough to play Double A ball and that they cut Majias because they did not want to keep only one black player on their team.[40] To Hall and other black patrons of the Pelicans, that excuse made no sense. The Pelicans, as local black fans pointed out, traded Stevens to the Hollywood Bears, a higher-ranked Triple A team that would also pay him more money, and Majias was one of the best prospects in the Pirates organization and had success against major league pitching in spring training. The two men could have easily handled Double A play, and besides, Pelicans protesters pointed out, a black player could succeed by himself. In reality, the Pelicans had recently been bought by local owners who did not want any black men on the team, because the racist owners believed black players would drive white customers away. The exact opposite, however, happened. Black fans started the most successful boycott in sports history and shut the team down.[41]

From the onset, the boycott constituted a collective effort from the *Louisiana Weekly* and black fans from across the state. In its first editorial about the Pelicans' decision entitled "Phoney as a Wooden Nickel," the *Weekly* complained, "Negro citizens are not going to pay to be segregated to see a team that does not represent the things which we preach in our democracy." The writer also added, "If Nowak is not interested in using one Negro player, then we aren't interested in supporting a team that does not represent democracy in action."[42] During the boycott, Jim Hall, its sport's columnist, led the fight and used his column to mobilize his army of boycotters, asking fans to "sacrifice their personal pleasure to protect their principles," and also turned his column into a forum in which fans could share their disgust with the team.[43] In his first plea to protest, Hall wrote a column entitled "Will They Pay to Have 'Jim Crow' Kick Them in the Face During the Pel Season?" and ended the column urging "Negroes shouldn't pay to have 'Jim Crow' kick them in the teeth."[44] In another column, he told his readers to "stop the flow of the George Washingtons and Abe Lincolns (dollars) into the coffers" and predicted an economic boycott would force the people "who haven't been able to see 'eye to eye' in the past will begin to see things in a different light."[45] When he learned that the boycott frustrated the Pelicans' front office, he told his readers, "This is the thing which has frustrated the Pelican front office, for most whites are of the opinion that achieved unity among Negroes is an impossibility. It's taken a long time for the Tan fan who follows baseball in New Orleans to put his feet firm on the ground and stand up for democracy in baseball here. Because of the great stand taken by Negroes, it's quite evident that the 'jig is up' so far as supporting Jim Crow in baseball."[46] And after Hall learned that the Pelicans were going to hire black ticket agents to try and encourage black fans to come to the game, he shot back, "If Negro ball players are not good enough to play on the Pelican team, Negro dollars or any other kind of support should not be good enough for the Pelicans coffers, even if the ducats are sold at the window by Negro personnel." Hall finished that observation with a call to action and arguing, "Anyone who supports such a program," he argued, "upholds Jim Crowism and he or she is a traitor to the American way of life. Negroes don't have to pay to have someone slap them in the face with discrimination."[47]

Throughout the first phase of the boycotts, thousands of black fans proudly stayed away from the stadium and nearly bankrupted the team by the end of the summer. In a letter to the *Weekly*, a group of 200 black Korean War and World War II Veterans wrote in solidarity, "If we cannot see a tan face on the field—it is not uncommon to see one in this era—it is unjust to the tan citizens' cause to support such an organization." The Veterans asked the *Weekly* to "inform the uniformed Negro public of this outrage and urge them to refrain from attending any Pelican ball games so long as Negroes are barred from its roster."[48] Another fan wrote, "I am one of the many who laud the position you took. It is high time that we wake up and refuse to patronize those who persist in denying Negroes their constitutional and God-given rights." And a woman pleaded, "I hope that every red-blooded race man here read what you wrote and I hope that every man who has an ounce of race pride will govern himself accordingly." She ended her stance by urging Hall, "My husband and I like that kind of journalism. Give us some more."[49] And a month into the successful boycott, the field secretary of the NAACP, Clarence Laws, added support from the branch and said, "Whatever happens you and the *Weekly* can take much of the credit because of your strong and incessant fight to eliminate segregation from sports and other areas of community life. Congratulations and keep up the good work."[50] By midsummer, the boycott and letter-writing campaign had taken hold all throughout the South, and black sportswriters in Atlanta, Birmingham, and Memphis advised their readers to stay at home too. If white owners did not want black players to play for their teams, or black fans to sit in integrated seating, then black fans would bankrupt their teams. In New Orleans, the ability of black fans to financially bankrupt a team became a reality within two years.

By 1957, the boycott had financially crippled the Pelicans, making it nearly impossible to have a successful team. The numbers did not lie. The estimated black attendance dramatically dropped from an estimated

40,000–50,000 fans before the boycott to 3,000 in 1956. Overall, the average attendance dropped from 1,300 a game in 1956 to 900 by 1957. And in 1956, the club had only 90,000 fans attend games, a dramatic decrease from the 400,000 in 1947, their best year.[51] The team had to fold in the 1959 season. But the damage had been done. As Hall stated in 1957, "The poor showing at the turnstiles here is a result of the Dixiecrats tossing their seeds of bigotry into sports. For years, the race haters have tried to narrow the broad concepts of sports to their small concepts of human dignity. They have been so busy scheming to preserve segregation in sports in Dixie, that they have forgotten their financial obligations." Even the Pelicans' GM Vince Rizzo complained, "Give me the 40,000 Negro fans we lost last year and we're out of trouble."[52] By this time, however, even if the Pelicans wanted to sign a black player, they could not. The previous year, the state passed a mixed sports ban, denying all integration in sports.

In 1956, the same racist forces that developed after the *Brown* decision also touched Louisiana and made their presence known in the first state-wide election they touched. That election, the White Citizen's Council sent a number of diehard segregationists to the state house and also helped elect Earl K. Long as governor. Although Long received a significant number of black votes—some estimate as high as 100,000—almost immediately after he won the governorship, in July 1956, Long, as the *Weekly* put it, "sympathized with Hitleristic 'pro-seg'—hate groups and tossed righteousness into the winds by giving his stamp of approval to ban interracially mixed athlete contests in Louisiana."[53] House Bill 1412, which went into effect on October 15, included a ban on athletic training, games, sports contests, social functions, dancing, entertainment, sanitary drinking water, segregated seating, and other places that blacks and whites would gather.

As expected, the black backlash to the bigotry was swift and condemned the state legislator of racism and refusing to move along with mainstream America. In its first editorial after the ban passed, the *Weekly* told its readers that the politicians bowed "to the wishes of the white supremacy extremists," and the paper scoffed, "It's laughable and tragic at the same time to see men of assumed intelligence and character in the legislature pass such crackpot legislation." In its main argument, the editorial suggested that this law would impact the white athletes more than blacks, because it would fill white men up with a sense of false racial superiority. In another editorial entitled "A Dire Reflection on Democracy," a writer suggested, "The simple, pathetic absurdity of those afflicted by ideas of white supremacy is becoming increasingly obvious and almost unbelievable. In their racial superiority fanaticism they appear to be losing their minds. Instead of acting and thinking like Americans who believe in democracy, fair play, Christianity, and the 'the Golden Rule' they are in their dull, ignorant way accepting and promoting the fascist-Hitlerite philosophy."[54] And, of course, Hall, took his shots at the new law and racist politicians. In his first full-length comments about the mixed law ban, Hall complained, "They say 'HITLER IS DEAD', that's hard to believe for in these days of racial restrictions in Louisiana, Hitlerism seems to be in mass productions in the Pelican State." And Hall correctly pointed out that, "The mixed ban is a delaying action to try and slow down the integration program in the Pelican State. That is the big issue— A slow down."[55]

In order to fight the ban, Hall recommended that blacks sue the state and boycott sporting events. He ordered that whites and blacks who favored integration should take their fight to the court and battle "the race-baiting politicians, who have rammed through laws forcing racial bans." And if the white institutions that made money off integrated sports were not willing to fight for fairness, Hall knew his people would fight back. He predicted, "It is almost certain that Negroes here and there in Louisiana will be as noticeable at any white promoted sports attraction as Gov. Long and the law-makers would be at [the] 'Free-The-Negro' Convention."[56] Hall's prediction almost came to fruition. The same set of folks who had been boycotting the Pelicans for more than a year discussed boycotting the upcoming lightweight championship bout between local black fighter Joe Brown and his black opponent Bud Smith. The fight represented the first major contest after the governor announced his support of the mixed sports law, but also the first championship contest in the Crescent City in more than 30 years. To test the potential of the boycott, Hall took to the streets to ask local black residents their opinions on the matter. Allen D. Torregano, an electrician, argued "We should boycott the fight," and added, "I don't know how much effect a boycott will have, but I think it's time we did something to protest the manner in which we are being treated. We have to be 100 percent strong to prove our point." Another man, indicating the urgency of the boycott, asserted, "Boycotting is an effective weapon . . . this we have observed in other Southern Cities. Let's use our 'Stay at home' weapon, proving to others that we can be united here in New Orleans." But in the end, most blacks went to the fight, sat in segregated seating, and supported one of their hometown heroes as he won the championship. They followed the assumptions of Leroy L. Porter, a clerical worker, who noted: "The irrational minds responsible for the passage of this bill care not one iota how many Negroes refrain from investing in the price of an admission ticket to this, or any other athletic affair staged in the state."[57] To be sure, Brown's rise from poverty in the segregated city to champion of the world gave local blacks hope. Brown won his title, but eventually made Houston his hometown. He wanted to fight the more lucrative integrated fights.

While the black press placed the blame where it should have been, with racist white legislators, local white writer James Keefe of the *Times Picayune* ignored the legacy of Jim Crow in his state, and the fact that Governor Long also passed 13 other Jim Crow laws that session, and instead blamed Jackie Robinson for the law. Keefe's main argument? Robinson refused to remain silent. In attacking the baseball pioneer, Keefe concluded, "The NAACP can thank Jackie Robinson, persistently insolent and antagonistic trouble-making Negro of the Brooklyn Dodgers for the law. . . . None of the most rabid segregationists accomplished as much as Robinson did in widening the breach between the white people and Negroes. He has been the most harmful influence the Negro race has suffered in the attempt to give the Negro nation-wide recognition in the sports field." Robinson, who refused to hold his tongue about racism, hit back hard. In an open letter, Robinson noted, "I really am proud that a man like Keefe dislikes me and what I stand for. It's the kind of an American that is losing prestige for us all over the world. . . . I as a Negro can stand all the lies and slurs he can dish out but as a Negro American I hate to see what he is doing to our country." Robinson scolded Keefe, "Am I insolent, or am I merely insolent for a Negro (who has courage enough to speak against injustices such as yours and people like you)?" Robinson also told Keefe that he was "deeply regretful" that the state passed the law because of "the damage it does to our country" by further eliminating the equal rights of black Americans. In his hallmark tone, Robinson ended his letter saying, "I am happy for you, that you were born white. It would have been extremely difficult for you had it been otherwise."[58] But, to be clear, some white people rejected the bill. They were not openly concerned with racial equality; however, they cared only about their economics.

The shortsighted sports law garnered immediate response from white sports businessmen who stood to lose money and prestige. The president of the Texas League, Dick Butler, pleaded with Governor Long to repeal the bill, because, as Butler argued, the bill would bankrupt the Shreveport baseball team, and because teams in the integrated league would not be able to bring their black players, and thus black fans would boycott the games. His prediction came to fruition. In less than a year after the bill passed, Shreveport had to financially fold because black fans boycotted the games. Paul E. DeBlanc, president of the Mid-Winter Sports Association, the group that oversaw the Sugar Bowl, also begged Governor Long to reconsider his position. The Sugar Bowl leaders knew that if the bowl went back to segregation, Northern teams would refuse to play in the game, thus cutting out a significant revenue stream. In order to avoid the economic consequences of the law, DeBlanc and his associates tried to push through a special exemption for the Sugar Bowl. The state legislature voted it down. Integration would affect everyone. State senator Willie Rainach, who spearheaded the bill, boasted, "Regardless of what these institutions may have to say, I think the people of Louisiana still want segregated athletics." Not to be outdone in his short-sightedness, state representative Lawrence Gibbs, who wrote the bill, argued that these universities were just bluffing and argued that "money and prestige will be a strong inducement for Sugar Bowl teams to leave their Negro players at home."[59] He was wrong. When the bill became law, integrated teams immediately withdrew their names from consideration, including Pitt and Wisconsin, who also withdrew from a planned home-away series with Louisiana State University. As Jim Hall stated, "These universities (Wisconsin and Pitt) only recognize the academic and athletic competence, not the color of one's skin in determining who shall represent their respective schools and meeting another institution in athletic events."[60]

The law also impacted the boxing ring. The National Boxing Association (NBA), for example, refused to sanction any bouts in the state as long as the law remained and called the law "completely repugnant to the spirit of America and the principles of freedom so clearly enunciated by the Supreme Court of the United States."[61] The NBA boycott would potentially economically cripple New Orleans, a hotbed for fighting, if the NBA stopped sanctioning fights in the state, because by 1957, the majority of champions and top contenders were black men, including local champion Joe Brown and local favorite Joe Dorsey, who had already felt the financial sting of having to fight in a segregated state.

In fact, Dorsey, looking for a fair chance to work in his home state, knocked out the mixed sports law. Although unheralded in the civil rights movement, Dorsey won one of the biggest battles against Jim Crow, as the destruction of the mixed sports ban paved the way for the end of Jim Crow in the state. Dorsey's fight against state segregation started a year prior to the passage of the mixed sports ban, when in 1955, Dorsey, the top 10–ranked lightweight, sued the Athletic Commission for discriminating against black boxers. In his suit, which never made it to court, he stipulated that the Athletic Commission's ban on mixed bouts violated the equal protection clause of the Fourteenth Amendment. Before

1956, Louisiana did not have a law restricting black and white men from fighting each other; rather, the Athletic Commission banned the practice and would not sanction mixed fights. According to Dorsey, the Athletic Commission's Jim Crow policy severely restricted his income, because he could fight only a handful of black boxers, doing so for a smaller purse. If he could fight white fighters, he estimated, he would make roughly $10,000 a fight opposed to $600 against a black opponent. Without fair compensation, Dorsey, who dropped out of school at the age of 15 to get married and support his family, had to work extra jobs, including a $45-a-week job as a night janitor. Dorsey also had to borrow money from his manager, putting him in further debt. "Sometimes you want to run away," he told *Jet*. "You get tired always fixing things around somebody else's house, but you're afraid if you ask them they'll put you out. You get tried worrying if the rats will eat up your kids. You get tired killing termites all the time."[62] Therefore, Dorsey sued for the right to fight white men. But the original case never made it to court, because as he waited for his case, Louisiana passed the mixed sports ban.

In 1957, Dorsey sued the state again. This time, however, he sued the state claiming that Act 579, the mixed sports law, violated his civil rights and the equal protection clause of the Fourteenth Amendment. In November 1958, three federal judges declared Louisiana's mixed sports ban unconstitutional.[63] Dorsey believed he would no longer have to ponder the what-ifs, as he told *Jet*: "If I could just get a few good fights under my belt . . . if I could just make enough money to buy a home . . . If I could just put my family in a decent home, I wouldn't mind fixing things. I'm a good man with my hands."[64] The state appealed the decision, but in 1959 the Supreme Court threw out the appeal, citing the law as unconstitutional. Unfortunately for Dorsey, the big integrated paydays in his home state never came. The Athletic Commission did not authorize a mixed bout until 1965 when Kenny Lange and Eddie Perkins battled in a 10-round bout. This match came on the heels of black professional football players, collectively for the first time, channeling the political activism of the civil rights movement.

In January 1965, just a week after the Crescent City hosted its first integrated Sugar Bowl since 1956, 21 black players in the American Football League (AFL) made a political decision that exposed a still segregated city when they refused to play in their upcoming all-star game in response to the persistent discrimination they faced leading up to the game. Hall, who called the 1965 Sugar Bowl "sweeter because some brown coloring has been added to the mixture," concluded that the game allowed New Orleans "to start the New Year right, that is, the American way."[65] Although most shared a similar sentiment about progress, had they listened to the eight black Syracuse football players, rather than using the players as props to suggest New Orleans was moving past racism, they would have known New Orleans remained stuck in its racist ways. Syracuse players struggled to get cabs on the streets, had businesses refuse them service, and were called "niggers" by onlookers.[66] Yet, because of their college status and the historical importance of the bowl game, they had to endure the bitter hate and play in the Sugar Bowl. But the pro players, who had grown accustomed to better treatment as professional football players, were not going to put up with discrimination.

Emboldened by the civil rights movement, the black football players banded together to boycott the all-star game to protest the daily racism they faced while in New Orleans. Although they were allowed to stay at an upscale integrated hotel, the rest of the city felt off limits to the players, and equally as embarrassing, they were dehumanized, including being called "Niggers." When they realized this racism would not cease, they decided to leave the city. One player, who remained anonymous, asserted, "It's easy to see how New Orleans could have given birth to the blues, even if it didn't. This place is an 'illegitimate mother' in its race relations." Running back Cookie Gilchrist reflected, "The city rolled out the red carpet and jerked it from beneath us. Then it got mad when we didn't fall." Running back Clem Daniels added, "We went to New Orleans to put on a great game and relax a little. We were refused, abused, and not wanted. So we left."[67] Art Powell, a star wide receiver who had a history of standing up against Jim Crow, said, "We know we aren't going to change these people. But neither are they going to change us. We must act as our conscience dictates." In 1960, as a rookie trying to make the Philadelphia Eagles, Powell quit the team after the team hotel in Norfolk, Virginia, denied him a room. Five years later, in New Orleans, when confronted with racial hostility, he boycotted the all-star game.[68]

Black sportswriters and athletes celebrated the activist spirit of these athletes and also chastised the mayor for suggesting black players "role with the punch." Countering the mayor's insensitive words, the *Weekly* bluntly stated, "It is impossible for any white person to completely place himself in the position occupied by any Negro. Any white person who attempts to do this must allow his imagination to travel back to the days of his earliest remembrances—to childhood days to being relegated to inferior and jim crow schools . . . to be refused certain jobs because of race . . . to being placed in inferior, segregated housing ghettoes." The editorial went on to assert, "If there is any white person who can pass this test, then and only then, is such a person psychologically prepared to imagine how he would react if he were subjected to the indignities experienced by the 21 Negro AFL players."[69] And Hall hailed, "We think the Negro players were right for not bowing to racial discrimination. That jive of the 'Players should have 'rolled with the punch' is for kookaburras. For more than one hundred years, Negroes have been rolling with the punch. The case in point, proves that the Negroes today, will not take the Sunday hate punches anymore."[70] Jackie Robinson proclaimed, "Personally I think the Negro stars deserve a great deal of credit. They are unwilling, as the Negro people are unwilling, to accept half a loaf. . . . We have been through centuries of that kind of thing." From Chicago, Superior Court judge Duke Slater, an all-American player in the 1920s when he played at Iowa, claimed, "All Negroes were lifted and inspired by the stand they took. The city of New Orleans lost more than a million dollars in tourist trade because of the disgraceful treatment accorded these Negro athletes. And when you hit them in the pocketbook, there is a good chance of getting results." Sam Lacy of the *Afro-American* asserted, "My grandfather and yours 'rolled with the punch' and their grandfathers before them did the same. . . . Today's grandfathers of the future are asking why it is that colored people are destined to be the only ones in this country showing the Christian attitude of turning the other cheek." Lacy closed, "They're interested in knowing why it is that we must content ourselves with being first class citizens only when the bugle blows for war and at income tax time."[71] And in the *Philadelphia Tribune*, an editorialist agreed with their actions, summed up what many felt in the civil rights movement, when he ordered, "The days of tokenism are on the way out. Men and women of intelligence must set an example. These young men did that."[72]

Until that moment, nobody had seen professional athletes united in mass to protest, and boycott, racial discrimination. One letter writer to *Ebony* celebrated the players while using this moment to challenge black athletes who remained content to leave things as they were. "I hope that other Negro celebrities in any field will follow the glorious examples of those football players," he said, "especially one silent baseball player who was being toasted in the Polo Grounds [Willie Mays] while he seemed to be oblivious to Negroes being washed in gutters by powerful fire hoses, bitten by ferocious dogs and beaten by even more ferocious cops in his and my hometown, Birmingham (Alabama)."[73] Most important for the players, their bosses had their backs. With the support of the AFL and, apparently, a number of white teammates who were willing to boycott with them, the game moved to Houston. Three years prior Houston had integrated its sporting facilities, a fact largely due to the tireless work of the local black press and citizens willing to boycott Jim Crow sporting events.

Houston

Houston's transition from a segregated Southern city—in December 1961 UCLA coach John Wooden deemed it the most segregated city his team had played—to a major league integrated sporting metropolis in 1962 was made possible by black activists taking advantage of local white businessmen's desire to push Houston as a modern city. Houston's vision of being a modern city with a major league team could be achieved, black activists demanded, only if the city integrated sporting facilities. At the head of the fight stood Lloyd C. Wells, a black sportswriter for the *Houston Informer*, who used his platform in the paper, and his position in the community, to rally black citizens around the cause of integration. In his first major battle for local sporting integration, one that took nearly five years to achieve, he pushed the local minor league baseball team, the Buffs, to integrate their seating. In 1961, after years of protesting the squad, the team finally integrated the stadium. That year, in early January, Wells and other activists also pushed the mayor to eliminate the city ban on integrated play in the parks and recreation basketball league to allow black teams to enter a local tournament. A black team won the tournament, and four black players made the all-city team.

But Houston still presented major problems for black fans and athletes. In April, when the Houston Golf Classic played at a public facility and denied entry to Charlie Sifford, the *Informer*'s editorialist fired back, "It must be that segregationists seek humiliation and domination more than separation of the race. The fact that more negroes than not have white blood in them shows that separation is the very last thing in the world that some people are interested in." The rebuke slammed white men for their hypocrisy; white men did not mind "integrating" with black women. Moreover, the editorialist moved past miscegenation and placed the segregationist snub in a Cold War and civil rights movement context, adding, "While Americans are spending their time keeping Charlie Sifford out of golf tournaments and Negro students out of the best schools in the segregation states, the Communists are having a field day promoting their cause and building their fences among the colored people of the world."[74] Local black Houstonians also faced the problem of segregated seating at the public football stadium and the sporting facilities at the University of Houston. Despite their segregation policy, these institutions courted black fans to fill their coffers. But soon, black fans would not put up with this treatment.

The first collective boycott by black athletes in America occurred in June 1961, when several black athletes refused to participate in the Meet of Champions hosted by the University of Houston. At this track and field meet, the University of Houston refused to remove the racial barriers placed on black fans. With leading black athletes set to attend, including high jumper John Thomas and world-record long jumper Ralph Boston, and eight leading athletes from one of the top track teams in the nation, Texas Southern University of Houston, meet officials expected a large turnout of black fans. Of the nearly 8,000 black fans officials expected to sit in segregated seating, only a handful—one count noted three— attended the event. How did this happen? Wells used the power of the press to organize local black residents and black athletes in a boycott. Thomas and Boston, however, were not easily convinced. The Olympians were still stuck in their beliefs that athletics offered the best means to push integration, and it took public pressure for the two stars to realize that by withholding their athletic bodies, they could also have an impact on race relations. Irritated by the star athletes' unwillingness to boycott the event, a local activist said that the two were "insults to the Negro race" and added they had been "brainwashed" by local whites. Eventually, however, when Thomas and Boston arrived at the stadium and saw the picket lines, they refused to cross. Thomas said, "I'm not going to go in there as long as these people are out here picketing." Celebrating his handiwork, Wells applauded, "One thing for sure, Negroes did unite and stick together as one in this matter. . . . I'm going on record here and now as saying that WE (Negroes) should never attend another segregated sports event here again."[75] In remarks that revealed the utter inflexibility of white segregationists, however, instead of looking to solve their racist problem, a meet official suggested to create a whites-only meet. After reading that suggestion, the editorialist for the *Informer* replied that racism helped "Russia to get ahead of the United States in trying to win the minds and hearts of the colored peoples, who make up three-fourths of the population of the world."[76] That astute proclamation boldly connected the civil rights struggle to the decolonization efforts, and reflected a new attitude in black Americans, an attitude quickly becoming noticeable in black athletes.

The boycott sparked immediate response from famous black athletes. Jesse Owens, however, did not like that activists bullied Thomas to boycott and argued it was "a pretty silly thing to withdraw young athletes who are college students because of a social structure," concluding, "Competition in athletics has broken down more barriers than almost any other thing."

In opposition to Owens, Jackie Robinson encouraged the athletes to "do your part" and noted that other college students were already risking

Jesse Owens (left) with Ralph Metcalf, before competing in the 100-yard dash during the Olympic tryouts in New York on July 11, 1936. (Library of Congress)

their lives in the "ongoing Freedom Rides movement."[77] This would not be the last time the two icons sparred over the role of black athletes in the civil rights movement. Robinson believed athletes had to use their platform to exact change, while Owens continued to believe athletic success alone would be enough to fight Jim Crow. Other black athletes, however, gained inspiration from the Houston protests.

Importantly, the successful track boycott garnered national attention and gave black athletes across the nation a blueprint with how to deal with segregated seating. In August, Virginia's NAACP asked the 19 black play-ers on the Baltimore Colts and the Pittsburgh Steelers to boycott a game in Roanoke, Virginia, because the public stadium had segregated seating. In a phone interview, Colts star player, Lenny Moore, told Wells that they did not know what they would do, but "we definitely don't want to play before a segregated audience. We have played before them before, but times have changed now." Moore noted that he read what happened in Houston and added, "What Ralph Boston and John Thomas did was right and the only thing they should have done under the circumstances as we know of them." He also invoked students in the civil rights movement and stated, "I am fully away of the sacrifices, Negro students strikes, and freedom rides. All of these things will be taken into consideration when were arrive at our decision." And Steelers defensive standout "Big Daddy" Lipscomb proudly stated to the press that he would "stick by my race." Eventually the other 18 black players decided to stick with their race and not cross the picket line. The threat of a boycott forced the city to integrate the sta-dium.[78] This important victory gave Wells some hope that he could accom-plish the same monumental feat and integrate Houston's football stadium. He had his work cut out. For that to happen, he would need the owners to willingly drop their racist bars or black players to boycott.

In Houston's first year in the AFL, 1960, the Houston Oilers signed black players—Julian Spence and John White—but they refused to com-pletely integrate their stadium and they barred black reporters from the press box. Wells spent the inaugural year campaigning against the racial exclusion and trying to get black fans to boycott the games. He had little hopes, however, the black residents would follow his lead. He derided, "It's no use urging Negroes to not attend the Oiler games here from the attitudes of several I've talked to, they will be out there like the white man wants them." In a presumed attack on the local black middle class, Wells also noted that local apathy to the growing civil rights movement, and complained, "Those who don't believe in the Sit-movements of Negro Col-lege students throughout the USA and the Alabama Bus Strikes and all the other protest movements made by Negroes throughout the USA in the past few years, then I'm quite sure you will feel no qualms about going out there and sitting in 'your place.'"[79] But to his surprise, 50 black fans attended the first game—in comparison 6,000 black fans sat in integrated seats in Dallas to see the Oilers play the Texas—and the numbers dwin-dled from there. Of those 50 who showed up, Wells winced, "They were the fifty biggest fools in Texas."[80] Despite the fact that Wells pushed owner Bud Adams to reconcile this racism, Adams would not even meet with the sports journalist to discuss the problem.

To make sure this racism ceased in the second year, Wells went on the attack. After placing a call to the ticket office, and learning that "colored tickets" would be limited to a section of the stadium—they were not allowed on the east side of the stadium—Wells quickly passed on the information to his readers. In a powerful editorial, Wells, the World War II veteran, appealed to "four freedoms" and the democratic ideas that garnered patriotic support to fight in a brutal war against racism and fascism. In a heartfelt letter, he said "Making me sit in a penned off area and depriving me of the same privileges that another person has because my skin is of a darker hue than his, makes me wonder what type of person and people these are who will contrive to do this injustice to me that the 'Four Freedoms' of our nation and the constitution of the USA states is unlawful." He added, "I hope every Negro in Texas will stay away from the Oilers games until they start treating all of the people as citizens."[81] To keep the black fans out of the stands, he used CORE, the NAACP, and the locally powerful Progressive Youth Association (PYA), a civil rights organization of young activists who had worked tirelessly to bring integration to the community. Unlike the NAACP, which reportedly did not picket the games—the organization did not hold picket signs until December—the PYA protested every home game that season.

The boycott lasted the whole season, but as the season progressed, more and more black fans started to cross the line, prompting Wells to challenge their insubordination, arguing, "Any Negro that goes out there and sits through a ball game under such conditions that exist is a little lower than a snail."[82] In reality, the picket did not work as well as the boycott of the Meet of Champions, because the Oilers compromised the protests by using other leading voices in the black community to encourage black fans to attend the game and by keeping Wells away from opposing opponents. When the Oakland Raiders came to town at the beginning of the year, for example, the Oilers sent a police escort to shield the black players from Wells and whisked the players away from the protesters.[83] But even those who learned about the boycott balked, and for that they caught the ire of Wells. In November, Wells complained, "Every Negro in the American Football League that has played here against the Houston Oilers is an insult to the actions of the hundreds of Negro youth who have made great personal sacrifices for the principles of human rights and gave up their chances at completing their education and in some cases the right to attend school and served jail time in fighting for these principals [sic] that benefit all Negroes." In other words, Wells tried to tell the players that the black community sacrificed their lives for integration and it was time that the black athletes sacrifice a little, too. But in 1961, most would not hear of that critique. When Abner Hayes, the star running back for the Dallas Texans, crossed the line, Wells charged, he "could have gained the admiration of the nation by refusing to play here, but just like a coward he went out and looked worse than he ever has in his entire football career."[84]

In his most successful boycott, for a game against San Diego Chargers, Wells managed to disseminate the protest information to the Chargers' black players weeks in advance of the planned boycott, to give them time to prepare. For this move, Wells even included the local black press in the Los Angeles and the San Diego branches of the NAACP to spread the word, and contacted the coach of the team, Sid Gilliam. Although Wells thought it would be possible to convince the nine black Chargers to join the protest, he still understood the reality that it would not happen. So just in case, he fired off words meant to sting the black players' pride, saying that if they played, "they are an insult to every Negro in the nation, a slap at every kid who has made a personal sacrifice by going to jail for participating in sit-ins and a mighty poor example of a man." He closed his weekly editorial, optimistically stating, "I can't believe that these fine young athletes are rank to the extent they would go against their race for the matter of personal gain and such. It remains to be seen."[85] But, in reality, the past attempts to boycott the Oilers, only to see the black players cross the picket line, should have given Wells a hint; these young men were not going to risk their economic livelihoods to fight stadium segregation.

Despite a massive picket, with signs that read "Enter Here: The Gutless," black players crossed the line and observed their contracts. Wells did not miss his opportunity to shame them by comparing the apathetic players with young civil rights activists. "At the time Negro Chargers were walking into the segregated Jeppesen Stadium," he reported, "Negroes were going to jail in Mississippi and Maryland for fighting the very thing these men were upholding, many of these sit-in strikers were leaving their jobs knowingly without any idea, if ever, when they would be able to return to them." Despite the fact that Wells and his activists did not get any of the players to join the picket, the prolonged fight produced one positive; the San Diego players said they would never play in a segregated stadium, and the Chargers' brass supported their players, agreeing to avoid segregated stadiums in their schedule. But for that to happen, Houston would have to integrate, or the Chargers would have to keep their black players home.[86]

The continued racism in segregated seating, and racist fandom—UCLA played in a winter tournament in December in an integrated arena after they demanded integration to play, but the racism from fans, players, and officials was so bad John Wooden held his black players out a game— raised an important question: would the city treat Ernie Banks, Willie Mays, and Hank Aaron this way? In 1960, Major League Baseball (MLB) approved a new franchise in Houston (Colt 45s), and leaders in the black community used this as leverage to integrate not only sporting facilities but also the city itself. Local white businessmen and city boosters believed that bringing a major league team to the city would signal that Houston was a modern metropolis due the respect of other major cities in America. But to achieve this goal, they needed a new stadium in order to prove to Major League Baseball that the city had the facilities to attract a team. In order to build a new stadium, what would eventually be called the Astrodome, the Houston Sports Association (HSA) got a bond placed on the ballot for the 1958 election. To pass that bond, however, it knew it needed all the votes it could get, so it tapped black business leaders to generate the black vote. As a stipulation to getting the black vote, however, black leaders, like Quentin Mease, demanded that the stadium and hiring practices of the team be integrated. HSA agreed and the bond passed. With a bond and stadium plans in place, HSA went to the MLB to get a team, and in 1960, MLB awarded Houston a franchise. Before the meeting, however, just to make sure HSA did not cross the local black leadership, Mease sent a letter to the chairman of the league, Walter O'Malley, that told O'Malley that the stadium had to be integrated. The following year, however, with projected costs for the stadium exceeding expectations, HSA needed the city voters to approve another bond. Once again, with the help of the black vote, city voters approved the bond. And the black community got what they were fighting for. In 1962, with the start of its first baseball season—the Astrodome would not be ready until 1964—Houston integrated all of its facilities to avoid public humiliation. The combination of sports and activism broke down barriers in Houston.[87]

The city had progressed so much in the field of sports and integration that the University of Houston, which integrated in 1963, also gave its athletic coaches full permission to pursue black talent. Houston, a school that was fighting for recognition among the highly touted schools in Texas, decided that it would use sports to boost its profile. Getting a jump on the top black athletes, coaches reasoned, would help them do the trick. In 1964, the football team signed Warren McVea out of San Antonio, the best running back in the state. In order to recruit McVea, Houston's football coach Bill Yeoman used Houston's leading black businessmen, lawyers, and doctors to sell McVea on being a black barrier breaker. As Yeoman told *Sports Illustrated*, "When I met with some of our Negro leaders, I told them that I'm prejudiced. I'm prejudiced against bad football players. If I didn't think Warren McVea had more ability than any kid in the state, I wouldn't want him."[88] Behind the promise of fair treatment, and a supportive black elite, McVea took the plunge. Although injuries limited his career—he still made second team all-American his senior year—McVea's success forced other Texas schools to recruit black athletes. That same year, the basketball team signed high school stalwarts from Louisiana, Don Chaney and Elvin Hayes, who would eventually lead the team to the Final Four in 1967 and 1968. During the duo's freshman year, Texas Western's basketball team famously started five black players in their championship game against the all-white starting five of Kentucky, a school that at that time refused to integrate, in what many people believe was the most important game in college basketball history. In fact, sports historian Charles Martin argued that the game "stands today as a watershed in the social history of college basketball."[89] Indeed, the game helped further open the gates of integration.

When Texas Western coach Don Haskins made a conscious decision to start five black players and also only play his two black reserves in the game—the team also had one Mexican American player and three white players—he quickened the integration of big-time Southern college sports. Viewers watching their televisions, and fans in the stands, could not help but notice the racial optics of the game. As Bill Nunn Jr. noted in the *Pittsburgh Courier*, "This was a game that featured the Old South and the new," with Texas Western representing what black people hoped was the New South, where color did not count. Much like Houston did when they signed McVea, Hayes, and Chaney, Texas Western, as a smaller Southern school, intentionally recruited black players to compete with the bigger Southern schools, like Texas or Kentucky, who refused to integrate. But the most renowned player on that team, rim-rocking David Lattin, a Houston native, who had previously played at Tennessee State, was the only black Southerner, because Haskins, who received the job in 1963, broadened his recruitment and signed his other black players from Northern cities, including Gary, Indiana, Detroit, and New York, and convinced them to return South in a reverse migration.

Beyond Haskins's remarkable ability to convince Northern black players to return to the South, the Texas Western's victory holds social significance, because white Southern schools learned that if they wanted to continue to compete at the highest level in college sports, they had to sign black players. L. I. Brockenbury, of the *Los Angeles Sentinel*, accurately predicted that the victory symbolized "a harbinger of things to come" and noted "the fact that more and more Southern 'white' universities are

Their white teammates, who felt ashamed by what they saw, offered to eat with their black teammates, but the black women, understanding the racial politics, gave them their out; they said they could eat where they wanted. The white women ate in the Jim Crow restaurants. Upset about what she saw, newly minted citizen Olga Fikotova Connolly, from Czechoslovakia, told the white press exactly how America treated its black athletes. Acting in the role of a white ally, Connolly said, "The Negro girls are not being served downtown. Earlene Brown has had to eat out of cans. We have found one lunch counter downtown that will serve us in a separate room."[2] Witnessing Jim Crow firsthand shocked the new citizen, who believed in the idea of American democracy. In her response to the criticism, Francis T. Kaszubski, the chairwoman of the national track and field committee argued, "Mrs. Connolly is not quite adjusted to our American way of doing things and she acted hastily." In other words, in America, black women who wanted to make the Olympic team and represent their country had to adjust to indignity. Hitting back at this blatant insensitivity by Mrs. Kaszubski, a black writer critiqued, "Mrs. Connolly did not act 'too hastily.' It may be the old American way to discriminate and segregate Negroes, but let's hope the motto of the new American way is to treat all Americans equally. America can ill afford the luxury of this or any other kind of discrimination."[3] As this support for Mrs. Connolly concluded, the presence of the black Olympians internationalized the problem of American race relations and forced the black athletes to look internally concerning their status in America as second-class citizens. For the Olympic qualifiers in Abilene, however, the Olympic committee made sure the athletes did not have to face Jim Crow. For the athletes, the city integrated all the facilities, housing, and restaurants. After all, how would it look if the athletes who qualified for the American Olympic team did so in segregation?

For the black athlete, participating in the Olympics during the civil rights movement raised the specter of what W.E.B. Du Bois called the "double consciousness" of black Americans. As Du Bois articulated, "It is a peculiar sensation, this double-consciousness, this sense of always looking at one's self through the eyes of other, of measuring one' soul by the tape of a world that looks on in amused contempt and pity. One ever feels his twoness—an American, a Negro; two souls, two thoughts, two unreconciled strivings; two warring ideals in one dark body, whose dogged strength alone keeps it from being torn asunder."[4] Black Olympians had a difficult question to answer; should they be proud of their opportunity and freedom to pursue their prowess, or should their status of celebrated heroes in a segregated society make them wary of American democracy?

Certainly, these great athletes enjoyed the opportunity to compete at the highest level and represent their country internationally. In fact, between 1948 and 1964, very few black athletes openly complained about the internal struggles they faced while representing their country. Most of the black athletes came from poverty, struggled to survive the exploitive amateur sports model that asked them to compete for free, and viewed athletics, and the Olympics by extension, as their main way to escape poverty. Although many black Olympians hated the situation, they dared not complain, understanding that to buck the system would bring personal problems. Instead, they chose to do their part, win and celebrate America as a beacon of democratic hope in the Cold War, and stand as symbols of progress. As Marion E. Jackson of the *Atlanta Daily World* proclaimed, "Negro athletes are becoming Uncle Sam's best diplomats abroad."[5] Uncle Sam used his black athletes and used them well.

With the backdrop of the Cold War and the civil rights movement, this chapter explores the meaning of the black Olympians from 1948 to 1964 and how their presence represented a dilemma for democracy. While the presence of black athletes allowed Americans to celebrate American exceptionalism and convince themselves that opportunities and victories for black athletes proved that the American way of life would triumph over internal racism and external evil, alternatively the optics of black Olympians in a Jim Crow society forced many Americans to reflect on the deep-seeded roots of racism in their own country. Could black Americans continue to represent their country abroad, yet live as second-class citizens at home?

A Prelude to the Games: Race, Jim Crow, and the 1946 AAU Championships

In 1946, black track athletes received their first tastes of the slow pace of American democracy in a postwar world, when in January 1946, the AAU chose San Antonio as the next site for the national track and field meet. This marked the first time since 1914 (Baltimore) that they held the meet in a state with legal segregation. In 1927, the AAU had scheduled its meet in New Orleans, hoping that the Southern city would temporarily erase Jim Crow, but when it became clear the city would not drop the color line, outside organizations pressured the AAU to move the event. In short, the organization did not want to force its black athletes to endure segregation. Thus, when the AAU decided to host the contest in the segregated South in 1946, the black press immediately tapped into its protest tradition and went after the amateur organization. It did not come as a surprise that the same radical left-leaning newspaper that had forced

Branch Rickey to try out Negro League players the prior year, the *People's Voice*, led the attack against the AAU. Rick Hurt, of the *People's Voice*, a pro-labor black-owned newspaper in Harlem, started his fight against the AAU in support of Joe Yancey, the track coach of the Pioneer Athletic Club, who said his team of 50 competitors would not compete in the South. In Hurt's first editorial—he fought the AAU in the press for nearly two months—which led with the words "TO TEXAS, WE WON'T GO," he vividly described the indignity of riding the Southern rails and how the substandard food, accommodations, and racism hampered the black athletes mentally and physically, ensuring that they could not perform at their best. When informed by the AAU that black athletes in the North could buy first-class Pullman tickets and ride unmolested to San Antonio, he quickly reminded them that Southern conductors would never let that happen and that if blacks were allowed to make it toward the dining room, they would "either be flatly refused service or stuck in the corner behind a curtain, lest your breath play upon the air being breathed by the fair and noble white citizens of the South." Hurt closed his first editorial, suggesting, "For my part, the games should never be held in the South. The games are national, encompassing the best track and field men in America. When the south decides to become part of America, then they can enjoy sharing in something that is American."[6]

The debate over the potential boycott, however, was one of the few battles the black press split on. While some leading writers like Wendell Smith and Sam Lacy agreed in principle with the boycott, other influential writers, like Dan Burley of the *New York Amsterdam News*, believed that in post–World War II America, an integrated event in the South would be the right remedy for the second half of the "double victory." The black soldier helped win the war, and now the black athlete could help defeat Jim Crow at home. Burley, the leading black advocate to propose blacks go to San Antonio, argued that black Americans in general, and black athletes in specific, could not run away from the problem. Burley concluded, "You'll be carrying the fight to the enemy if you show up. You'll be running away if you don't." To this point, Hurt countered, "What I should like to know is this—what fight is he referring to? He should mean the over-all fight that all Negroes are engaged in right now, a fight for complete democracy as quickly as effectively as possible."[7] Burley also added that if no blacks showed up, then there would only be white champions, a problem for black Americans who counted sports titles as racial advancement. Of course, Burley did not advocate the Jim Crow policies; he just wanted to make sure black athletes did not give up their opportunity to compete. In a similar fashion, another black reporter from New York, Don Deleighbur, deemed black participation essential to helping solve the race problem in America. He pleaded, "The race issue today is paramount in this country," and urged, "We need everybody to bring about better understanding and a relaxation of the tension that is gripping whites and blacks over inequalities of the American economic, political and social structure." These instructions from both camps of the black press, as it turned out, weighed down on the black athlete.[8]

Like the black press, black athletes drifted into two camps; go South and prove their humanity to the racist South, or stay home and preserve their dignity. In the first camp, Eddie Conwell, the world-record holder at 60 meters, said he had no worries about going and saw his presence as an opportunity to break barriers and prove black people are willing to challenge problems: "Negroes never solve race prejudice by running away from it. I don't like to go South under present conditions, but I am going because I believe that the more often we go the quicker we will help to break down undemocratic barriers."[9] Elmer Harris, a 600-meter champion, saw this as an opportunity to show solidarity with his Southern brothers. Believing the black athletes from the South would help Northerners navigate the racism, Harris claimed, "I am willing to undergo humiliation this time if it will help my Southern friends to see more clearly the injustice of it all." The most ardent support for the San Antonio meet came from 1932 Olympic sprint champion Eddie Tolan, who had also competed in a similar, integrated AAU meet in Dallas in 1936. Tolan made his passionate plea to both Russ Cowans of the *Michigan Chronicle* and Dan Ferris, the national secretary for the AAU. The Olympic champ concluded that having the meet in the Jim Crow South would be good for race relations, because black success at the meet would help advance race relations by creating interracial goodwill and argued victories by black athletes would "symbolize the beacon of interracial understanding and good will, freedom and victory over the theory of 'WHITE SUPREMACY,' of Democracy in action." He also reflected that the war "taught us the danger in not realizing the destiny of one people effects that of all others," and believed that a black boycott would "keep alive Hitler's theory of sharpening racial differences in order to establish forceful rule." Chastising some black writers, he pointed out that some in the black press were "too quick to cry discrimination or raise questions of inequalities and then do nothing to eradicate or remedy the evils that cause them." Instead of attacking the AAU for forcing black athletes to accept Jim Crow, he congratulated the organization as an "agency symbolizing Democratic activists, appearances below the Mason-Dixie [*sic*] line strengthens the fight for an America from racial bigotry, free from fear, free from want, free from oppression or free from special privileges for a few."[10]

But in their support for breaking barriers in the South, the athletes missed an important point: white Southerners knew black people had talent and ability. The problem, as most pro-boycotters understood it, was that white Southerners did not care about equality, only about athletic entertainment. In other words, a meet in San Antonio in which the best black athletes acquiesced to Jim Crow would not change Jim Crow. Herbert Douglas understood this well. Douglas, who 22 years later supported the proposed 1968 Olympics boycott by black athletes, said that he had no intentions on going and that he would "gladly take part in any open meet staged in the North."[11] Douglas's disdain for discrimination, along with other athletes who felt the same way, sparked a movement for an alternative racist-free event.

At the beginning of the boycott movement, white ally Stanley Woodward, the sports editor of the *New York Herald-Tribune*, offered another solution. Labeling the San Antonio meet the "Nordic Championships," if black athletes boycotted, Woodward ordered that a better, and more democratic alternative, would be to host an event for everyone at Randall Island in New York. In his editorial he attacked the AAU for its shortsighted vision of democracy and argued, "The AAU, glorious organ that it is, has fumbled the ball again in a day when the USA is attempting to represent itself as the ideal democracy. . . . The AAU's action was particularly ill-timed and this department trusts that no Negro athlete will submit himself to what would be forthcoming should he undertake to enter the Bilbo Belt," referring to the pro-segregationist senator from Mississippi, Theodore Bilbo. In solidarity with this proposal, white writer Joe Cummiskey argued that white athletes who competed with blacks as equals should support their black brothers in this boycott and bemoaned, "The white boys who for years have competed against these same great Negro stars should react the same way anyone ought to who isn't wrapped up in a warped mind and hates people because their skin is black or because they're Protestant, Catholic or Jew. And I have a hunch they will. It would be a great lesson in Americanism for everyone if there was a mass exodus from Texas even before they start and all of them show up at Randall's Island." Cummiskey made a strong point. Plenty of white runners in the North had black teammates. Pioneering black track coach Joseph Yancey, who coached the elite Pioneer Club, an integrated unit, gave his white athletes no choice. They had to do the right thing. Yancey immediately pulled all of his runners, black and white, out of the meet. He would not subject them to the humiliation of Jim Crow and expect them to perform at their best.[12] The pressure from the black press and the potential to create an alternative meet had its intended effect, forcing San Antonio to accommodate the black athletes or lose the expected revenue from the event. To be clear, the black athletes were the show, the stars, and their presence drew the crowd.

Both black and white sportswriters in San Antonio, however, attacked the Northern press, for what they deemed was a "carpetbagger" mentality trying to shame the South and their ways, but San Antonio still capitulated. Specifically, an unnamed black writer noted that the leaders in the city, white and black, would call every top-notch black athlete and personally guarantee them that they would not have any problem with Jim Crow in the city. He also attacked Northern writers by singing the praises of his city. "San Antonians," he said, "who have gone to eastern schools and lived in the East and North, avow to the fact that there is less discrimination in San Antonio than in many cities of the North."[13] And the black millionaire, Valmo Ballinger, who owned the black newspaper the *San Antonio Register*, guaranteed that he would make sure the black athletes had the best black hotels or stayed with the top families in the city.

For many, especially the athletes, these assurances from white and black leaders in San Antonio were enough to get them to forgo the counter-meet and try their luck in the South. Of course, they still had to live in segregated accommodations, and black fans—about 1,000 a day attended—had to sit in a segregated facility, but no black athletes were confronted with Jim Crow. Most important, for observers, the black athletes performed well. Collectively, it was the best black athletic performance since the 1936 Olympics, when the "Black Auxiliaries" taught Hitler an athletic lesson about racism. In San Antonio, black athletes broke multiple records and shamed Jim Crow at the same time.

Of course, Hurt never wavered on his commitment to the alternative meet and his insistence that black athletes should never have to bow to Jim Crow. In his final editorial on the event, he argued, "I hold that as long as the South chooses not to act like a part of this democracy that it should be allowed to 'act like the South'—at the same time being denied the honor of participating in something that embraces these United States." He also pointed out, moreover, that regardless of location, the black athletes would have won their races. Thus, they could have held the event in the North, and produced the same results. Hurt, however, still saw a small silver lining. Hosting the event in the Jim Crow South, he hoped, "called the attention of the country to the evils of segregation and discrimination that would await the Negro athletes in Texas."[14] Two years later, these same athletes would challenge the principles of American democracy.

1948

For black America, the 1948 London Olympics offered a new athletic opportunity to prove their equality in a changing society. In the first Olympics after World War II, a war fought for the ideals of democracy and freedom, their athletic performances would take place on an international stage, for their country, thus displaying athletic patriotism that they thought would help win their cause for equality. Moreover, this team had the most "tan talent" to date, including 9 of the 11 women runners and 7 of the 16 boxers. Black Americans had always used their participation in the Olympics as proof of their patriotism, but these games were different; they carried greater importance, because they occurred at the beginning of the Cold War and at a time when the federal government made its first commitment to civil rights, with President Harry S. Truman desegregating the military and also issuing the president's "To Secure These Rights" study, about the need for the federal government to provide civil rights. Thus, in this context of the government's early commitment to containment of communism and to civil rights, the 1948 games acted as a proving ground for America internationally and internally about ideas of race and racism. For those invested in projecting and protecting America's democratic image abroad, the presence of the black athlete somehow proved to other nations—especially those that fought for freedom from colonialism after the war—that America's system of democracy and capitalism offered the best opportunities for black people.

For black athletes, however, in regard to race and representation, the 1948 Olympics could not have gotten off to a worse start. A year prior to the games, the U.S. Olympic committee, led by the racist Avery Brundage, selected the University of Southern California (USC) track coach, Dean Cromwell, as the head track coach. Cromwell, as black people already knew, held racist views about black athletes. During the 1936 games, for example, a reporter overheard Cromwell saying, "We should not have Negroes on our team; they discredit our country." And when he returned home from the games, he told a crowd at the National German-American Alliance rally, "Only one in seven New Yorkers is American-born. Oh if I could only be that handsome Hitler in New York for one hour." Moreover, Cromwell did not restrict his racist attitudes to the Olympics. During his tenure at USC, he had only a handful of black runners on his team, and none since 1930. It was clear to any objective observer that Cromwell's prejudiced attitude about black athletes had no place on a team representing America. Adding to the insult, local Los Angeles reporters discovered that Cromwell wanted his neighborhood to reflect his racist attitude, too. In 1943, Cromwell signed a racially restrictive covenant that excluded "occupancy by any person whose blood is not entirely that of the Caucasian or white race."[15] What type of unifying message about democracy and equality would it send if the United States Olympic Committee hired a racist to coach the predominately black team?

Black sportswriters across the country immediately denounced the decision to hire Cromwell. A. O. Prince, of the *California Eagle*, complained, "Negro athletes will get about as square a shake from old Dean as they would from [Mississippi] Senator Bilbo."[16] Prince admitted that Cromwell was an excellent track, but also called him the wrong man for the job because "he is incapable of fully coordinating Negroes into his track patterns."[17] And Leslie Matthews of the *People's Voice* complained, "Dean Cromwell, should not be chosen as the Olympic coach. He does not want a winning team, but an all white team to represent the U.S." Matthews's paper also encouraged black readers to write the AAU and protest the decision to hire Cromwell.[18] In his editorial condemning the decision, Arthur Kirk, of the *St. Louis Argus*, referenced Brundage's overhanded tactics during the 1936 games when he kicked Eleanor Holmes off the team for drinking alcohol on the team ship. Kirk urged, "This one is bigger and it affects the Democratic standing of the United States. Let's get busy and clear this up faster than you put Eleanor off of the Olympic swim team for drinking champagne in 1936."[19] Brundage, however, could not have cared less about black America's complaints about a racist coach. He held those same views. When Brundage, who black athletes would later dub "Slavery Avery," stepped down as the head of the USOC during the games, a black writer urged, "Let's hope that some person who has a better sense of judgment of what Civil Rights mean, [than] the fleeting [Brundage]."[20]

Just as expected, at the games Cromwell openly treated his white athletes better than their black counterparts. Black sprinter Barney Ewell complained that Cromwell intentionally had him practice his starts the wrong way to throw off his rhythm, all in favor of Cromwell's "pet" Mel Patton of USC.[21] And after Harrison "Bones" Dillard defeated the "white hope" Patton to win the 100m gold, instead of congratulating Dillard, Cromwell refused to shake the black man's hand. Irritated by Cromwell's un-American racism, the black press used black athletic success to take shots at Cromwell's racist remarks. Arthur Kirk stated, "If the Negro discredits this country then let's take away the places that Sepia stars have won so far in this Olympics game and see what would happen."[22] The following week, after black athletes added more medals to their glory, Brink took another shot at Cromwell and concluded, "These athletes deserve more credit than just winning, because they had to face all of their events under a narrow-minded, color-blind, individual who couldn't see anything by [sic] White." Kirk closed by asking, "Just how did the Negro athlete disgrace the United States in any Olympic game? The only thing that I am able to see is that they helped in many ways."[23]

Beyond Cromwell's racism, black athletes' success gave the black press a chance to brag about black brilliance while shaming America for racism. On the track, black runners accounted for 68 of the nation's 196 points, which included victories by Tuskegee Airman, Mal Whitfield, in the 800 meters, and Tuskegee track legend Alice Coachman in the high jump. Meanwhile, strong man John Davis, a Brooklyn native and a World War II veteran, dubbed the "Brown Giant from America," owned the tag of strongest man in the world, and his feats of strength and his magnificent black body graced the pages of black newspapers as a reminder to readers that he represented a symbol of black power. And then there was Harrison Dillard, the so-called fastest man in the world. Bragging about Dillard's victory, a *Baltimore Afro-American* editorial reported that his victory "gave us ample cause to stick out our chest."[24] And black writers also bragged that black athletes won acclaim for other countries, too. The same writer that celebrated Dillard concluded, "With more and more of our representatives—men and women—yet to be heard from and with competitors from Panama, Jamaica, Bermuda, British Guiana, Puerto Rico, et al, entered in the games, we can be assured of our share of the world's top athletic rewards."[25]

Although overshadowed by the male athletes on her team, Alice Coachman's record-setting performance stood out as one of the most significant stories of the games. The black press ran stories on Coachman's victory, showed pictures of her leaping over the high jump bar, and showed her standing on the medal stand. In addition, the NAACP Youth Organization held a ceremony in her honor; she met President Truman—she called this her "greatest moment" of the year—and sportswriters voted her the ninth best black athlete in 1948. Equally as important, her victory had potential implications for race relations in the South. Coachman hailed from Albany, Georgia, the Deep South, and her segregated hometown celebrated her accomplishments with a parade that brought out community leaders, including the mayor, a clear sign that, at least for the day, she represented more than just menial labor in the South, and that quite possibly, whites and blacks could get together and celebrate. In the *Chicago Defender*'s piece on the parade, the writer acknowledged that the parade had been Jim Crowed, but still felt "the whole affair must be put on the credit side of the race relations ledger." He added, "Here was evidence that good impulses were at work and that there was a spark of decency in the leadership. They were afraid to stand up and be true Americans, true lovers of democracy, true Christians but they gave us some reasons to believe the day is going to come when the color line is going to lose its magic in Dixie."[26] Unfortunately, as Martin Luther King Jr. found out 14 years later when he helped lead efforts to integrate Albany in 1962, the color line did not "lose its magic." In fact, Albany remained one of the few "failures" King had in the movement.

Besides the hope for integration in the South, Coachman's victory set the stage for black women to represent America on an international stage. As scholar Jennifer Lansbury notes, "Coachman's story is important not so much because she was 'the first,' but because she represented a defining moment in the history of black women athletes."[27] Coachman became the first black woman athlete to win acclaim on an international level, thus showing that black women athletes' importance would transcend the black sports pages. Black women who ran track became the international face of American athleticism, a future full of pitfalls and promises.

The mass participation of black athletes also gave black sportswriters an opportunity to criticize American racism and point out the hypocrisy that allowed black athletes to wear "U.S.A." across their chest, provided black athletes equal treatment overseas, but forced them to come home to Jim Crow conditions. "Anyone who would like to get democracy in sharp focus," Russ Cowans suggested, "would do well to attend the Olympic Games. . . . Here a boy or girl is not judged by his or her color." But this was not the case at home, as black American writers were quick to point out.[28] After Coachman told the *Afro-American* that she "felt good for my family, for my Albany, Ga home, for my school and for my fellow Americans who are privileged to live in this land of opportunity," the paper asserted, Coachman "was born and raised in a small Georgia community, where members of her race are treated with scorn by the other group. To meet the nation's leader and shake his hand might well have provided a memory she will carry to death."[29]

The father of black sports history, Edwin B. Henderson, provided the loudest attacks on American racism. In his column about the Olympics, pointedly entitled "Tan Stars Shame USA in Eyes of the World," Henderson gloated that white readers who picked up papers during the games saw their white hope, Mel Patton, losing to "four colored boys" which must "have added points to the blood pressure of the American fascists." After further boasting about the exploits of black runners, including noting that white women had shied away from track because black women had dominated the sprints for the past decade, Henderson closed, noting, "The thousands who witness the Olympic games, the millions more who listen in and read about these exploits must sense the shame of keeping colored citizens in semi-slavery in a so-called free country." When the games ended, Henderson went down the line, celebrating every black victory, and asked, "Now what does this all mean? Well, it weakens still more the claim of the racists that colored people are inferior? Inferior in what? Surely not in these exhibitions of neuro-muscular skills where every white boy in America was straining his heart's muscle to get on a team." The black athlete, Henderson huffed, had hurdles to jump before he even made the team. "The colored athlete not only has to train, and compete, but he has to master the art of over-coming the 'not wanted' sign he sees in most white American eyes and in places and [have] courage to compete against these psychological odds and still win." For Henderson, black success proved that if "given a chance, we can do as well if not better in those things where the barriers are down."[30]

Even the British press noticed the great paradox in black participation. One British article, entitled "The Ban and the Banner," remarked that three black runners swept the 100-meter race and told its readers, "The two who are Americans will face the color problem on their return home." And in the *Reynolds News*, a reporter blasted, "Is it too much to hope that colored victories in the Olympic Games, and the uninhibited interracial fraternization of Wembly [England], will be of some education value in the Southern States of the USA?" The writer answered his own rhetorical question, "Probably it is. The white supremacy diehards will rationalize the colored athletes' victories discovering biological differences to account for them."[31] Of course, the British press did not look inward to deal with its own racism, and colonial legacy, when celebrating sprinters like Jamaican Arthur Went, but it gladly took the opportunity to knock America for its Jim Crow practices. Sadly, as the black athletes found out when they got home, being an Olympian and representing their country could not defeat Jim Crow back home.[32]

Norvell Lee learned those lessons the hard way. In November 1948, Lee, a Howard University student, who represented the United States as a heavyweight boxer in the Olympics, purchased an interstate train ticket in his home state of Virginia. Legally, since 1946 and the *Morgan* decision, which ruled that state segregation laws did not apply to interstate travel, Lee, who purchased an interstate ticket, should have been allowed to ride where he wanted. But when the Olympian sat down in the white section, the conductor immediately asked him to move. He could ask the heavy-weight to move, of course, but he could not force the heavyweight fighter to budge. Without the courage to try, the conductor quickly tracked down a sheriff, who told Lee to move to the "colored section" or get off the train. The proud Olympian got off the train, and at the next stop he purchased another ticket home. This time, like the last time, he plopped down in the "white section." Instead of ordering him to the "colored section," however, the sheriff arrested the Olympian and charged him with violating state laws. Lee, the proud Olympian, college student, and World War II veteran, challenged the arrest on grounds that it violated his civil rights. Although lower courts ruled that Lee was in the wrong, the state's highest court reversed the lower court's decision and dismissed the case, and ruled that Virginia's segregation laws "did not apply to Lee since he was an interstate passenger." Lee, who did not win Olympic glory in 1948— he won gold in the 1952 games—won the biggest fight of his life, a legal battle for his dignity.[33] Unfortunately, by the 1952 games, Lee, like the rest of black athletes, would have to fall back in line.

The 1950s, the Black Olympian, and the Politics of the Cold War

For the black athletes, the omnipotence of the Cold War in 1950s' American society shifted their perception on how to measure their athletic achievements while living with the reality of a Jim Crow America. If the 1948 games stood as a test of the limits of racial democracy, the 1952 and 1956 games became a show of American solidarity. The 1952 games saw the entrance of the Soviet Union to the games, and historian Damion Thomas notes, once that happened "the Games became a crucial arena for Cold War contestation."[34] For black America, the Cold War in the 1950s, with the specter of the Red Scare and McCarthyism looming over America, changed black politics, forcing many activists to shift their so-called left-leaning special grievances toward the center to avoid being tagged as a Communist. As leftist black leaders Paul Robeson and W.E.B. Du Bois quickly learned, and civil rights organizations found out, challenging the status quo of American racism had consequences. The government confiscated Robeson's and Du Bois's passports, and in the South, a number of states, including Louisiana and Alabama, tried to outlaw the NAACP as a pro-Communist organization. This did not end the civil rights movement by any means; rather, the tag of communism forced mainstream black organizations and leaders to tweak their tactics. The increased political scrutiny also had an impact on black athletes. Under the veil of hyper-patriotism, the black Olympian had to play a new role and help America battle the Cold War on two fronts. As kinesiology scholar Jamie Schultz wrote, "As sport became an important state on which to act out Cold War politics, athletes became players in international diplomacy."[35] Thus, the black athletes who lived with the daily indignities of discrimination also became the global face of American democracy and fairness. Their athletic success proved American might and, by extension, that America was in the right.[36]

Understanding the magnitude of these games, black Americans did their best to help promote these Olympiads as an opportunity for black athletes to help America put on a good face for the rest of the world, thus prompting black outlets to celebrate America's reliance on "tan talent." For example, *Jet* ran the headline, "America's Track Hopes Placed with Negro Stars," to get their readers up to speed with the Olympics.[37] The 1952 team was flooded with black stars, including repeaters Harrison Dillard, Mal Whitfield, John Davis, and Norvell Lee on the men's side, and Mae Faggs, the champion sprinter, on the women's side. These athletes—all college educated—symbolized the hope for black integration, as they represented some of the best and brightest of black America. As one editorial in the *Chicago Defender* suggested, "More than the United Nations, more than the international meetings of labor unions, yes even more than the religious conclaves, the Olympic games can dispel the racial, religious and national misconceptions that are the causes of world unrest." And that meant black Americans were the ones who were going to "dispel" the "misconceptions" of America. The author also pointed at that the games constituted "a gathering where democracy is not talked about but where it is a living reality," and closed by articulating his vision for the future: "We'd like to see the Olympics, the greatest demonstration of democracy we know, be held in Jackson, Miss., some day."[38] In a similar gesture to racial goodwill and promoting American democracy, one of the leading black track coaches, Joseph Yancey, told a group of attendees at the Interracial Forum, "The example of American athletes of all races, creeds and colors living and working together will show the world the strength of our democratic convictions."[39]

Like the past games, black athletes brought home their fair share of gold medals—Dillard, Whitfield, and Davis all repeated as champions, boxers won five gold medals, and the women's relay team, which had three black women, won the 4 × 100-meter relay—but they still came home to Jim Crow conditions in the South and to ghettoes in the North. After the games, in an article entitled "The White Man's Burden in the Olympic Games," Henderson critiqued, "The Negro, frequently alluded to as 'the white man's burden' carried on strong arms and legs the balance of athletic power in the 1952 Olympic Games. . . . Without the points contributed by Negroes, Soviet Russia would have been an easy winner in terms of the unofficial system of scoring." Henderson also added, "The Olympic Games demonstrated the worth of Negroes as true Americans. They are a people who come through 'when the chips are down.' They have always made their contributions to meet our country's needs." With that, Henderson implored, "It is time for those who consider the Negro as a 'burden,' or as a negligible factor in the affairs of our nation to consider the cost of 'killing the goose that lays the golden eggs.' To the extent that injustice is done the Negro, to that very same extent is America's margin of greatness impaired."[40] But beyond their moments of glory, and notches on the medal count, their medals meant nothing for social change back home.

European countries, including a paper in Finland, quickly pointed out the inconsistencies and made it a point to black athletes about how America used her "second-class citizens." *The People's Democratic Front [Finland]* said, "American colored persons, which at home live as bad pariahs, now in the Olympics are good for saving medals for the American banner." The writer continued, "We are happy about their victories but they should do it for their own part of the world—Africa." But this critique of America gave black athletes an opportunity to respond and show their loyalty and profess patriotism. In his response to the slander, John Davis, the strongest man in the world, said, "This is ridiculous. What do they mean? Do they think Italy should get the American gold medal in the 100-meter dash because Lindy Remigino was born of Italian parents? If you followed that theory, the United States wouldn't send anybody over here but Indians." Boxing gold medalist Norvell Lee claimed, "Why, my American ancestry traces back five or six generations." And speedster Harrison Dillard added, "We won the right to represent the U.S., in a fair competition with athletes of other races. We came here as representative of the county where we make our homes: where we live and breathe and work and eat and are happy with our families, the same as other people are in other solid nations of the world. That's all there is to it."[41] When he got back home to Cleveland, Dillard, the 110-meter hurdles champion, also told a banquet, "All of us went to Helsinki to win, but just as important, we went as Americans. We found that the Russians were human—they were interested in us as we were in them. They wanted to talk about America, and we told them the truth. They were a friendly wholesome group." He also told the audience that the Russians, at first, separated from other athletes, but "after a few days the imaginary 'iron curtain' fell and friendliness prevailed."[42] Dillard, who grew up in the segregated ghettoes of Cleveland, sold the American narrative, that sports, no matter how unjust a society, remained the surest way to democracy and equality.

Within the four years between the 1952 and 1956 games, America went through significant changes regarding civil rights and the growth of the civil rights movement. In 1954, the Supreme Court ruled separate but equal education unconstitutional in *Brown v. Board of Education*, and two years later, after nearly 50,000 black people boycotted buses in Montgomery for more than a year, the court ended segregation on city busing. With a civil rights movement now in full bloom—in 1956 Martin Luther King ascended to international notoriety—and the still powerful Cold War propaganda machine operating, black sportswriters' points about patriotic participation and athletics became even more poignant. Emphasizing the irony of America's reliance on black athletes to prove its democratic ideals, Bill Matney of the *Michigan Chronicle* quipped, "Whether America again can ride to victory on the shoulders of its 'second class' citizen in this tense period of ideological warfare is indeed an interesting thought."[43]

Despite the sharp critiques of the great athletic paradox, black sportswriters and athletes once again understood that they had to show their loyalty to country and prove democracy could work. For example, Arthur Kirk of the *St. Louis Argus* argued, "The job will not mean just winning the gold medals, but it will help show the rest of the world just what freedom means as the boys and girls on our team will be watched closely. All of them are ladies and Gentlemen in every sense of the word and on top of that they are good athletes who will fight every inch of the way."[44] And the *Louisiana Weekly* printed a political cartoon celebrating Olympic glory with a sketched billboard that read "American Sports: Democracy in Action" and a caption suggesting "The Olympics Will Show the World Our Better Side."[45] While this sketch hinted at the reality that "our better side" consisted of equal opportunity, it also revealed the fact that black Americans believed that black people represented America's "better side." This was especially the case for black women.

To be sure, the Olympic Games gave black Americans an opportunity to celebrate black women on an international scale. In doing so, black writers pushed back against the stereotypes that depicted black women as "mammies," "jezebels," and "sapphires" and instead situated black women in the traditional fold of white Western womanhood.[46] Black writers depicted their women as the embodiment of American womanhood, and they could do this, they felt, because black women represented the overwhelming majority of the team in the most important and attention-grabbing sport, track and field. In other words, as scholars Susan Cahn, Jamie Schultz, and Jennifer Lansbury suggest, black women dominated the sport that the majority of white women athletes tried to avoid. As these scholars point out, the insults of being "Molly Molls," "lesbians," and too manly, and also consistently losing to black women, had driven a number of white women away from the sport, leaving black women to fill the void.[47] In 1952, while observing the women's Olympic team, the black sportswriter Sam Lacy pointed out how the white media tried to ignore black women's dominance: "Since the gals from Tuskegee, Tennessee State University, etc., have begun to so completely dominate the feminine track picture, there has been a marked decline in American Olympic interest in that direction." Lacy lamented. He continued, "The action is reminiscent of the way the emphasis was switched from the dashes to the hurdles, then to the middle distances and the mile, and later to the jumps, vaults and weights, as tan faces progressively invaded each event in which the other group had previously excelled."[48]

The black community, however, did not have the same cultural hang-ups about women's sport. Although black women felt the sting of these deplorable gendered terms that insulted womanhood, black culture celebrated strong woman's bodies. Susan Cahn concludes, "Black women's own conceptions of womanhood, while it may not actively have encouraged sport, did not preclude it. A heritage of resistance to racial and sexual oppression found African American women occupying multiple roles as wageworkers, homemakers, mothers, and community leaders." Instead of seeing their physicality as a flaw, Cahn asserts, black women celebrated "an ideal of womanhood rooted in the positive qualities they cultivated under adverse conditions: struggle, strength, family, commitment, community involvement, and moral integrity."[49] Moreover, Title IX (1972) forced schools to award women athletic scholarships, and black coaches recruited black girls to black colleges by offering them athletic scholarships. And in the North, a number of black women joined track and field clubs sponsored by factories or the Catholic Youth Organization, or joined the teams at their school. In short, because the black community had celebrated black athletic femininity, and schools offered opportunities for those who succeeded, the black community had no problem elevating black athletic women as the epitome of American womanhood.

Thus, during the Cold War, in which American propaganda promoted U.S. women as slender and beautiful—they meant white homemakers— and Soviet women as muscular and unrefined, black women on the track and field team became the symbol of American womanhood. While this might have been a reluctant realization for the white press—white writers quickly pivoted to celebrate slender white swimmers when they had their chance—black sportswriters took joy in pointing out the facts. For example, in 1948 Edwin B. Henderson pointed out to these differences when he wrote, "Colored girl athletes are as a rule effeminate. They are normal girls. . . . Eight of the eleven girls representing America are colored. All of them are normal girls. Whatever they win will be done as real female women and not as men temporarily masquerading as women."[50] Four years later, an article in the *Afro-American* asserted "London Calls Olympians Team of Glamour Girls" and gloated about how the European press treated our black women as beautiful beacons of democracy. Sam Lacy concluded, "Frankly speaking, our women's track and field team did look as though they had come to the games to represent the U.S. in some sort of fashion show."[51] Three years later, in an *Ebony* article about the top black women sprinters, after describing the "slender" Barbara Jones, a high school student from Chicago, the writer added, "These girls are now America's newest sports heroines, definite threats against the huskier, state-subsidized Russian women in next year's Olympic Games." The article also added that with young stars like Jones and Mae Faggs, "girls no longer shun track because they fear it will make them muscular freaks. And boys are learning that a girl track star can be as feminine as the china-doll type."[52] But a black woman did not necessarily have to be slender to be a model of American womanhood.

While, historically, most of the black women athletes that America has embraced as representative of America—this list includes, but is not limited to, Wilma Rudolph, Florence Griffith-Joyner, and Allyson Felix—have been deemed beautiful, fit, and heterosexual, the momentary celebration of Earlene Brown by the black press shows that there was a moment, and an opportunity, for America to embrace a "heavyset," athletic, black woman.

During the 1956 games, Brown was one of the most celebrated black athletes in the Olympics. The press touted the "robust" 222-pound 20-year-old as America's best hope at gold in the 1956 games, and because of her marriage, her new kid, and her job at a factory, the college-educated Brown became a momentary symbol of black womanhood. No doubt, a lot of this celebration stemmed from the fact that Brown was a housewife who had recently had a baby, thus assuaging black writers' fears that the increasing crop of black women athletes were lesbian. In 1954, for example, *Jet* ran an article, "The Truth about Women Athletes," where it celebrated black women athletes as "models of femininity contrary to all the whispered rumors about their private lives."[53] With Brown and her baby, there was no doubt about her heterosexuality. She was a black woman, housewife, mother, and champion shot-putter. Even though she did not win gold, she represented a face and figure the black press could parade as a symbol of womanhood.[54] But the white press did not treat Brown with the same reverence. As Maureen Smith and Rita Liberti note in their excellent work on Wilma Rudolph, the white media paid more attention to Brown's dark skin and size as a way to reinforce old racialized gender norms of black women. In Brown's case, white writers turned the American shot-putter into the mammy. She was their "colored foil" to the white women they loved to fawn over and the occasional black women they lauded. The white media's treatment of Brown was indicative of how America treated its black athletes, celebrated but still racially critiqued for their unforgiving blackness.[55]

1960 and 1964: The Backdrop of the Civil Rights Movement

While the Cold War continued to loom large during the Olympic Games of 1960 and 1964, the burgeoning civil rights movement inserted itself as an essential social backdrop to the global games. Certainly, during the 1952 and 1956 games, the world knew about America's racial problems with Jim Crow, but by 1960, with the development of the sit-in movement that featured an estimated 70,000 participants, the civil rights movement had moved beyond the focus of a singular city and spread throughout the nation. During the 1960 games, for example, racial confrontations broke out in Jacksonville, Florida, Buford, Georgia, and Memphis, Tennessee, which resulted in fist fights, rock throwing, one firebombing, and hundreds of arrests. And the movement to strike down the racist system had touched more and more athletes who represented America. A number of these black athletes, for example, attended Tennessee State, in Nashville, the epicenter of the movement. In Nashville, black students at Fisk and Tennessee State led sit-ins, boycotted the downtown businesses, and helped articulate a radical nonviolent agenda that spread to other college students throughout the nation.

Two of the biggest stars on the track team, Ralph Boston and Wilma Rudolph, attended Tennessee State, along with six other athletes. How could the movement not touch them? As their head coach Ed Temple reflected, "When they had the boycott about not buying, nobody went downtown and bought, and there wasn't no doubt about that. Everybody participated in that."[56] But most of the black college athletes who became involved in the movement or expressed social awareness about the movement said little and did little at the time. To be sure, U.S. track officials, and government officials who hoped black athletes' participation in the games would be a beacon of democratic hope for the rest of the world to witness, did not have to worry about black athletes embarrassing the nation by their public involvement in the civil rights movement. And the press made sure to sell black athletes' participation and performance to project a public image of American peace and opportunity. No two black athletes were more essential to this than Rafer Johnson and Wilma Rudolph.

Coming into the games, many considered Johnson the most popular athlete and essential athlete to propel the mythmaking machine that projected the story of American meritocracy. The greatest all-around athlete in the world, the star decathlete had a personal narrative that highlighted triumph over segregation, individual hard work, and the essential role of well-meaning whites. And the white press considered him the "good Negro," humble, well meaning, and well liked. As his pastor said, "This is a most remarkable human being. He is as gentle as a child, and yet he is tremendously competitive."[57] And a *Chicago Tribune* writer described, "Rafer has the poise and dignity of a king. He's not a talker, he's a doer, and he's apt to clam up completely when asked about his accomplishments. . . . There is a

Wilma Rudolph at the finish line during the 50-yard dash at a track meet in Madison Square Garden. (Library of Congress)

gentleness and honesty about him along with his competitive spirit which lifts your heart."[58]

Johnson, who grew up in segregated Dallas, before moving to the small farm town of Kingsburg, California, with his family, used his personal story to promote the promise of integration and what it held for black people. As he told *Time* magazine before the games, "I don't care if I never see Texas again. There's nothing about it I like. If my family had stayed in Texas, I not only wouldn't be representing the U.S. in the Olympic Games—I wouldn't even have gone to college."[59] But not every place in America mirrored the South. In the North and West, Johnson proved black people could have a true shot at equality. But, in truth, Johnson's family struggled economically. For the first year in California they lived in a boxcar by the local cannery, until a white man, Edward Fishel, gave Johnson's father a better job, employed his mother as a domestic worker, and helped the family move into a small house. In Kingsbury, the white people—except for the racist sheriff who told the family "I don't want to see the sun set on any niggers in this town"—treated the Johnsons as part of the community.[60] When the sheriff demanded Fishel fire the Johnsons simply because they were black, the well-meaning white man refused. When the prejudiced police officer demanded the Johnsons leave, they refused. Eventually, the police chief quit his job, and the town got along just fine with the Johnsons. Of course, it helped that Johnson was a star athlete who led their local track, basketball, baseball, and football teams. He matriculated to UCLA, concentrated on his education, integrated a fraternity, and became the "top athlete" in the world. Between 1957 and 1960, his world-record performances, and his epic battles with top Russian athlete Vasili Kuznetsov, Johnson became the leading athletic Cold War warrior, displaying American might and American racial progress, all at the same time. And then the USOC made him captain of the team for the 1960 games.

Johnson's captaincy also meant he would carry the American flag during the opening ceremonies, which worked to sell America as a place of progress, a nation that could push past prejudice. As white Olympic executive Louis J. Wilke, of Oklahoma, admitted, "We not only felt he was probably the greatest all-around athlete in the country, but also an example of our finest traditions."[61] The image of Johnson carrying the flag needed no explanation. As the white writer Arthur Dailey noted, "When Rafer Johnson, proud and straight, emerged from the tunnel with the American flag firmly in his grasp, the spine of every American in the stadium could not help but tingle."[62] For white America, Johnson's captaincy, and steady flag-bearing display, helped obscure what many had already tried to deny, that America had a race problem.

While Johnson's opening ceremony moment blinded white writers to American racism, it gave black writers an opportunity to reflect on the meaning of black patriotism and race relations going forward. Bob Hunter in the *St. Louis Argus* argued, "The rest of the world will undoubtedly consider this a show meant for propaganda purpose, but the fact remains that big Rafe (be he pawn or prince) is still out front, thus displaying to the world that the Negro athlete has made a place for himself in the sports world."[63] *The Los Angeles Sentinel* called the moment "symbolic of the changing times" and claimed, "This is another step towards America's total democracy."[64] In the *Baltimore Afro-American*, a writer observed, "It was a fitting tribute to the world's finest athlete that he should display the colors of the world's greatest nation."[65] And an editorial in the *Michigan Chronicle* urged that instead of highlighting the fact that Johnson was the first black man to carry the flag, "we find it much more important to emphasize the normal acceptance of Johnson as an American rather than the spurious adulations about race." The editorialist also noted, "Many Americans are 'carrying the flag' in other fields of endeavor. They are doing so because of their competence and abilities and because they, too, are loyal Americans anxious to demonstrate the meaning and worthiness of American democracy." He closed by praising Americans, arguing, "Americans of every persuasion, section and color realize, that true democratic freedom is indivisible."[66] Of course, readers of the *Chronicle* had to understand that this was all hype and hyperbole. Right next to the editorial about Rafer, the paper placed a political cartoon about segregation in local Detroit public schools. Rafer might have brought momentary hope, but his flag carrying or athletic feats would not end the harsh reality of segregation.

Like Johnson, Wilma Rudolph's glory offered an opportunity to celebrate an individual accomplishment of a black athlete as a way to congratulate America, while ignoring racism, and, in Rudolph's case, sexism too. Nobody could deny that while Americans rejoiced over women's victories in track and field, and pushed these amazing athletes to compete with the Soviets, the country, and the USOC, did not adequately fund women's track programs. In one of the most poignant statements about the twin evils of sexism and racism in sport, Sam Lacy headlined a column before the games, entitled "How Come Uncle Sam Ignores His Nieces?" Led by the Tigerbelles of Tennessee State, black women made up the majority of the team; thus, Lacy fumed that the lack of funding stemmed from the fact that they were black, especially since other sports, white-dominated sports, received more funding. "It may be interesting to note," Lacy lamented, "that the United States, as in the past years, is devoting very little attention to the women athletes of its track and field contingent." Lacy pointed out, however, "Swimmers, fencers and other distant stars invariably get the full treatment from Uncle Sam's Olympic committee." He reminded his readers that during the 1952 games he had argued, "The subordination was probably caused by the traditional American practice of minimizing the importance of any venture in which colored contestants supplied the big effort."[67]

But the continued success of black women in track and field, combined with the prolonged Cold War and the growing civil rights movement, meant that black women could no longer be ignored. Accomplished athletes, regardless of race, had to be promoted and propped up, and Rudolph had the perfect story to sell. When Rudolph won Female Athlete of the Year in Europe, an editorial in the *Houston Informer* praised, "It is good to have a Negro girl win this kind of world recognition, and to have this kind of inspiration come to other young women of Miss Rudolph's racial group. American racial segregation and discrimination have closed so many doors in the faces of Negro women, that it becomes easier for them to say, 'what's the use,' than other American women; and any encouragement like that which comes from a Wilma Rudolph is always highly welcomed."[68] Rudolph gave black women, the most marginalized American citizens, hope. And she gave America hope.

Born in rural poverty in Clarksville, Tennessee, Rudolph's rise to the top embodied the classic "rags-to-riches" individualist bootstrap story Americans loved to sell. As Smith and Liberti contend, stories about Rudolph and other black athletes "provided the US mainstream media and government with a narrative of opportunity contrasting with those that underscore racial inequality, oppression, and brutality."[69]

Rudolph's story is well known by now, but worth a brief retelling. Rudolph, one of 19 siblings, contracted polio at a young age, which severely limited her mobility and forced her to wear a big clunky metal brace around her leg. Miraculously, the poor sickly kid recovered and eventually starred on her high school basketball team, and within five years of taking off the brace she made the 1956 Olympic team as a teenager, and followed that up by earning a spot on the 1960 team as the top athlete, when she won three gold medals. After she won, the white press celebrated her as a model of womanhood. "Her manners are of a natural delicacy and sweetness as true as good weather," said Barbara Heilman of *Sports Illustrated.*[70] *The New York Times* called her a "young lady of charm and poise," and presidential candidate Richard Nixon used Rudolph's star power for a photo-op to sway the black vote, despite the fact that most black people could not vote in the South, including her family.[71]

But on their way to telling the tale about the polio-stricken Olympic hero, most accounts, especially white accounts, left out the rides to the all-black hospital sitting in the back of a Jim Crow bus; they omitted the teeming poverty rural blacks faced in the South, the indignity of domestic labor black women had to take, the segregated education, including the underfunded track program at Tennessee State where the men and women's teams had to practice by the school's pig farm, or the preparation she and her track mates had to have just to avoid the sting of embarrassment eating at Jim Crow restaurants. These stories of racism missed the medal ceremony, unless, of course, they served a greater good of American mythmaking. But black writer L. I. Brockenbury did not miss the irony. As he made clear, after he watched Rudolph win in Rome, and the band played the national anthem, "I got to thinking about this girl from Clarksville, Tennessee and the great service she has rendered to the Negro race and America. . . . Here is a girl who might be jailed if she were to try to eat at a lunch counter in her home town . . . and if she went down to register for voting they would probably try to starve her and all the members of her family." The *Los Angeles Sentinel* writer then asked, "How is it that our athletes can represent the United States before the world and then have to come home to be treated like dogs? When is America going to awaken? How much longer can our leaders continue to feel that they are fooling the world by their doubledeal treatment of Negroes."[72]

As Brockenbury's critique suggests, despite the adulation from both black and white writers, black athletes came from segregated spaces, and most, especially those from Tennessee State, a school that brought home seven gold medals, would return to segregation.

Gold Medalists, American Heroes, and Second-Class Citizens

Mississippi governor Ross Barnett, a racist segregationist, applauded long jumper Ralph Boston and noted, "All Mississippians are proud of him for the great honor he won," which prompted Medgar Evers, the head of the Mississippi NAACP, to retort that Boston "will be returning as a second class citizen because he cannot compete at Ole Miss or Mississippi State in a field in which he has won world-wide acclaim."[73] In his column after the games, Sam Lacy, while celebrating the great achievements of black athletes, also reminded his readers of the racial hardships they faced before representing their country. Lacy lamented that long jump record holder Ralph Boston, a biochemist major at Tennessee State, and two-time hurdler champ Lee Calhoun grew up in the violent segregated town of Laurel, Mississippi, "a place where if a Negro can get out he gets out," Rafer Johnson's family had to survive the racist local sheriff, basketball star Oscar Robertson was the grandson of a slave, and Wilma Rudolph could not even get into Vanderbilt or the University of Tennessee due to Jim Crow.[74] Thus, while America celebrated American athletes as Cold War warriors, it ignored the daily indignities that black athletes had to face.

But the black athletes could not forget them; they were returning to them and would be reminded quickly of their place in the Southern racial order. Cassius Clay, the gold medal winner in the light heavyweight division, received Jim Crow treatment at a restaurant in his hometown of Louisville, even while wearing his medal around his neck. Clay liked to tell the story of when he threw his medal in the bottom of the Ohio River to protest the prejudice he faced. Although false, it boldly made the point the struggles the celebrated black athletes had when they came home as second-class citizens. And Wilma Rudolph, with three gold medals to her name, showed open trepidation about returning home to Tennessee. She told the *New York Amsterdam News*, "It's going to all but kill me to have to go back home and face being denied this, that, and the other, because I'm a Black American. In America, they push me around because I'm Negro, here in Europe, they push me to the front."[75] And although her hometown of Clarksville hosted its first integrated parade to celebrate her feats, this showing of support, was, according to Smith and Liberti, a move by "white leaders to construct a mythical image of Clarksville for the track star's homecoming, one in which racial inequalities ceased to exist and where white and black citizens lived without incident."[76]

In reality, prejudice permeated Clarksville, and whenever the star returned home, she had to confront these assaults on her human rights. By 1963, Rudolph had drawn the line. No longer could she stand by while the city treated black folks like second-class citizens. On the day she returned from her goodwill tour where she represented the United States, as the face of democracy and opportunity, Rudolph and other black residents protested a local restaurant that refused to integrate. As one observer noted of Rudolph, who received a key to the city in 1960, with that key she could not "unlock a restaurant that was shamefully padlocked in her face."[77] After two days of protests, and a week of meetings with local black civil rights leaders, white businessmen, and local politicians, the city decided to desegregate all restaurants. This was obviously a step in the right direction, but in the realm of civil rights, more had to be done. America had to stop treating black athletes like stars abroad, but second-class citizens at home. Black Olympians understood this well, especially Mal Whitfield.

The 1964 Olympics in Tokyo went the same as the previous games; black athletes won gold for America and came home to be treated as second-class citizens. But according to Mal Whitfield, the three-time Olympic gold medalist and ex-Tuskegee Airman, the black athletes should not have been there. Whitfield, like a number of black athletes of his generation, had become more publicly involved in the plight of his people. For Whitfield, his decision to get involved in the civil rights battles derived from a combination of African independence movements and the slow pace of black liberation at home. Whitfield, who following his retirement from track in 1956 went on to coach in Africa as part of a goodwill gesture, had been inspired by the African liberation from colonialism, but saddened by his lack of equality at home. According to Whitfield, white America celebrated him for his speed but hated him for his skin. "I was still loyal and dedicated to my country, but I was upset, because there had not been equality, even before and during my time of being a popular personality while waving the red, white, and blue flag around the world." Whitfield returned to the States in the spring of 1963, after coaching Nigeria and knew the time was now. After experiencing the joy of seeing independent Africans, and the sorrow of second-class citizens at home, he remembered, "I felt I had to do this, because I had seen all these positive changes in the governments of Africa when they became independent. I expected similar progress here at home."[78] Whitfield believed that his best hope rested in attending the 1963 March on Washington with the masses, and inspired by the potential of the event, he tried to get other athletes to attend the March in a mass. Although several athletes attended the magnificent March, by the beginning of 1964, with the slow pace of the civil rights progressing, he believed he needed to do more. Tired of the second-class citizenship of his people, Whitfield took to *Ebony* to offer his suggestion to end racial prejudice—boycott.

In this radical statement in *Ebony*, Whitfield told black athletes to stay home from the Olympics "if Negro Americans by that time have not been guaranteed full and equal rights as first class-citizens." In other words, he wanted black athletes to boycott the Olympics. The Olympic champion claimed he made the statement for two reasons. First, black athletes had to join the fight for civil rights. He argued black athletes had been "conspicuous by their absence from the numerous civil rights battles during the past year." Second, the champ also charged that America had to "live up to its promises of Liberty, Equality, and Justice for all." In examining the potential impact of the boycott, Whitfield ascertained that America put a lot of emphasis on winning the games, and knew that the withdrawal of black athletes would make that impossible, thus hammering home the point about how important black Americans were to America's global image. Whitfield also understood that besides losing medals and esteem as a powerful nation, the protest would make America look bad in the eyes of the world.[79] How could this nation profess democracy, justice, and equality, if black athletes refused to participate for their country? After giving his reasons for the boycott, the star athlete used the next few pages to briefly detail the plight of black athletes and the second-class treatment they received. For him, it should have been a no-brainer for black athletes to follow his lead. Continued Jim Crow and economic depression trumped the potential Olympic glory gained from winning in the games.

Although Whitfield made a compelling case, no athlete followed his lead. With the civil rights legislation making its way through Congress—President Johnson signed the Civil Rights Act the summer of 1964 and the Voting Rights Act on the agenda—and most black athletes believing sports offered them their best way out of poverty, few would take the risk. Despite the fact no black athlete boycotted the games, Whitfield's plea for protest, and his contempt for second-class status, had already manifested itself in other black athletes. The activist-athlete had arrived.

CHAPTER SIX

African American Athletes and Activism: Everybody Has a Part to Play

Assessing the change in public attitudes of the black athlete in 1967, *Ebony* magazine observed, "The demigod of the 60s is more militant and less accommodating to racial injustices." To make his point clear, the writer suggested, "Compare heavyweight titlists Joe Louis with Muhammad Ali. Joe's frustration were never unleashed outside the ring. He didn't identify with unpopular causes, although there were plenty. His image blended perfectly with what the white public thought the heavyweight champion should be. . . . Twenty-seven years later, despite improvement in all services, Muhammad Ali does hold it against the entire nation that Negroes aren't free."[1] That 20-year transition from safe protests to bold proclamation of black rights, or the transition from "shut up and play" to the activist-athlete, touched every black athlete.

By the 1960s, with the civil rights movement growing into a national movement, in the North as well as the South, black athletes had to have something to say about the civil rights movement. Reporters demanded athletic activism, and their people struggling in the streets expected black athletes to use their platform. To be clear, every athlete did not want to engage in politics; they believed their play and performance would do enough to win the day, but they had to address the issues. As Arthur Ashe said in 1967, "I'm no militant Negro, no crusader. I want to do something for my race, but I figure I can do it best by example, by showing Negro boys the way."[2] The transition of Arthur Ashe in the 1960s, from a tennis "phenom," who believed his individual success would break down barriers, to an athlete activist exemplified the transition a number of leading black athletes went through as individuals trying to come to terms with their special privileges as superstars and their people's plight as second-class citizens.

Early in his career, Ashe represented an enigma to the black press: an isolated Negro in a prestigious white-dominated sport, a man they celebrated for his grace and game, but a man who seemingly did not want to weigh in on the race issue beyond what it meant to Arthur Ashe. Before he became an activist-athlete, for example, Ashe told the white press that being the lone Negro on the tennis circuit gave him an economic advantage. As he told one writer, "Look, man, being billed as the lone Negro in the game probably means a $100 or so a week more for [me] than the others in market value."[3] To be clear, the black press loved Ashe and celebrated his accomplishments for what they meant for black advancement; however, they wanted him to show more consciousness about the civil rights movement. The black community demanded a new assertive athlete.

Ashe, the great-grandson of slaves, grew up in segregated Richmond, Virginia, playing tennis on the segregated parks and recreation courts his dad maintained as the safety officer of black parks and recreation facilities in Richmond. When somebody discovered young Ashe, that is to say, another black person recognized his tennis talent, he or she sent the young black protégé to Dr. Walter Johnson in Lynchburg, Virginia, just as they did with Althea Gibson. Under Johnson's training, Ashe quickly became the best black player in the South, a problem for a young talented black tennis player. As a black man, in the Jim Crow South, his competition was limited to other black players and usually restricted to private black-owned tennis courts. The best white players, and the best white courts, were off limits to him, even in his hometown.

Even after 1963 when he became the first black player to represent the U.S. Davis Cup team, Southern tennis courts, except in Miami, Jim Crowed him. Despite facing racial rejection, Ashe appeared unconcerned. In October 1963, just months after the March on Washington, Ashe told *Ebony*, "I have not heard, or been subjected to, a single racial rebuff at any tournament although I am the lone Negro in most of them." He also admitted, "I sometimes allow my friends to call me 'shadow' because I'm the darkest thing in sight."[4] The next year, he told Claude Harrison Jr., of the *Philadelphia Tribune*, "It's true that I have been turned down by many southern tournament officials. But I'm not going to press the issue.

Officials have the right to invite whom they please." He continued, "Most of the players and people don't look upon you as a Negro. Yet deep down inside, you know you are different. You feel like you are a part of a tennis group, yet a part [sic] from it." Ashe, at that moment, could not articulate the rage of isolation that simmered inside him. Dr. Johnson had trained him, as he trained Althea Gibson, to shut up and play. Johnson taught Ashe, like he taught Althea Gibson, that playing hard and winning would be his contribution to the movement. As Ashe told Harrison, "I cannot stop other Negroes from deifying me or from being motivated now to reach the top in tennis. But all I have accomplished I have accomplished for myself, not for a race." To which Harrison told his readers, "Whether Ashe likes it or not he is a Negro player."[5] And being a black athlete at that time meant that people expected Ashe to get involved in the movement.

At first, however, Ashe was a reluctant athlete activist who believed that his singular success would help advance the race. In 1964, for example, he told the *New York Times*, "I want to do something for my race, but I figure I can do it best by example, by showing Negro boys the way." He also took a shot at other activists when he said, "I don't want to spend my life fuming. What good would that do? It's like beating your head against a brick wall. If you go looking for discrimination, you can find it places."[6] Arthur Ashe just wanted to be "Arthur Ashe," and although other black youth his age had risked their lives to end segregation in the South, while he played tennis at UCLA in the West, none of that registered with him. Activism? That was not for him. In his first autobiography, *Advantage Ashe*, published in 1967, he doubted Martin Luther King's nonviolent mass protest and instead asserted, "It looks to me as if a Negro's best chance to advance is to get himself an education somehow and prove his worth as an individual." Ashe also believed, "By crusades and protest marches and rock-throwing we seem to try to ram ourselves down people's throats. . . . We'll never advance very far by force, because we're outnumbered ten to one."[7] But Ashe knew these sentiments would not sit well with most black Americans at that time. As he asked, "Does this make me an Uncle Tom? If so, okay. I'm not the crusader type. I pay my $3 yearly dues in the National Association for the Advancement of Colored People, and tend to my tennis." He also related his activism, or lack thereof, to Joe Louis, and added, "I feel the way Joe Louis does. When somebody asked why he wasn't active in the civil rights fight, he said 'Some people do it by shouting, some march, some give lots of money.' I do it my way—behaving. All ways help."[8] By this time, however, most famous black athletes, except Willie Mays and Jesse Owens, had expressed an open contempt for racism and had been involved in the movement in some shape or form.

Simply paying NAACP dues, an organization that had largely been pushed aside during the nonviolent protest phase of the movement, and an institution that had largely been considered obsolete in a Black Power era—that summer Stokely Carmichael of Student Nonviolent Coordinating Committee and Floyd McKissick of Congress of Racial Equality, once integrationists, had advocated for Black Power—did not count as activism. In fact, at a time when the black community demanded their athletes be aware and involved in the movement, Ashe's apathy further proved that he was aloof about things that most mattered to the black community. But people change.

By 1967, the movement changed Ashe, pushed him further to the left and to the edge of activism. "I'll be the first to admit I arrived late," he told *Life*. "I've got a backlog of unpaid dues."[9] Ashe moved from a man believing that his athleticism alone could solve racism to an activist. On his newly vocal activism, he told *Ebony*, "It's changed mostly because I'm older and wiser. Then there's outside pressures. What was liberal five years ago may be moderate now." Clearly, activists like Carmichael pushed Ashe to see the world in a different light. Being the isolated Negro now meant something more than perhaps extra endorsement dollars and instead meant he had a responsibility to his community to wrestle with the same struggles they faced. As Ashe told *Life*, he had become aware of "a social revolution among people my age. I finally stopped trying to become part of white society and started to establish a black identity for myself." Admitting that his father sheltered him from racism, he continued, "I heard about police brutality, but never saw anything like that. There were places we couldn't go, but we just accepted it. Now I realize that has a deep affect. You grow up thinking you're inferior and you're never quite sure of yourself."[10] On Carmichael and Black Power activists, he told an interviewer, "We need aggressive militants, the Stokely Carmichael and Rap Brown and Leroi Jones figures. You need men with charisma who can appeal to emotions."

For Ashe that meant that guys like himself, more moderate—Ashe had plans to work with Whitney Young and the Urban League in the summer of 1968—had to offer a safe alternative to Black Power or the movement would be "dead." As an integrationist, Ashe looked at the Urban League as moderate and not militant, but activist enough to get the job done. He believed in the notion of Black Power, but only so far as political power, and urged that blacks should vote in a bloc. On helping the ghettoes, he told the *Chicago Tribune*, "The only way to advance materially this whole human rights struggle is to have us hold out a hand to the slums, saying, 'Look, I'm going to help you!' And keeping the hand out until we've proved it." He continued, "Meanwhile the other hand is out, raised up toward the white establishment steadily insisting, but also slowly building up confidence."[11] In March 1968, he also proudly gave his first civil rights speech, a speech that reflected his moderate bootstrapping approach but words that also showed his commitment to equal rights. In line with his politics-of-respectability attitude, Ashe told a black crowd in Washington that black poverty partly stemmed from "one-half laziness" and implored black people to get active to change their world, "a do-it-yourself blood-and-guts, Me Power kind of philosophy."[12]

In many ways, Ashe's commitment to activism and economic uplift mirrored that of famed football player Jim Brown, who also took a "can do" attitude to civil rights, and backed his attitude up with the Negro Industrial and Economic Union (NIEU). Though Ashe was coming along slowly, and clearly stood behind giants like Brown, Jackie Robinson, and Bill Russell at the time, he had at least come to the conclusion that athletes had to be activists. "A long time ago," Ashe told the *Washington Post* in 1968, "I was standoffish about everything. I wasn't aware that what I said carried any weight. It obviously carries weight now; it would be almost sinful not to throw it around in the right direction."[13] Ashe knew that black athletic excellence also demanded activism.

During the post–World War II civil rights movement, while athletes like Joe Louis, Jackie Robinson, and Sugar Ray Robinson lent their names to civil rights issues in the late 1940s and throughout the 1950s, until the 1960s, most athletes remained silent on social justice issues and preferred to let their play act as their politics. In other words, caught up in the notion that their success promoted democracy, black athletes would rather shut up and play. But as the sit-ins commenced and the civil rights movement expanded to include more activists, especially college-aged activists, collectively black athletes started to use their platform to speak out. The Freedom Riders and participants in sit-ins gave black athletes strength while also reinforcing that being a superstar athlete—many of them faced discrimination when they tried to buy houses in white neighborhoods—did not afford them protection from discrimination. In 1965, after being arrested for protesting Jim Crow at his University of Kansas alma mater, star halfback Gale Sayers captured this sentiment when he said, "They [white people] accept me as a football star, but not as a Negro."[14]

Along with activists in the movement, moreover, black sportswriters pushed athletes into activism. In 1963, for example, one black writer argued, "If ministers and people of other professions, and even children, can take part in protest demonstrations and sit-ins and subject themselves to police dogs and fire hoses as well as arrests, Negro athletes could at least lend their active support to the campaign for racial justice."[15] The writer implored his readers to put pressure on athletes to join the movement and force the athletes to use their platform and comfortable levels of economic success to help the fight. But, of course, even as the movement grew in the 1960s, many athletes, like Willie Mays, continued to preach athletic participation over political activism. The cheers they received from the crowds, especially from white fans, drowned out the cries for help in the movement. For them, their behavior, on and off the field, both as role models and as visible representations of the race helped lead to racial reconciliation.

While paying special attention to leading black athletes, this chapter follows the transition of black sportsmen and sportswomen from athletes to activists. While not every athlete made this move, the majority of elite black athletes from Joe Louis to Jim Brown transitioned from a model of shut up and play to one that required activism. For the first time, starting in the 1960s, black athletes collectively used their platform to help shape society around them. In an era that lacked guaranteed contracts, this move required these athletes to risk their careers to join the movement. But the magnitude of the movement, and the reality that their brothers and sisters across the nation risked their lives for civil rights, required the black athlete to do so. As Lloyd C. Wells, of the *Houston Informer*, noted in 1961, "In these changing times and with Negroes new trend toward demanding social equality and acceptance on individual merits, instead of being treated as the part of a whole, that whole being a stereotypes group, we, as members of that group, should look with respect and admiration toward the Negro athlete who isn't the 'grinning Tom,' that who by his skill and ability has reached the pinnacle of success in his sport, but lacks the character and personal integrity to stand up for all important principals of social and economic equality."[16] The black community demanded a black athlete willing to fight for rights off the field. The days of shut up and play were done.

Shut Up and Play

Black Americans loved Joe Louis. He made it. As James Baldwin observed, this love for Louis stemmed from the fact that Louis "succeeded on a level that white America indicates is the only level for which it has any respect."[17] Political activist James Boggs reflected, "Whenever he was talked about by white society for what he meant to Negros, they always talked about his role in relation to Negro behavior and that he advanced his race from his personal conduct. His personal conduct I never cared for. He had a 'place.'"[18] In other words, whites liked the black hero, Joe Louis, because he was acceptable to them. He stayed in his place. And white politicians, especially Republicans, used the acceptable Louis to their political advantage. Believing that Louis had considerable pull in the black community, leading Republican candidates often sought him out for an endorsement.

And Louis often obliged. But he did so at his own peril. With Louis rejecting the Democratic Party, during a time when more blacks in Northern cities had shifted their political allegiance to the Democratic Party, many in the black community openly complained about his involvement in politics, calling him a political patsy and demanding he stay out of politics.[19] After Louis supported Republican Thomas Dewey for governor of New York, for example, a group of black GIs wrote Louis, lamenting, "To us, you are a symbol of the talent and ability of Negro youth when given an even chance to show it. You have been tops as a fair fighter. Don't let the Republicans put rosin on your gloves, Joe!"[20] Two years later, during the 1948 presidential campaign, after he endorsed Dewey, an editorial in the *Cleveland Call* complained, "Our advice to Joe Louis is to stay out of politics. He is physically well equipped to be a champion boxer. He has achieved immortality in his profession. However, for politics, he has neither the training or experience."[21] To be sure, besides the fact that Louis remained Republican, most of the contempt with Louis stemmed from the black middle class who saw Louis's slow speech patterns and his famous deadpan stare as signs of lack of intelligence. What does he know, they asked? But lack of syntax was not a sign of intelligence. And Louis did not remain in his place. The heavyweight champion always looked for ways to knock out Jim Crow.

Although he might have been a political patsy earlier in his career, by the late 1940s Louis used his platform to fight Jim Crow. In 1947, he wrote a piece in *Salute* entitled "My Toughest Fight" and used the magazine to discuss his battles with Jim Crow and told his readers that he was going to do his part to fight racism. He admitted, "That's the one match I'd like the best. Just to get Jim Crow cornered in the ring. And to get in one good sock. It might be another one of my lucky nights. But I guess it can't be done that way. Prejudice is a funny thing. You can't knock it out of peoples' hearts and minds with KO punches. It's buried deep inside. Like cancer." Louis, however, believed that along with legislation, black athletes could "help win this fight against Jim Crow."[22] The following year, in 1948, as he prepared for a championship fight against Joe Walcott, Louis hosted the controversial Paul Robeson at his training camp and endorsed Robeson's National Non-Partisan delegation heading to the nation's capital to push for civil rights legislation. Of his support, Louis said, "We have been trying to get the Anti-Poll tax, Anti-Lynch and F.E.P.C, bills through Congress a long time. This delegation will help and I support it."[23] In September of that year, when asked about the presidential election, he noted he would campaign for the person he believed would do "the most in the nation for civil rights."[24] In the end, he supported Dewey over Harry Truman, because, as Louis suggested, Dewey hired blacks in his cabinet, pushed and supported New York's Fair Employment Practice Committee (FEPC) law, and displayed the "kind of action that America's one-tenth [i.e. its black population] is in dire need of if he's to be lifted to the level of all other free people throughout the world."[25] Dewey, of course, lost, but Louis continued to use his platform to get involved in civil rights politics. Equally as important, Louis's public politics put other professional athletes on notice; much more would be expected of those who achieved the most fame.

In 1951, Sugar Ray Robinson, the greatest "pound-for-pound" fighter in the history of boxing, learned this lesson quickly. Just months after he lost his welterweight crown to Randy Turpin, a top black contender from England, the black press hit Robinson for his inaction in an incident involving famed black entertainer Josephine Baker. The Stork Club, a famous night spot in New York that was known for Jim Crow policies—the owner once said he "didn't want niggers" at his club—had just recently refused Baker service at the club. The discrimination upset Robinson, her good friend, who then issued a public statement that condemned racism and suggested he would use his platform to demand a change. In a pointed letter, Robinson, who sat on the same board of the Damon Runyon Cancer Fund with Sherman Billingsley, the owner of the club, and reporter Walter Winchell, the organizer of the cancer fund, said, "I can't tell you how it makes me feel being a member of a committee to feel that you are fighting cancer, and you have a cancer right there in your own committee." He concluded, "None of us very seldom get in position that we can do but so much, according to the way things are, coming from a minority group. But I promise you that the entire organization, Mr. W.W., and Mr. Billingsley and everyone will know just how I feel about it, if I have to resign from the cancer fund."[26] In other words, Robinson threatened that if the club did not end its Jim Crow policies, Robinson, the star boxer, would quit his position on the cancer fund, thus limiting the potential for the fund to raise money. This declaration against discrimination, where he decided to take an active role and fight back, demonstrated a shift in his previous apolitical thoughts that asserted that hard work and dedication would "help to break down some of the stupid racial prejudices barring our way."[27]

But being an athlete activist required a commitment to causes and the ability to block out naysayers, and Robinson lacked those qualities. Very quickly, Robinson changed his political tune on the Stork incident. While other black celebrities and activists picketed the club, Robinson backed down from his commitment to join the pickets. While maintaining that he would still fight the club's policies, he told the black press, "I'll be the first to help the NAACP or any other group that's trying to do a worthy job. But I'll have no part of this demonstration against Walter Winchell." He also argued that even if Winchell was guilty of allowing Baker to face discrimination, "I don't believe he's guilty, but even if he was, does it erase all the good things he has done before for minority people?"[28] After receiving much flack for his inaction, Robinson donated money to those fighting the club but did not quit the Cancer Fund. But his first foray into politics, combined with a growing national civil rights movement, meant more people expected Robinson to do his part.

By 1954, while Robinson continued to raise money for research, it became apparent to those in the black community that he did not give the same attention to the NAACP. His apparent lack of acknowledgment of "race funds" irritated many in the black community who called into question his race loyalty during a time of increased civil rights action. A saddened Robinson heard their calls and argued that the hits on his racial loyalty "wounded the deepest." Robinson argued that he gave money to the NAACP and Urban League but did not advertise the fact. He also told his critics that the money he helped raise went to more than 100 black doctors working on cancer research and implored black people to "stop looking at things with Jim-Crow eyes just as they expect the white man to stop doing." He urged, "We have to stop thinking in Jim-Crow terms if we [are] expected to be thought of in democratic and American terms." Moving beyond race, he also noted that he did not support any organizations unless "they respect the rights of the people and ignore the nature of their religion."[29] Despite his insistence that he gave charitably to race organizations, the people demanded more and continued to challenge him on his charitable race consciousness.

The public challenges worked. After the Montgomery Bus Boycott started in December 1955, Robinson announced that he would donate a portion of his fight proceeds to the NAACP and other black "charities."[30] With more people openly willing to sacrifice their lives for their civil rights, Robinson knew he had a part to play. Unfortunately for Robinson, he did not pay the same attention to his taxes. After years of not paying income taxes, the federal government garnished most of his prizefight wages and property in 1955, leaving him nearly broke and unable to raise funds for civil rights causes.

Jackie Robinson

Unlike "Sugar Ray" Robinson, nobody had to jab Jackie Robinson to join the fight for civil rights. The legendary athlete had a rebellious reputation for hitting Jim Crow back. His willingness to engage social justice issues and risk his reputation in an era where whites demanded black silence paved the way for other black athletes to be fully free. As black writer Charles Livingston told his readers, before Jackie Robinson signed with the Dodgers, "The Negro athlete then was expected to be a star on the one hand, and a submissive individual on the other hand." But

Jackie Robinson, leading North American baseball player, demonstrates batting techniques to Bob Allison, Voice of America sports editor, while preparing for a special English-language interview to be heard on VOA's *In the Sportlight*, in the early 1950s. (National Archives and Records Administration)

Livingston lauded a change came with Robinson. "From the start," Livingston said, "Jackie made it clear that he wanted to be accepted and respected not only as a ballplayer, but as a normal human being as well. He wanted none of that bowing, pleading, scrapping and groveling role. And he got none." If Jackie remained docile as expected, Livingston concluded, "the progress of the Negro athlete after him would have been slowed by the inconvenience of unequal status."[31] But for Robinson, being an activist was not always in the cards. When he signed with the Dodgers, Branch Rickey asked his barrier breaker to hold back his tongue and turn the other cheek when confronted with racism. For a proud man like Robinson, who prided himself in fighting back, this request was easier said than done. For nearly three years, Robinson had to internalize all the racial abuse, until Rickey gave him his figurative freedom papers. Once free, Robinson refused to hold back.

Before Rickey gave Robinson permission to fight back, however, the star player gave America a taste of his verbal eloquence to denounce discrimination and injustice. In what Robinson would deem one of his lowest public moments, Congress asked Robinson to appear before the House of Un-American Activities Committee in 1949 and denounce Paul Robeson, the athlete-turned-actor-turned activist who had questioned black America's willingness to fight in another war for America. For the last two decades, Robeson had used his celebrity platform to lash out against injustice, especially in America, and Congress feared that his ability to speak truth to power would damage America's reputation around the world as Americans prepared to battle the Soviet Union in the Cold War for the hearts and minds of decolonizing nations.

Congress also feared that Robeson's rebuke would become contagious among other black Americans. In their desperation, they dragged Robinson into this political battle, so Robinson, the most famous black American, could denounce Robeson and encourage other black Americans to support America's slow progress toward true equality. As Malcolm X later angrily told Robinson, "You let them use you to destroy Paul Robeson. . . . Your White Boss sent you to Washington to assure all the worried white folks that Negroes were still thankful to the Great White Father for bringing us to America, that Negroes were grateful to America (despite our not being treated as full citizens), and that Negroes would still lay down our lives to defend this white country (though this same white government wasn't ready nor willing to defend Negroes) . . . even in those days, Jackie!"[32] Unfortunately for Robinson, he did just that and at one point told the audience that Robeson made a "silly statement" and concluded, "I can't speak for any fifteen million people any more than any other one

We Will Win the Day

person can. . . . I and other Americans of many races and faiths have too much invested in our country's welfare, for any of us to throw it away because of a siren song sung in bass." Robinson later regretted these words and the fact he let Congress use him for its own political agenda. But all was not lost with Robinson's testimony. Despite ridiculing Robeson, Robinson also told Congress that most black Americans agreed with Robeson's frustration with the slow pace of civil rights. Robinson testified, "If we are to make progress in this matter, the fact that it is a Communist who denounces injustice in the courts, police brutality, and lynching when it happens, doesn't change the truth of his charges."[33] And Robinson ended his testimony warning that black Americans would not "stop fighting racial discrimination in this nation until we got it licked." Thus, when Rickey finally gave Robinson permission to publicly protest prejudice, he shamed baseball for many teams' unwillingness to integrate, he protested for black voting rights, he picketed Jim Crow businesses, and he urged President Eisenhower to end lynching. In short, Robinson became the model for the activist-athlete, and soon others would follow. It took nearly a decade, but by 1960 a noticeable changed had occurred in black athletes.

For the first time in significant numbers, in the 1960 presidential election, a number of black athletes discussed civil rights. They did so via their endorsements of politicians based on those candidates' civil rights track records. During the Democratic nomination process, for example, the party used a number of black athletes to appeal to the black voters. These men included Gene "Big Daddy" Lipscomb, Buddy Young, Ralph Metcalf, Hank Aaron, and Willie Galimore. In voicing their opinion, Lipscomb, Young, and ex-track star Ralph Metcalf traveled to Milwaukee to endorse Kennedy as the right choice for blacks. Lipscomb applauded the Massachusetts senator for being moderate on civil rights and argued, "They [Congress] can pass any bill they want to but people have to go out and enforce the bill and fight for their rights." Kennedy, he believed, was the right man for the job to change the hearts and minds of Americans. Young, the famed running back, acknowledged that Humphrey had a better record on civil rights but thought that Humphrey was "too loud" and thought that Kennedy's "moral conviction" would suit blacks better than his lack of record on civil rights.[34]

After reading their endorsements, however, Robinson had some choice words for the black athletes. Robinson, who voted for the Republican Party in most elections, urged: "If their choice is Kennedy, all well and good, but please fellows, find some more realistic grounds upon which to champion his cause. For 'in this day and age,' with Negro youngsters in the South bravely facing beatings, fire-hoses, tear gas, clubs and guns, and still insisting upon going to jail to win rights for all of us, we have little patience with this kind of Uncle Tom."[35] To be sure, Robinson, who supported Nixon because he believed that the vice president was sincere in his thoughts on civil rights, stayed with him the entire election, even when it became clear that Nixon courted white Southerners and the nominee had stopped making inroads into the black community. Propelled in part by the black vote, Kennedy won the election by the narrowest of margins.

During the Kennedy presidency, Robinson used his star power, and the stage that he held in his weekly columns, to continuously challenge Kennedy on the latter's lack of interest in civil rights. In 1962, in a column entitled "Kennedy Insults Negro Community," Robinson called out the president for refusing to meet with 100 ministers who supported Martin Luther King's struggling nonviolent battle for integration in Albany, Georgia. Instead of meeting with the ministers, Kennedy, as Robinson pointed out, met with an unrelated youth orchestra. After reading about this lack of regard for black lives, Robinson blasted him for this move: "We believe this incident shows quite clearly where the President stands. We are more than ever convinced that we were accurate in 1960 when we accused him of insincerity on the race issue in America."[36] The following year, in March, when Kennedy still showed few signs he cared about civil rights, Robinson attacked him, in an article entitled "Mr. Kennedy Is Doing Nothing for Civil Rights." Robinson told his readers, "He has achieved nothing—and has fought for nothing—in the area of civil rights legislation. He has made beautiful statements and fine appointments but he has failed to lend the great legislative executive and moral weight of the Presidency to the just cause of bringing about laws to help make the Negro a first-class citizen."[37] President Kennedy, in fact, did not give a speech about the need for civil rights legislation until June, after the Birmingham campaign.

Importantly, while Robinson called out President Kennedy, he also used his platform to push other black athletes into the movement. He understood that black athletes had a unique freedom afforded by their income and their celebrity status, and had a responsibility to speak out. In 1962, at an NAACP event in Mississippi, he met with star centerfielder Curt Flood, boxing legend Archie Moore, and heavyweight champion Floyd Patterson to address the freedom fighters in the movement. Moore, who was born in Mississippi but raised in St. Louis, told the audience that he was there to help ensure that his kids would "grow up in a better world than the world of my own childhood." Patterson told the congregation that he felt "guilty" watching the events from New York but decided to "stop watching and do something about it."[38] As of that moment, however, doing something about injustices meant showing up to meetings. Neither fighter had enough courage to remain nonviolent, as movement leaders like King called for, if white racists attacked them. They were prepared to fight back, but King and other nonviolent leaders did not want people willing to fight back; they wanted protesters willing to withstand the abuse in hopes that the racists would ultimately see the error in their hateful ways, leading to a truly democratic America built on love and not violence. The following year, while he prepared for a rematch with the new champion Sonny Liston, however, Patterson traveled to the heart of the movement in Birmingham with Robinson to participate in the movement. All eyes of America watched the city where King made his latest stand against integration, read with awe and apathy when he wrote a "Letter from a Birmingham Jail," and viewed with horror when Bull Connor allowed his police department to abuse child protesters. When Patterson arrived, the fighter noted that being part of the movement was more important than training for the championship fight and promised that he would have the courage not to fight back if violence confronted him. During their tour of the destruction caused by black residents who rioted against continued racial oppression, and the damage of the black-owned Gaston Motel, where King and other civil rights leaders often stayed, caused by dynamite, Patterson and Robinson presented a powerful image of black solidarity. Of his trip to Birmingham, Patterson told writer A. J. Liebling of the *New Yorker*, "You feel like an animal walking in the jungle. . . . It is not like part of the United States." Other athletes, however, skipped out on the trip. Sonny Liston reportedly said, "I ain't got no dog-proof ass," referring to photos and film of Birmingham police siccing dogs on civil rights protesters, while Bill Russell, who would soon join the ranks of activist-athlete, said, "If I went down there to Birmingham and let someone spit on me and didn't do anything about it, it wouldn't be me."[39] Instead, Russell organized a protest in solidarity with Boston's black community.

But not every athlete supported Patterson and Robinson's decision to get involved in politics. Jesse Owens used his platform to criticize Robinson and Patterson. From his residence in Chicago, Owens, the 1936 Olympic hero, gave the press what would be a standard tune from naysayers of the movement and called the pair outside agitators. Owens critiqued, "I can't see where they're going to be of any great help." He also claimed that locals would have to solve the Jim Crow problem on their own and added, "To have people from the outside go in, for some things

I don't think that's a good idea." When a reporter asked the Olympic star if he had been asked to help, he answered, "No. I haven't been asked because I haven't allowed myself to be asked."[40] Upon reading this, Robinson hit back. He reminded Owens that he had a duty to participate. "We must keep these youngsters aware—and especially we who have been fortunate like Floyd, Jesse and myself—that no Negro has it made, regardless of his fame, position or money—until the most underprivileged Negro enjoys his rights as a free man."[41] Later that month, Robinson issued a challenge to every black baseball player to participate in a "Freedom Day Demonstration" in the upcoming off-season. Upon hearing this call for solidarity, the black sportswriter Charles J. Livingston announced, "If the current colored major league players fail Robinson, they'll also be failing their race as well."[42] For whatever reasons, the demonstration never materialized.

As a sportswriter, Livingston was one of the first black writers to openly hold black athletes accountable for their lack of commitment to the civil rights movement. Nearly a decade prior, in 1955, Livingston suggested that the top black boxers should donate money to the NAACP, and he argued that even if they did not make as much money as Louis or Sugar Ray Robinson, "many of them can well afford to make a contribution to another kind of cancer that is eating at the vitals of American democracy . . . the cancer of racial discrimination. And so doing they would be performing a great service for a great cause and a great nation."[43] In 1963, Livingston put the full-court pressure on black athletes. During the Birmingham campaign, he ordered that since the black community had battled for the black athletes' right to compete and earn a living—he listed pickets in boxing, baseball, and football—black athletes should return the favor and "show their gratitude by leading picket lines and other campaigns against racial bigotry on behalf of their less fortunate 'brothers'." Livingston noted that everybody had a responsibility to fight for justice, but he also believed that because athletes made it big, they were the "most obligated to directly lead the civil rights fight."[44] In July, after few athletes heeded the call to fight for justice, Livingston again called them out and complained that too many black athletes lacked the "courage or conviction to stand up and fight with their less fortunate brothers."[45] In particular, Livingston lambasted leading athletes like Oscar Robertson, Wilt Chamberlain, Jim Brown, and Willie Mays.

While the aforementioned athletes would eventually use their platform, Mays, the greatest player of his generation, ducked his responsibilities throughout his career. Just a month after Sheriff Bull Connor sicced his dogs on black children in Birmingham, Mays, the Birmingham native, told one reporter, "Sports has helped tremendous in race relations, and I mean with both the southern and northern white man. Prejudice can work both ways, you know. You can prejudge a white man just the same as he can prejudge you." Instead of getting involved, Mays believed that being himself, the likeable "Say Hey Kid," would be enough. "I think I can make one contribution. I think I can make it easier for the next guy. In San Francisco I go anywhere I want to go. My face is so well known that people recognize me. If I carry myself in a way, the next guy is accepted easily. I mean the next Negro guy, just walking in off the street. If I'm rowdy, it will be bad. So I just go in and have fun."[46] A year later, as Congress debated civil rights legislation, and activists risked their lives in Mississippi, Mays told *Jet*, "Reporters are always asking me why I don't sit-in or demonstrate for civil rights. I try to make my contributions for racial harmony in the best way I know how—on the baseball field." Mays reasoned, "The Rev. Martin Luther King can't play baseball, so he doesn't try. Now how would I look trying to preach to people. I try to do my best with in my abilities and I think I've helped my people. I don't criticize the movement, person or action because I'm no statesman man. I am only a ball player."[47]

His aloofness on civil rights became even more unbearable for many, considering the fact that when the Giants moved from New York to San Francisco, white neighbors tried to bar Mays from moving into their neighborhood. The racism became so embarrassing for the city of San Francisco that the mayor had to step in and help Mays buy a house. But instead of publicly condemning restrictive covenants and the racist housing market, forces that maintained segregation, Mays shrugged and suggested, "I feel if you build a house you're entitled to sell it to who you want," a remark similar to future California governor Ronald Reagan's racist rhetoric during an equal housing campaign, when he infamously said if a white person did not want to sell a house to a black person they should not have to.[48] Mays felt, however, that since he, the great Willie Mays, could live anywhere he wanted to in San Francisco in 1963, racial progress had been made. Mays's unwillingness to fight for civil rights, however, forced Jackie Robinson to call him out. In 1968, Robinson told the white *Los Angeles Times* reporter Charles Maher, "Willie Mays has a personality that is loved by white Americans and I think he will be one of the first negroes to move into a front office positions."[49] And on a television show filmed in San Francisco, Robinson questioned Mays's commitment to the movement, prompting the great outfielder to retort, "I can't go out and picket. I can't stand on a soap box. People like Mr. (Martin Luther) King and Mr. (Roy) Wilkins are better equipped than I am. But that doesn't mean I have not been doing anything for race relations."[50] But while Robinson criticized Mays, Jim Brown, the great running back, understood Mays's success as a necessary strategy. As he told *Ebony* in 1964, "We need street demonstrators. We need Negro celebrities lending their names to the cause and we need a Willie Mays quietly setting an example of greatness."[51] The black writer "Doc" Young agreed with Brown's earlier assessment and supported Mays in his battle with Robinson. Young retorted, "Willie Mays has proven that he is a man. He is one of the all-time great major leaguers, in the fullest sense of the term. In his own way, doing what he does best, he has contributed far more to the cause of racial equality than MOST loudmouth critics who run around the world putting people down."[52] For Mays, his contribution to the civil rights movement consisted of giving speeches to audiences about staying clean and working hard and giving money to causes and organizations. But for most prominent black athletes, by 1968, during what many would label the revolt of the black athlete, they knew they had to get actively involved in the fight for racial equality.

Bill Russell

Whereas Mays stayed away from the movement, by the summer of 1963, most prominent athletes knew the time was now. Many were pulled to participate by the great swell in racial pride gained from the March on Washington in August, including the outspoken Bill Russell. In fact, Russell met with King the night before the event, and the civil rights leader invited him to stand on stage. Russell declined the invite and instead sat in the second row.[53] From his vantage point, however, the legendary center for the Boston Celtics concluded, "The March on Washington was brilliantly conceived and badly executed. . . . I think they were in error right at the outset when the idea was compromised by including whites . . . this was one time—the first time—when Negroes should have stood together alone—representing all Negroes." According to Russell, by integrating the march, and thus making it tame because they stripped away the powerful block of a solid black base, it killed the momentum of the civil rights movement and allowed the "status seekers," and "not the fighters," to come to the forefront.[54] Russell was a fighter and not a status seeker.

To be sure, Russell was one of the few athletes who could match Jackie Robinson as an activist. This is not a line meant to keep score; rather, it is to highlight his commitment to activism and his use of his platform to attack prejudice. The bitterness of the years of bigotry he battled while being a barrier breaker had built up inside him, and he wanted white

America to know his frustration. He once told a reporter, "I don't like most white people because they are white. Conversely, I like most Negros because they are black."[55] These sharp words stirred up a heap of controversy, but Russell did not care. He did not aim to please. And he told the *Saturday Evening Post*, "The first thing we [as Negroes in sport] have to get rid of is the idea that this is a popularity contest. I don't work for acceptance." Unlike Mays, Russell had no pretensions that sports, and more specifically the black athlete, would push America past racism. "They tell me, 'But you've had more success than most Negroes, you have a large earning capacity.' And I tell them to go to hell. Nobody said, 'here's a nice little Negro boy I should give a break to.' I have what I have only because I have the ability."[56] Russell, like Robinson, did not let his star status blind him. And he would not let white people define him and dictate his behavior. "I used to love to read how Jackie Robinson was 'surly and oversensitive,'" Russell said, "because he had the audacity to think he was a human being."[57]

One of the greatest gifts Russell gave to the movement was his willingness to forsake a reputation for being likable in order to publicly attack racism. No athlete was more eloquent about his or her assertion of equality, or more forceful about how, as a black person, he or she would be treated in an unjust America. In interviews and written articles in *Sports Illustrated*, *Sport*, the *Saturday Evening Post*, and his two well-received books, *Go Up for Glory*, and *Second Wind*, Russell asserted the "new Negro" attitude of the black athlete. Russell articulated the feeling that white America had created a racial divide and, as a black man, he asserted he should not have to put up a façade to appease white fans and their feelings. His job was to confront racism. He dictated stories about the racism he faced in the National Basketball Association (NBA), especially in the league's southernmost city, St. Louis. He boldly told readers that the NBA had a quota system to keep black players off the teams to ensure white fans come to the game. He attacked racism in the South and the North, he praised Dr. King but also criticized nonviolence, and he openly discussed his appreciation for Malcolm X. After Malcolm's assassination in 1965, Russell said the controversial leader, "spoke more truth, with less pretenses, than any other black leader. Dr. King may have inspired more people, but Malcolm opened eyes. His sense of injustice was so keen that he pointed out areas of cultural bias that even its victims had been unaware of."[58]

Most important, Russell's critiques about American racism carried weight, because he got involved in the movement. In 1958, after having to stay in a Jim Crow hotel in Charlotte, North Carolina, even though team officials had told their black players they would not be Jim Crowed, Russell and his black teammates, Sam Jones and K. C. Jones, and Lakers star Elgin Baylor, publicly complained about the situation and promised never to play under Jim Crow conditions again. The Celtics and the rest of the NBA supported this decision, and a few months later the league passed a resolution that teams would sign nondiscrimination assurances before they traveled down South. But these nondiscrimination assurances did not completely protect the players from racism on the road. In 1961, in Lexington, Kentucky, after a coffee shop refused to serve four of his black teammates, Russell, the de facto leader of black players, made the decision that he and his black teammates, and the black players on the St. Louis Hawks, would not play in the game.

Every black athlete, at some point in his or her career, had to play in a Jim Crow town. Black athletes knew this and seemingly put up with these conditions as part of their role to improve race relations. But during the civil rights movement era, most started to challenge the system. As Russell once stated, "For a great number of years colored athletes and entertainers put up with these conditions because we figured they'd see we were nice people mostly. . . . I'm not insulted by it. I'm not embarrassed. I'm of the opinion that some people can't insult me. But it was the greatest mistakes we ever made, because as long as you go along with it, everybody assumes it's the status quo. The way I feel about it, if I can't eat, I can't entertain."[59] Black athletes grew tired of the excuses the media and the athletes made for playing in these horrid conditions. They said it would make things better, that entertaining whites in this manner would help prove blacks belonged, but playing under these conditions just appeased the racists.

By 1963, Russell was fully involved in the civil rights movement. Russell believed that blacks had to keep pushing whites on the issue of civil rights or else equality would never come. "We have got to make the white population uncomfortable and keep it uncomfortable, because that is the only way to get their attention," he told the *Saturday Evening Post*.[60] If blacks kept pushing, he believed, then society would reach a point where "either there will be a really integrated society or we will understand, absolutely and finally, that we will never become part of society."[61] This meant that he had to join the movement. He could not stand on the sidelines. In fact, at one point in 1964, he claimed he would retire from basketball if it helped advance civil rights. When asked about this, he concluded, "Yes, but only if it would make a concrete contribution. There'd be no choice. It would be the duty of any American to fight for a cause he strongly believes in."[62]

During the Birmingham protests, while Robinson and Patterson were down South, Russell led a march in solidarity with residents of Boston's predominantly black neighborhood, Roxbury, through the streets of the city. That same year, Russell and his wife, Rose, who sat on the board of the local Boston NAACP, joined the local fight to integrate the public school system.[63] The following year, he received a call from Charles Evers, the brother of the slain civil rights hero Medgar Evers, asking him to go down to Jackson, Mississippi, and help with the movement. Russell knew this move would be dangerous, because black life in Mississippi meant nothing to white racists. White Mississippians would not think twice about killing an NBA MVP. But despite the daily fear of death, and a struggle within himself questioning if he could be nonviolent, Russell traveled to Jackson to give integrated basketball clinics in the most dangerous state to blacks in America. When asked why he risked his life to go to Mississippi, Russell responded, "This is a burden that must be shared by all."[64]

Jim Brown

During the civil rights movement era, no black athlete was more feared or forceful than Jim Brown.[65] Although Brown, who had been a star running back at Syracuse during the mid-1950s and the best back in professional football since his rookie year in 1957, had not publicly positioned himself in the movement until late 1963. Still, behind the scenes, Brown had fiercely fought for black dignity, especially for his black teammates and among his white teammates, coaches, and his team's white owner. Brown organized his black teammates and operated as their unofficial spokesperson, even taking up their segregated rooming situation with then owner Art Model, who went out of his way, and spent extra money, to ensure blacks and whites stayed separated on the road in hotel rooms. "I organized the black cats," Brown remembered. "If the brothers were going to be separated, I wanted us separated on our own terms, not the team's. I told my teammates we had to maintain our pride and dignity."[66] For Brown, black pride and dignity, also meant that black players could not "shuck and jive," or openly smile at every white man, especially coaches. Whites expected them to be happy-go-lucky, but Brown demanded blacks be serious. On these sentiments, Brown said, "Generally, he expects you to be a jolly fellow, always laughing. When he wants to talk foolishness he comes to you, but when he wants to talk seriously, he goes to a white man. Cut this off from the beginning. Let [the] white man know you're interested in the same things—getting ahead, having a nice life, a home, a family."[67] In other

Football player Jim Brown, whom many consider the greatest running back in football history, with his children. (Library of Congress)

words, if black players showed that they were serious and did not defer to whites in conversations, it would prove their equality.

Brown, like Russell, ignited a new attitude in black America in general, and the black athlete in particular. In his interviews, and his writings, he told whites that his dignity and manhood counted and would not be compromised. In a 1964 interview in *Look*, he opened up many white eyes when he told white America he was dissatisfied with their discrimination. "I may very well make more money this year than any Negro athlete in the world, yet I want just as deeply as the poorest sharecropper to be a free man." More important, he told whites he did not care what they thought. This was an important revelation, because since the rise of Jesse Owens, Joe Louis, and Jackie Robinson, whites demanded black athletes' docility and public humility. Brown bruised white egos. "I do not crave the white man's approval: I crave only the rights I'm entitled to as a human being. The acceptance of the Negro in sports is really an insignificant development that warms the heart of the colored man less than it does that of the white man, who salves his troubled conscience by telling himself, 'Isn't it wonderful that Negroes and whites are out there playing together?'"

These words shocked white America, but as Brown told readers, "The fact is, the more successful a Negro is, the more difficult it becomes for him to accept second-class citizenship."[68]

In order to earn equality, the forceful running back believed that black people had to force the action. In one of his most controversial statements, just months after the Civil Rights Act of 1964 passed, he said he did not believe King's nonviolence would work, and he noted that he could not love someone that did not love him back. Instead of siding with King, Brown channeled Malcolm X's rhetoric when he noted that freedom had never been won peacefully. He estimated that at least 99% of black America agreed with the Nation of Islam and "the white man had better start trying to understand him."[69] In short, whites had to give black their freedom immediately. When asked about these controversial statements by the black writer Claude E. Harrison Jr., Brown asserted, "As a man, I am entitled to express myself on any issue without being taken to task by the fans, press, or anyone." He also doubled down on the immediacy of the situation and urged, "It's no secret that the Negro is in an explosive mood and that the sooner the white man makes a real effort to understand him the quicker the racial battle will be won."[70] A few months later, still trying to waken whites to the fact that blacks had to have their rights immediately, he told *Ebony*, "I doubt that the American white man realizes the time has come when he must make a move." Brown continued, "He must give us the laws that make us free men and he must enforce those laws."[71] But even if or when blacks had equal rights by the law, Brown also believed that blacks would not have true independence unless they had economic power. To that end, Brown put his money where his mouth was.

In 1966, after retiring from the NFL to pursue an acting career, Brown announced the creation of his new venture, the National Negro Industrial and Economic Union. As he stated in his retirement speech delivered from London—where he was filming *The Dirty Dozen*—Brown told the press, "My main ambition right now is to devote as much time as possible to the Negro Industrial and Economic Union (NIEU) project, which stresses full participation of Negroes in the mainstream of American economy."[72] With the help of Maggie Hathaway, Brown designed NIEU to give black people economic independence by helping them secure small business loans, offering professional advice, and helping existing black businesses to grow. In other words, he wanted to create self-help opportunities and promote "green power" in the black community. As Brown told one reporter in 1966, "We just want Negroes to participate in the economy of the country so that they can stand on their own feet and won't have to beg anybody to give them a little of this and a little of that. What could be more dignified than that?"[73] Brown believed if the civil rights movement had concentrated on economics more than producing marches, then the American ghettoes would have not seen as much rioting as they did. While one could argue with this assertion, Brown truly believed green power would lead to black liberation. But to liberate black people with green power, Brown also believed that blacks had to emancipate themselves from their own insecurities and ineptness about economics. To that end, Brown advocated that black people needed to stop wasting their money as consumers and instead look for ways to be producers. The NIEU, as Brown saw it, would be the bridge to black freedom.

Black economic liberation, Brown believed, could not be achieved without the black athlete. When Brown said "we," he was referring to his other athlete activists, nearly 100 black athletes, like teammate John Wooten, Bobby Mitchell, and basketball great Bill Russell. Athletes like Wooten, the executive director of the NIEU, had the ability to go into the ghetto and get the hardest guy in the street to listen, and to help residents organize. The black sportswriter A. S. "Doc" Young noted these athlete activists "struck out on a course which very well may be, in the long run, if not in the short dash, the most important move made toward equality by any group in the history of Negroes in this country." To support his claim, Young cited the fact that athletes had the most prestige and money in the community and put it all on the line to help prop up 23 million of their brothers and sisters.[74]

Within five years, Brown expanded the NIEU and went down South to rural communities, including at one point in 1970 traveling with a group of black football players to a small rural town in Mississippi to help a poverty-stricken black community fight and survive a long history of economic exploitation. As Brown told the athletes on that trip, "None of you is asked to give a lot of your time. The mistake most make is one of great thrust with a program, then they go back home and the project falls on its face. As athletes, you represent one of the highest income groups in the country. There isn't another black group whose income average could approach yours."[75]

Beyond the belief that business success would bring black liberation, Brown also emphasized that seeing black businesses succeed would instill pride and dignity into the community. In other words, mirroring Malcolm X's prior claims to black psychological power as part of his Black Power strategy for black liberation, Brown believed that part of the struggle for black freedom came from within and that if blacks did not help prop each other up and instill pride, they would not have the courage or energy to continuously fight for freedom and maintain that newfound status. To that end, the NIEU launched youth programs. In 1967, it created "Operation Soul Brother," a program featuring black athletes visiting ghetto communities and helping local youths establish leadership skills. It also built community centers, helped find summer employment for youths, and provided job training. By 1968, the program had secured a half a million-dollar Ford Foundation grant to continue the development of youth programs. While he seemed radical, Brown did not revolt from the system. His belief in capitalism relied on a fundamental belief that black capital could solve issues of social justice.

CHAPTER SEVEN

The Revolt of the Black Athlete

With an impressive leap of 5 feet, 2½ inches, Eroseanna Robinson had just tied for first place at the 1958 AAU Track and Field Championships. As a photographer got ready to snap a picture of the champion, Robinson snapped back, "I'm not interested." Robinson did not mind the picture; she was talking about something bigger. She did not want what was coming next, a trip to Russia. Why? Most athletes would have been excited about the feat; after all, the winners of the meet were headed to Moscow as part of a U.S.-U.S.S.R. goodwill track meet between the two Cold War nations. Black athletes—12 were on the team that traveled to Moscow—played an important role in these state-sponsored meets. Their success, and no doubt their smiles, gave the U.S. government an opportunity to show people of color across the globe that America, and not Russia, had their best interests in mind. Who would pass up a chance to travel, compete for their country, and prove their patriotism? Eroseanna Robinson. She wanted no part of this propaganda. "This is a political maneuver," Robinson ranted. "But I don't want anyone to think my athletics have political connotations. In other words, I don't want to be used as a political pawn." U.S. officials, including famed Tennessee State track coach Ed Temple, did not understand her politics. Temple suggested that the track meets represented a "goodwill gesture" and that it was better to settle political differences in sports than to fight real battles in wars. Robinson, however, held to her convictions and boycotted the meet. Robinson, a pacifist, was not going to let her country use her during the Cold War.

She competed for competition and not for country, especially not for a country that would use her athleticism but not free her people.[1]

Two years later, Robinson was back in the news again for her activism and not her athleticism. This time, in 1960, Robinson sat in the Cook County Jail in Chicago, because she had refused to pay taxes since 1954. A supporter who helped lead a protest in solidarity outside of the jail told the *Chicago Defender*, "She does not want her money to go for mass slaughter, war, and killing. Eighty percent of U.S. tax money is spent on wars past, present, and pending. It is money used for military preparations, military foreign aid or interest paid on past war." She would rather her tax dollars go to "housing, education, and public welfare."[2] To show her seriousness, Robinson fasted and refused to eat until she was released from jail. If not, she argued, she would die for her beliefs.

To be sure, the track star did not come to these radical ideas on a whim; Robinson had been active in politics and the battle for civil rights and justice since the 1940s. As she pursued her athletic career, she was an active member in the Fellowship of Reconciliation and later the Congress of Racial Equality (CORE). During one protest for CORE, she reportedly had her arm broken during a demonstration against a Jim Crow skating rink in Chicago. At the 1959 Pan-American Games in Chicago, she refused to stand for the playing of the national anthem. One wonders what Robinson might have done if she ever earned a trip to the Olympics.[3] Would she have boycotted the games or used her opportunity to protest at the games? But the 33-year-old never qualified in previous years, and her fast during 1960, which she ultimately ended to save her life, combined with her imprisonment, ruined her chances to properly train for the 1960 Olympic Games.

While Robinson's story has largely been lost to history, her protest and willingness to withdraw her labor from competition as a political statement against American oppression anticipated the changing attitudes of black athletes by nearly a decade. To be sure, her activism and her willingness to use her athletic status as a powerful lever against uneven racial justice places her in the pantheon of those celebrated athletes in the era marked by the "revolt of the black athlete."

By looking at Muhammad Ali's political transformation from the lovable "Louisville Lip" to an activist who battled with the U.S. government over his refusal to fight in the Vietnam War, the planned boycott of the 1968 Olympics, and the protests of black college athletes in 1967 and 1968, this chapter will explain the meaning behind what many called the revolt of the black athlete. How does one distinguish between the activist-athletes and those athletes who are lionized as part of the revolt of the black athlete? While athletes who are considered part of the revolt of the black athlete were certainly activist-athletes in the mold of Jackie Robinson, Jim Brown, and Bill Russell—Russell's writings and interviews hinted at this revolt—much of what is considered the revolt of the black athlete occurred after the integration phase of the civil rights movement, which, many scholars say, concluded with the passage of the 1965 Voting Rights Act. Thus, the activism during the revolt of the black athlete occurred during the Black Power phase, mostly after 1966, when young activists like Stokely Carmichael publicly challenged the usefulness of an integrated society that continued to oppress black folks socially, economically, and politically in America.

As Harry Edwards, a leading architect of the movement when he worked as a sociology professor at San Jose State University, declared, "The revolt of the black athlete in America as a phase of the overall black liberation movement is as legitimate as the sit-ins, the freedom rides, or any other manifestation of Afro-American efforts to gain freedom."[4] Even though most black athletes who revolted challenged American democracy from so-called privileged integrated spaces on predominately white college campuses, their position as athletes gave them a powerful perspective from which to criticize the promises of integration. These athletes were tired of being marginalized on campus as isolated black athletes, upset with the all-white coaching staff racially berating and mocking them, and fed up with their continued segregation in society. How, many of these athletes contemplated, could tens of thousands of people cheer them in the arena, the stadium, celebrate their Olympic glory, yet refuse to rent an apartment to them, deny them an opportunity to pledge a fraternity, forbid them to date who they wanted to date, or stare at them as human pathogens when they walked in the library? In short, they learned that sports in America were a dubious democratic design that deterred black people from full participation in America. "It was inevitable that this revolt should develop," Edwards wrote, "with struggles being waged by black people in the areas of education, housing, employment and many others, it was only a matter of time before Afro-American athletes, too, shed their fantasies and delusions and asserted their manhood, faced the facts of their existence."[5]

Black athletes, and the racially marginalized people they represented, were supposed to be happy with the old beliefs that suggested isolated individual athletic success marked the best path toward freedom. But these athletes who revolted felt the full weight of integration's inadequacies and decided to fight back. And they had a lot of power. They realized their campuses and their country depended on them, so they used the most powerful weapon they had, their bodies, to challenge the system.

To be sure, the revolt of the black athlete was a brief moment in history where black athletes publicly challenged the shortcomings of integration and democracy, and willingly risked their careers to bring about change. Like Eroseanna Robinson before them, they threatened to withdraw their participation from a system that exploited their black bodies. These athletes, however, quickly learned that challenging the system was not easy. There were consequences to pay. Ali lost three years of his career and millions of dollars, other college athletes lost their scholarships and their shot at the pros, and they all took unnecessary hits in the press that wanted them to shut up and play.

Muhammad Ali

Nobody thought that the loquacious lad from Louisville would lead the revolt of the black athlete—nobody. Born in 1942, in the segregated Kentucky city, for the first three years of his professional career, Cassius Clay, the Louisville Lip, was known more for his mouth and moves in the ring—sportswriters hated his style of fighting and said he ran too much—than for his politics. In fact, until 1963, when he dragged the National Association for the Advancement of Colored People (NAACP) through the mud for its civil rights platform, Clay's most important political statement followed his 1960 Olympic triumph when he told a reporter who had asked him about intolerance in America, "Oh yeah, we've got some problems. But get this straight—it's still the best country in the world."[6] Until his first real political statements in 1963, most writers were enamored with his ability to brag first and then box. Writing in 1966, James L. Hicks, of the *Amsterdam News*, reflected, "When Clay first came on the scene he played the role of a white man's Negro. . . . Ole Cassius started out playing the role of a clown. He became a Clown Prince of stupidity and the white people loved him to the extent that he could do no wrong."[7] After his victory over the veteran Archie Moore, in 1962, a fight many had hoped Moore would win to shut Clay up, Lawrence Casey of the *Michigan Chronicle* wrote: "It would do well since you have proven yourself with victory over Ol' Archie, to temper your egotistical statements."[8] Casey's words rang similar to a number of black writers who thought Clay had the opportunity to be one of the best boxers in his division, but he had to silence himself.

Still, other black writers believed Clay's bragging was beautiful—black and beautiful. Alex Poinsett, writing for *Ebony*, declared, "Lingering behind his words is the bitter sarcasm of Dick Gregory, the shrill defiance of Miles Davis, the utter contempt of Malcolm X. He smiles easily, but, behind it all, behind the publicity gimmicks and boyish buffoonery, behind the brashness, Cassius Marcellus Clay—and this fact has evaded the sports writing fraternity—is a black furnace of race pride." Poinsett proffered, "His is a pride that would never mask itself with skin lighteners and processed hair. . . . He does not talk publicly about racial discrimination, preferring instead to leave protests to race leaders. But a hint of feelings, searing the very depths of him, surface even in his most jocular

Muhammad Ali wearing the 24-carat gold-plated championship belt in 1964. (Library of Congress)

moments."[9] In other words, Poinsett knew early on that Clay used his gift of gab to masquerade his politics.

While he played the role of clown prince, the man who would soon be "the greatest" had secretly attended meetings of the Nation of Islam (NOI), a branch of Islam that held strong black nationalist beliefs.

In 1963, the revelation that Clay attended NOI meetings and that he had a burgeoning friendship with Malcolm X shook the foundation of the sports world and eventually changed the landscape for the black athlete.

Politically, as it was for other black athletes, 1963 was a pivotal year for Clay. It marked the first time the public heard his position on integration and the civil rights movement, the year the public found out about the NOI meetings and his close friendship with Malcolm X. In March, when asked about the civil rights movement, Clay told a white reporter from the *New York Post*, "I have no use for the organizations like the NAACP. I'm a fighter. I believe in the eye-for-an-eye business. The NAACP can say, turn the other cheek, but the NAACP is ignorant. You kill my dog, you better hide your cat." In regard to James Meredith, the black student who bravely integrated Ole Miss, Clay remarked that Meredith showed "guts" and then added, "But I don't want to meet him. I don't like people like that. I believe it's human nature to be with your own kind. I know what rest rooms to use, where to eat and what to say." He finished his rebuke on integration, noting, "I don't want people who don't want me. I don't like people who cause trouble."[10] While white newspapers mostly ignored the comments—there was a major newspaper strike at the time in New York—the black press could not ignore what Clay said. The Louisville Lip had poked holes in their hopes that sports, and by extension black athletes, would help lead the cause for integration. At this moment, for example, Ollie Matson, the star football player for the Los Angeles Rams, headed the NAACP's athlete outreach division, and Matson's dinner banquet in Los Angeles in June attracted nearly 100 black athletes and sports personalities willing to support the organization. Clay wanted nothing to do with that. According to historians Johnny Smith and Randy Roberts, Clay's "comments provoked fear that one of the most famous black athletes in the country had forsaken the ideals of integration and embraced the separatist ideology of the Nation, an unsettling thought for those who had built him up as a hero."[11] When he had the opportunity to apologize to the NAACP, and then buy a lifetime membership as a sign of solidarity, he refused to do so and remarked that it should pay *him* to join the organization.

Clay's public statements about integration, and growing rumors that he belonged to the NOI, sent reporters scurrying to find evidence of his political/religious affiliation. They soon found it. In July, a reporter saw him leaving Mosque No. 2 in Chicago, one of the most important mosques in the NOI, and in September a reporter cornered him after an NOI meeting in Oakland, California, to ask him about his involvement with the NOI. Clay easily evaded this questioning and told the man, "I'm not a politician. I don't talk against anything. I'm a peaceful man."[12] But just a few weeks later, in Philadelphia, at the largest meeting for the NOI of the year, the press caught up with him again and asked him to address rumors of his affiliation with the group. The talkative Clay stunned the reporters when he declined the opportunity to speak and instead told them, "If you want to interview somebody, interview Malcolm X. He's really got something to say."[13] Clay's assertion that the media interview Malcolm X, a man most whites associated with hate, shocked the establishment. How could the onetime patriotic Olympian, the kid who joked too much, and the fighter who wrote poetry predicting the defeat of his opponents have a serious political thought that would indict America as a racist nation and also be associated with a man of hate? This upset the press, but soon, it believed it would get its revenge. In order to shut Clay up, it turned to the one black athlete it thought it hated more, Sonny Liston, an ex-convict with a well-known criminal record of physical violence and supposed Mafia connections. In short, America both hated and feared Liston because he was a so-called big-scary black man who had no fear of white power and had no intentions of conforming. He wanted to be left alone.

The Clay–Liston bout, scheduled for February 1964, marked the second time within the previous two years that a heavyweight championship battle between two black fighters symbolized a political divide in America and how Americans, both black and white Americans, projected political implications, hopes, and worries on such a bout. Prior to the Clay contest, Liston's first championship match against Floyd Patterson, in 1962, marked the first time Americans assigned racial and political symbolism to an intra-racial contest. For that match, most Americans assigned Liston the role of the bad black man, or the black man who was ready to "do whites in," as Amiri Baraka described him. Patterson, for his part, perfectly played the role assigned for him; the good-reformed black man who put on a positive face for the potential of an integrated society. Born poor in Brooklyn, the onetime juvenile delinquent found religion in juvenile detention, reformed his life, became the youngest heavyweight champion ever, and lived modestly and spoke eloquently. The press, and even the president, suggested that Patterson was the perfect role model for a new integrated society. And Patterson understood this well. For two years, he refused to fight Liston, suggesting that Liston, the man who had been in and out of prison, did not live up to the expectations of a champion. But he could not continue to duck Liston; the American public was pressuring Patterson to defeat the so-called black beast for integration's sake. But everybody who followed boxing knew Patterson had no chance. Liston, for lack of better words, was a "bad dude." He knocked out Patterson in the first round. In a rematch the following year, he knocked him out in the first round again. Nobody thought he could be beat, which is why many people wanted Liston to fight Clay. Liston, for the first time in his life, became the "good guy." To be clear, he was not good like Patterson; Patterson was the acceptable Negro for integration, but Liston was good because he was not linked to the NOI.

At a time when Congress had started working on the Civil Rights Act of 1964, it became imperative, many thought, that a black Muslim not get his hands on the heavyweight crown, the most important title in sports. In fact, the public became so enamored with Clay's friendship with Malcolm that when reports surfaced that Malcolm was at Clay's training camp in Miami, the fight promoter threatened to cancel the fight unless Clay denounced the NOI and Malcolm X. The bold boxer would do no such thing, and when he heard the demands that Malcolm leave, Clay started packing his bags. Instead, understanding the magnitude of the fight for young Clay, Malcolm X temporarily left Miami. But he would be back. Unlike most people, Malcolm believed Clay was destined to win the fight, and Allah would give him the strength.

On February 25, 1964, young Cassius Clay shook the world. And on February 26, he woke them up. The day after the famous fight, a subdued Clay publicly admitted to his membership in the NOI. When asked, "Are you a card-carrying member of the black Muslims," Clay jabbed back, "I believe in Allah and in peace. I don't try to move into white neighborhoods. I don't want to marry a white woman. I was baptized when I was twelve, but I didn't know what I was doing. I'm not a Christian any more?"[14] Toward the end of the interview he asked the white writers a rhetorical question, "I catch so much hell, why? Why me when I don't try to bust into schools or march around or throw bricks." They had no answer. Clay, however, knew the answer. Martin Luther King Jr. and other integrationists caught hell because they were black. Malcolm X caught hell because he was black. And Cassius Clay caught hell because he was black.

Just months after he won the championship, he dropped Clay, which he called his "slave name," and started going by Cassius X. Then NOI leader Elijah Muhammad gave him his new name, Muhammad Ali. On his name change, Ali once said "Changing my name was one of the most important things that happened to me in my life. It freed me from the identity given to my family by my slave masters."[15] As expected, the backlash to Ali's public affiliation with the NOI and his new name sparked fierce backlash, filled with vitriol from both whites and blacks.

The political transition from Clay to Ali tugged at the moral fabric of America and exposed the reality that a younger generation of black folks did not hunger to sit at an integrated lunch counter or live in integrated spaces. To whites who had never given much thought or concern about the plight of black America, Ali's political awakening was just another opportunity to deny black equality, but for black folks engaged in integration politics, Ali's political status enraged them because his boisterous politics knocked down what they had fought for. While a number of black people, especially working-class folks, showed support for Ali, those in leadership positions in the civil rights movement attacked him for what they considered Ali's betrayal of their integrationist ideals, his newfound freedom. An editorialist in the *Michigan Chronicle* supported his religious freedom but cautioned Ali about having "diarrhea of the mouth" while talking about pugilism and also politics. The writer also added: "Athletic achievement does not necessarily give a person credentials to speak authoritatively about crucial issues that affect the Negro masses."[16] In April, an editorial in the *Cleveland Call and Post*, chided: "It's too bad that Negroes can't flunk him out of the race. Just as his heavyweight title is a tainted one, so is his identification as a Negro tainted." The naysayer continued, "Mr. X may think he is a big man, but this delusion exists only in his ignorant head."[17] Early Battey, a catcher for the Minnesota Twins, who participated in the March on Washington, denounced Ali's affiliation as "ill-advised." Battey told a reporter, "I have always been brought up to believe in equality. That goes for everyone, Negro and white. I've seen prejudice against the Negro, not so much in baseball, but while traveling around. I don't think that can be solved though, by the theory of black supremacy which the Muslims preach."[18]

Even Martin Luther King Jr. took potshots at Ali. King claimed, "When Cassius Clay joined the Black Muslims and started calling himself Cassius X, he became the champion of racial segregation—and that is what we are fighting." He also added, "I think Cassius should spend more time proving his boxing skill and do less talking."[19] Ali did both. He spoke for his people and fought for himself, both done brilliantly. He would not be like previous black champs. "I've heard over and over, how come I couldn't be like Joe Louis and Sugar Ray. Well, they're gone now, and the black man's condition is just the same. Ain't it? We still catching hell."[20]

Unfortunately, for the newly crowned champ, things quickly changed in the NOI. Less than a month after he won the title, Elijah Muhammad kicked out Malcolm X for insubordination. Muhammad did not like Malcolm's increasing desire to move the NOI, a group that did not want to participate in politics, into a powerful political organization to realize the full potential of Black Power. Moreover, others believed, Muhammad started to grow jealous of his protégée's popularity. Malcolm was seen as the figurehead of the movement, not Muhammad, and this bothered the aged leader. In addition, Malcolm had recently questioned the leader about his infidelity. All of these things led to Malcolm's demise in the movement, and later his life. Showing loyalty to the leader, Ali remained with the NOI, while Malcolm X eventually started his own organization, the Organization of Afro American Unity. The two, Malcolm X and Muhammad Ali, never had a meaningful conversation with each other again. A year later, as Ali prepared to battle Liston for a rematch, members of the NOI allegedly murdered Malcolm X.

Those uncomfortable with Ali's new public politics had hoped that the first Clay–Liston fight was a fluke and that Liston would destroy the brash black Muslim in their rematch, but those hopes quickly evaporated when Ali shot a quick right to Liston's jaw, dropping the ex-champ in the first round. With Liston out of the picture, eyes turned to one overmatched man to carry the hopes of integrationists and white Americans, Floyd Patterson. For those who believed that the results of the ring had ramifications beyond the squared circle, the idea that Patterson could be a savior made complete sense. Patterson, as previously mentioned, was a well-liked nonthreatening personality propped up as a "good black" and represented the positives of an unjust America.

Patterson, the good black or the "black–white hope," played this role all too well after Ali won the championship. At the end of 1965, in fact, he penned a column in *Sports Illustrated* and suggested that he hoped that Ali beat Liston in their rematch, so that he, Patterson, would be the one to wrestle the championship back for America. In his column he wrote, "I say it, and I say it flatly, that the image of a Black Muslim as the world heavyweight champion disgraces the sport and the nation. Cassius Clay must be beaten and the Black Muslim's scourge removed from boxing." Patterson also jabbed, "He has continually damaged the image of American Negroes and the civil rights groups working on their behalf. No decent person can look up to a champion whose credo is 'hate whites.' I have nothing but contempt for the Black Muslims and that for which they stand."[21] To these attacks and more, Ali shot back by calling him an "Uncle Tom," promising him a vicious beating in the ring, and giving him a verbal lashing: "Patterson says he's gonna bring the title back to America. If you don't believe the title already is in America, just see who I pay taxes to. I'm American. But he's the deaf dumb so-called Negro who needs a spanking."[22]

The Ali–Patterson fight represented more than just two men battling in the ring; it constituted a political contest that highlighted political and social allegiances in the black community and encompassed the growing Black Power movement as activists separated from the integrationist civil rights ideas. Summing up this sentiment, black political activist Eldridge Cleaver observed, "Muhammad Ali is the first 'free' black champion ever to confront white America. . . . Floyd Patterson was the symbolic spearhead of a counterrevolutionary host, leader of the mythical legions of faithful darkies who inhabit the white imagination, whose assigned task it was to liberate the crown and restore it to its proper 'place' in the Free World."[23] Most young black activists who had pushed beyond integrationist politics harbored the same sentiments as Cleaver. And in the end, their man, Muhammad Ali, easily defeated an overwhelmed and overmatched Patterson. In fact, the fight was so brutal, writers chastised Ali for allowing Patterson to stay in the fight and absorb more punishment. Ali might have dusted off the black–white hope, but his public fight against racism also meant Ali would have more battles, even with his own government.

Nearly three months after he punished Patterson, Ali had to face his biggest opponent, the one that would make him hated and a hero all at the same time. While training in Miami for his next battle in February 1966, as the Vietnam War intensified, Ali received the shocking, life-altering news that his military draft status had been changed from 1-Y (not qualified for the military) to 1-A (reclassified as immediately eligible for armed services). Immediately, the media descended on him asking for an interview, and soon, he gave them what they wanted, a sound bite they could publish in their papers to sell copies. But this phrase was not solely for the reporters; his powerful words stood for the generation looking to combat what they deemed an unjust war in Vietnam. Ali, in his activist eloquence, chimed, "I ain't got no quarrel with the Viet Cong." With those powerful words, and his subsequent fight against induction, Ali became the first major celebrity to oppose the war, thus making him an icon and a beacon of hope for young Americans protesting American militarism.

But the boxer quickly found out that his toughest opponent would be his own government. After Ali first publicly stated his disagreement with his draft status, newspapers across the country pressured the Illinois Athletic Commission to deny him the right to fight in his scheduled March 29 fight against Ernie Terrell, in Chicago. The commission had caved to public pressure. And after Illinois said no, other states followed. Their decisions forced Ali to find another opponent, George Chuvalo, and fight in Toronto, Canada. And the government continued the onslaught by denying his petition to be reclassified based on his conscientious objector status. At a hearing in August 1966, after being twice denied, he told a board, "The Holy Qur'ran and the teachings of the Honorable Elijah Muhammad tell us and it is that we are not to participate in wars on the side of nonbelievers, and this is a Christian country and this is not a Muslim country."[24] After hearing Ali's pleas, the judge Lawrence Grauman surprisingly ruled to grant him conscientious status, only for the FBI to recommend the Appeal Board overrule the judge's decision. The Appeal Board listened to the FBI. A few days later, Ali griped: "How can I kill somebody when I pray five times a day for peace?" Then on April 28, 1967, in Houston, Ali had his final showdown with the Appeal Board after it ordered him to show up for induction.[25] As the date neared, the "people's champ" increased his public protests against the injustice of sending him to war. He asked, "Why should they ask me to put on a uniform and go ten thousand miles from home and drop bombs and bullets on brown people in Vietnam while so-call Negro people in Louisville are treated like dogs?" He continued, "If I thought going to war would bring freedom and equality to twenty-two million of my people, they wouldn't have to draft me; I'd join tomorrow." In his bravest stance, the heavyweight champion, on April 28, 1967, refused induction into the military. In his letter, he wrote, "I refuse to be inducted into the armed forces of the United States because I claim to be exempt as a minister of the religion of Islam."[26] With that bold stance, sanctioning bodies stripped him of his right to the championship, states denied him the right to fight—he had previously fought a few times in Houston—and naysayers labeled him a traitor. By 1969, moreover, with Ali unable to make money or bring the NOI money, the organization stopped supporting its champion.

Ali's refusal to join the military, however, represented black pride for many young people who had come to see the war as another manifestation of oppression. As Ali suggested when he quipped, "I ain't got no quarrel with the Viet Cong," and stated that his people were catching hell at home, many black people started to compare their plight to oppressed people, whom the United States treated as colonized subjects. On Vietnam and black Americans, Cleaver concluded, "The American racial problem can no longer be spoken of or solved in isolation. The relationship between genocide in Vietnam and the smiles of whites toward black Americans is a direct relationship. Once the white man solves his problem in the East he will then turn his fury again on the black people of America."[27] In 1967, Martin Luther King Jr. also strongly came out against the Vietnam War and publicly sided with Ali. "As Muhammad Ali has said," King noted, "we are all victims of the same system of oppression."[28]

Ali's refusal to be complicit in this colonization, both home and abroad, and the government's insistence that he join the ranks, galvanized young black Americans to view the war as linked to the historical oppression in their own lives. That he was willing to risk his livelihood for his beliefs meant that he would always be their champ. To that extent, activists protested boxing bouts featuring other black fighters angling to win Ali's vacated belt. In March 1967, for example, they led a boycott and a protest of the Joe Frazier–Buster Mathis bout in Madison Square Garden. Amiri Baraka [LeRoi Jones] said, "The winner might tell white people he's heavyweight champion, but black people would laugh him out of the streets. Muhammad Ali will always be champion."[29] Despite the fact that both men were black, the young black activist believed that Ali was the only true champion, and thus Frazier and Mathis represented the white man's champ. Regardless of who won, they would have no standing in the black community.

Black athletes also recognized the important struggle Ali faced in his decision to fight for his rights and looked for the best way to show solidarity. In June 1967, Jim Brown collected a group of black athletes to meet Ali in Cleveland to listen to his reasons behind his resistance and offer him advice. The group included luminaries like Lew Alcindor (later Kareem Abdul-Jabbar), Bill Russell, Bobby Mitchell, Willie Davis, and John Wooten. If any of them had doubts of Ali's sincerity before they met him, he quickly erased them when he eloquently spoke about his faith in Islam and clearly stated his reasons to reject induction. In a letter in *Sport Illustrated*, Bill Russell told the magazine, "I envy Muhammad Ali. He faces a possible five years in jail and he has been stripped of his heavyweight championship, but I still envy him. He has something I have never been able to attain and something very few people I know possess. He has an absolute and sincere faith."[30] With that, the athletes rallied around the champ and closed ranks with him in his battle against the government, boxing sanctioning bodies, and the public. In truth, however, Ali gave black athletes more than they gave him. He gave them the power to speak out, to believe in their convictions, and to fight the athletic system that oppressed them. No group of athletes was touched more by Ali than black college athletes. And, in a sign of solidarity, black athletes were prepared to carry Ali's rebel torch, even if that meant derailing their own careers.

Olympic Project for Human Rights

Just months after Ali refused to take a step toward induction in a Houston courtroom, in September 1967, Tommie Smith, the long-legged sprinter from San Jose State, stepped into his own controversy. And like Ali, Smith's bold stance for justice left a lasting mark on American society. What Smith had previously hinted at to a reporter in Japan, he made official in the States; black athletes were prepared to boycott the 1968 Olympics. Though Smith told a reporter the boycott was "unlikely at this time," he also surprised the scribe by suggesting that black athletes had been talking about the possibilities at track meets, and several athletes were "in favor of it." He also noted that before anything became official all athletes would have to be contacted and take a vote on the resolution.

That meeting would have to wait until Thanksgiving weekend, but hearing Smith's initial marks about the boycott elicited immediate reaction from journalists, white and black. Jim Murray of the *Los Angeles Times* argued that Smith was like a child holding his breath waiting to get his way from his parents and that most Americans did not care about the Olympics, and thus, the potential boycott would not have its intended effect. White people, in other words, did not care enough about sports to fight the continued oppression of black Americans. Black writers for the *Los Angeles Sentinel*, Brad Pye Jr. and L. I. Brockenbury, however, used their columns to defend Smith and enlighten Murray. Pye argued, "Negroes have been winning gold medals for this great country of ours for years. . . but these medals lose a little luster when you can't buy a home in Ladera Heights, Glendale, Anaheim and hundreds of other areas without an act of congress. . . simply because of your skin."[31] Brockenbury also took his friend Murray to task for being just another "fair-minded" white sportswriter who refused to understand the plight of black Americans. Brockenbury observed, "What most white Americans doggedly refuse to admit is that racism always has been—and still is—an integral part of the 'American way of life' . . . And what most white Americans don't know—or else close their eyes to—is the fact that American black men of today—especially the younger generations—simply are determined NOT to accept the status quo relationship of black to white any longer." Brockenbury closed by telling Murray, "Our white brethren sports writers—as well as all other Americans—are going to have to realize that a NEW DAY is here, and like it or not—all of us are going to have to adjust to it and accept it as an inevitable fact of life!"[32] Brockenbury believed that a "NEW DAY" was coming because he understood that the push from black athletes came from the college-educated athletes, like Smith, who would no longer put up with the status quo. He was right.

Smith's initial boycott remarks resonated with Pye and Brockenbury, and scared Murray, because the track star's words came on the heels of a successful, yet controversial, college protest in which black students at San Jose State shut down a scheduled football game between San Jose and the University of Texas, El Paso (UTEP). The successful shutdown constituted a culmination of years of racism black students faced. In short, black athletes on campus still faced the same daily injustices that the previous generation of athletes fought, yet the school continued to increase its recruitment of black athletes. Harry Edwards, the ex-San Jose State athlete who worked at the school as a sociology professor, and Kenneth Noel, another ex-San Jose State athlete, spearheaded the protest. Under Edwards and Noel, the newly formed United Black Students for Action (UBSA) proposed a list of 10 demands for the university to meet or else face a forced shutdown, "by any means necessary" of the season's opening game against UTEP. The demands included a ban on Jim Crow fraternities and sororities, an end to student housing discrimination, an increase in minority recruitment and enrollment, and civil treatment of black athletes. In the end, the university met their demands, but as a precaution it also canceled the football game fearing that the black students and outside agitators might blow up the stadium. After the cancellation, Ronald Reagan, the state's governor at the time, complained, "Young athletes are going to be victimized by such an action. Edwards is contributing nothing toward harmony between the races." To that criticism, Edwards shot back in his typical brazen fashion and called the governor "a petrified pig, unfit to govern."[33] Despite the brash words for the governor, it was in this moment that Edwards had clarity; athletics could be the one powerful lever blacks had to fight for equality, and he planned to use it to its fullest power, even if he no longer participated in sports.

With momentum from the UBSA shutdown, and talk spreading among black athletes about a boycott, Edwards decided to pull harder on that athletic lever and called on a group of black athletes to gather in Los Angeles during Thanksgiving break to discuss the potential boycott of the game. At the Black Youth Conference, while some of the top athletes on the West Coast attended, including basketball star Lew Alcindor and San Jose sprinters Tommie Smith and Lee Evans, many from the Midwest, East, and South, specifically black women, either did not get invitations or simply could not make the trip. Still, despite missing a few important faces, nearly 200 athletes (amateurs, professionals, and retired) attended the event. Those athletes who believed sports improved the condition of black life, like "Deacon" Dan Towler of the Los Angeles Rams, were shouted down when they explained how great sports had been to black people. This meeting was not a debate; it was going to be an affirmation of a boycott. The most memorable and most effective words came from the best collegiate basketball player in the country, Lew Alcindor. Alcindor matriculated to UCLA from Harlem, and already had a reputation for his dominating basketball skills and his political consciousness off the court, told the audience, "Everybody knows me. I'm the big basketball star, the weekend hero, everybody's All-American. Well, last summer I was almost killed by a racist cop shooting at a black cat in Harlem. He was shooting on the street—where masses of black people were standing around or just taking a walk. But he didn't care. After all we were just niggers." Alcindor then went on to explain the lessons from that encounter. "I found out last summer that we don't catch hell because we aren't basketball stars or because we don't have money. We catch hell because we are black," he said. He then implored his fellow athletes to take a stand. "Somewhere each of us has got to make a stand against this kind of thing. This is how I take my stand—using what I have. And I take my stand here."[34] For any members who stood on the fence, they quickly hopped off when they heard Alcindor's powerful words. At the end of the meeting, in a yea–nay vote, the overwhelming majority of participants decided to boycott the games. As Edwards told the press a day later, "It's time for the black people to stand up as men and women and refuse to be utilized as performing animals for a little extra dog food."[35]

A month later, with the help of civil rights activists Louis Lomax and Martin Luther King Jr., the newly formed Olympic Project for Human Rights (OPHR) formulated a list of demands, which included the restoration of Ali as the heavyweight champion, the hiring of more black Olympic coaches, an Olympic ban on the apartheid nations South Africa and Rhodesia, the firing of Avery Brundidge, head of the International Olympic Committee (IOC), and the integration of the New York Athletic Club (NYAC).

Although the Olympics remained nearly a year away, and no athlete had made the Olympic team yet, the reality that potential Olympians agreed to boycott the games put all black athletes on notice. The vote forced them to honestly assess America's racial progress during a time of continued racial discontent as cities across America continued to burn in rebellion. Even if they disagreed with the tactic, these star athletes, whom most Americans assumed were content with their lot in life, had to speak out on race and racism. No athlete could escape the conversation or controversy. Throughout the boycott movement, of all the potential Olympians, long jumper Ralph Boston, a Mississippi native who had lent his name to the civil rights movement in his home state and who had also boycotted a track meet in Houston in 1961 to protest the stadium's Jim Crow policies, became the leading athletic face for the nay vote. He did not want this unofficial title, but the media needed a black face to put in opposition to the boycott, and Boston, a graduate student at Tennessee State, and world-record holder at the time, represented the perfect vision of dissent: educated, articulate, and athletic.

Boston, who had already been to two Olympics, had two main reasons he wanted to avoid a boycott—one athletic and the other based on political practicality. First, Boston wanted to go to a third Olympics before his career was over. Nobody could dispute that desire. As athletes, they all wanted to compete against the best. A week after the Thanksgiving meeting, Boston told *Sports Illustrated*, "What boycott? I've put too much time and effort into track and field to give it up. If I felt there was a sufficient reason I would boycott, but I don't even know what the reason is." He concluded by hailing sports as a savior, "At least Negroes have this much: we can compete in amateur sports and we can represent ourselves and then the country."[36] In fact, throughout the year, including a piece in *Sport* entitled "Why They Should Not," Boston continuously hoisted sports as blacks' best chance to equality. Sports, according to Boston, represented merit and democracy, gave young blacks a chance to improve their education, and proved blacks could succeed if they received an equal chance. Boston urged, "I believe sports has generally afforded Negroes more opportunity to do good for themselves and for their people than any other area of our life."[37] But to Boston's point, ex-Olympic high jumper Gene Johnson asked, "What would be the fate of a Ralph Boston if he was not a 27-foot long jumper, of a Charlie Greene if he was not a 9.1 sprinter?" Johnson answered, "They would be 'faceless' black men caught in the same system of racial discrimination as many other black citizens."[38] Athletes like Tommie Smith understood that racial reality well.

For Tommie Smith, the greatest sprinter of his generation, sports represented a mirage. Sure, they gave Smith a chance to go to college and escape the farm fields that his family worked as migrant laborers in California, but Smith also knew that in sports he was a "fast Nigger" and outside of sports he was a "Nigger." And Smith had the hate mail to prove it. The moment he spoke up for his rights, the hate mail and the violent threats poured in. In truth, Smith touched a nerve in American society by exposing the long roots of racism. Smith received an education at San Jose State and was supposed to be satisfied with what sports brought him (he was), so people wanted him to shut up and play. But Smith also knew that the small gains he won were for himself and not his people. And still, even with multiple world records, he faced daily racism on campus.

Like other athletes across the campus, Smith struggled to find adequate housing and cringed when he heard students and teachers call him "Nigger." The Olympics, as he said, were his lever, his one tool of power to challenge racism. "If I give [the Olympics] up," he said, "it will be painful to me and probably cost me prestige that will affect me the rest of my life. But I am prepared to do just that if it will help my people gain full equality in their country." In another interview with *Track and Field News* he proudly proclaimed his broad aims: "We are a race of proud people and want to be treated as such. Our goals would not be just to improve conditions for ourselves and teammates, but to improve things for the entire Negro community."[39] The world-record holder articulated a sentiment that few athletes before or after him ever had. His successes had been individual, sports did not improve his community's situation, but through sports he could make a change by refusing to participate in the one avenue he was granted equality. Smith became the face of rebellion and risked his reputation for his people. For that he was vilified the discontented Negro. His country owed him more, but he expected that much, and he was prepared to fight.

Amateur athletes were not the only ones to weigh in on this debate; the ex-Olympians who had received adulation in the past had something to say too. After all, they had already experienced the realities of winning medals for their country only to come back home to be treated as second-class citizens. Mack Robinson, the brother of Jackie, won a silver medal in the 1936 games, attended the University of Oregon for three years on a track scholarship—like most black athletes when he finished his eligibility the school moved on from him and did not help him graduate—but could only find a job as a street cleaner in his hometown of Pasadena, California. In 1968, he admitted, "We were more or less used for our ability." To highlight this injustice, after he returned from the games, the Olympic hero performed his menial job wearing his Olympic uniform. Robinson, however, wanted the athletes to participate in the games, because, as he told *Newsweek*, "I've worked so hard to raise money for them to go."[40]

Norvell Lee came home from the 1948 games and had to ride on a Jim Crow train in Virginia. Lee, who won the Jim Crow case, believed that racial politics had no place in the Olympics. Calling the boycott "senseless," he argued, "Athletics is one area in which colored people have enjoyed complete freedom. Their success has been based on skill rather than color." Although he ruled out a boycott among amateurs, the two-time Olympian felt that professional athletes could make the most impact, because, as he cited, the revenues teams would lose if the professionals boycotted would force reform.[41] Milt Campbell, however, a Newark, New Jersey, native, who won gold in the decathlon in 1956, had a different take. The black nationalist pointedly argued, "We are simply kidding ourselves if we think winning Olympic medals is advancing our race as a whole." Campbell minced no words: "Remember, when you play ball you're only entertaining the white man. And whitey isn't going to give you something unless there's something in it for him."[42] Most athletes, however, sided with Robinson and Lee, and urged the athletes to participate. While most admitted to facing injustices, they also had been won over by the power of sport and still believed that sport, especially the Olympics, gave black Americans their best opportunity in life.

No ex-athlete fought harder to maintain the status quo than the great Jesse Owens. Owens, who was born to sharecroppers and grew up in a Cleveland ghetto, denounced the boycott decision, declaring the games apolitical and noting the Olympics gave blacks an equal chance to compete. Immediately, upon hearing about the planned protest, Owens shot back, "I deplore the use of the Olympic Games by certain people for political aggrandizement. There is no place in the athletic world for politics." Two months later, as the movement continued to pick up speed, the track star added his standard line about the potential of athletics to combat prejudice, "We have been able to bridge the gap of misunderstanding more than anywhere else," and suggested sports had been "a great boon because as far as our understanding; we cannot legislate man's heart."[43]

Throughout 1968, Owens continued this line of attack in the press, on television, and in his book *Black Think*, an up-by-the-bootstrap autobiography that situated Owens as a well-meaning moderate and took a number of swipes at so-called black militants. To be sure, Owens took a lot of flack from black activists, including Harry Edwards, who routinely went out of his way to label Owens an Uncle Tom. The despicable name-calling obstructed the reality of Owens: he came back from the 1936 games a celebrated hero who could not find adequate work. Owens had to humiliate himself and race against horses to earn a living. He found his medals could not break down the barriers of Jim Crow, and the Olympic legend found himself barred from many Jim Crow establishments. The black athletes who proposed the boycott did not want to be treated like Jesse Owens. If so, their medals would have little value.

Despite Edwards's constant framing of the boycott movement having the support of both men and women, in truth, black women's opinions were not considered. This movement, like much of the Black Power movement, got framed around rescuing black manhood, while ignoring the significant roles black women played in the political freedom struggle of black Americans. As the two-time Olympic champion Wyomia Tyus remembered, "They argued black athletes should definitely not go to the Games because of the unfair treatment of all black people in America. But as far as women were concerned, we were never approached to be part of that movement. It was more like 'We're doing it, so you should follow.'" Tyus, and other women, however, had something to say. Years later, Tyus remembered feeling both sorry for and supportive of the athletes. She knew that all Olympic athletes had sacrificed a lot for this one moment, and a boycott would strip them of their glory, but she also understood that the boycott, and subsequent protest by Smith and John Carlos, brought necessary attention to ongoing American racism. "I also thought it was the best thing that could happen," she recalled, "because it definitely exposed the world to what was happening to black people in America, how unfairly we were being treated."[44]

Like Tyus, her ex-teammate, Edith McGuire, who won silver in the 1964 Tokyo Games, thought the racism that persisted in America was enough to boycott the games. She told Walter Hoye of the *Michigan Chronicle* that she recognized the seriousness of the sacrifice and said, "More than likely I would boycott," if she was on the team.[45] Their teammate Willy White, however, strongly denounced the proposed boycott. White, who was seeking her fourth straight Olympics, argued that the boycott centered too much around San Jose State and lacked necessary specifics. A week after the initial meeting, she told the press, "I can suggest specific issues and more specific methods of protest in behalf of Negro status than this boycott proposal." Further elaborating, White argued, "The question could be brought up why don't we have Negroes on our Olympic swimming, gymnastics and many other Olympics units beyond track, basketball and boxing." A few months later, in an interview with Sam Lacy, she insisted that she believed that Tommie Smith and Lee Evans were "sincere in the aims they've set," but worried about outsiders like Edwards who convinced them to boycott. White noted that black athletes had been approached in 1956, 1960, and 1964 with the same requests, but after the games those asking them to sacrifice their careers did not support them. In essence, the politicians used athletes for their own gains. "These are the things that are suspect," she suggested. "Is it only when an Olympic year comes around that colored people in America suffer from racism and ostracization?" she asked. "If the campaign were a continued thing, rather than occasional, I'm sure there would be more of us willing to participate in the protest." She ended her rebuke arguing, "I have no sympathy what-soever with a move that is designed to give political strength to people with unmistakable ambitions."[46]

Like the athletes, the black press's opinions varied throughout the nation, with most asking the athletes to abstain from their plans. Some writers were still caught in the powerful web of the American democratic sporting monster that forced people to believe sports offered blacks their clearest victories, while others believed the black community was way past due for a change. A week after the initial announcement, an editorial in the *Philadelphia Tribune* rebuked the athletes and asserted, "The boy-cott, if it materializes, would leave the Negro athlete outside the interna-tional field and eliminate one of the real opportunities he has for display of his prowess in the athletic arena." The editorialist also suggested that these athletes were pawns in a game of men like Edwards and argued athletes had nothing to gain from such an action.[47] The *Louisiana Weekly* also denounced the initial boycott, arguing that it would not bring any real systemic changes. "A boycott of the Olympic Games now," it wrote, "is an anachronism." In its opinion, the boycott appeared "to be the last desperate attempt of a spotlight-loving individual to keep from fading into the obscurity from which—but for the American principles he now condemns—he could have never emerged." And Jim Hall, who led the successful boycott of the New Orleans Pelicans more than a decade prior to the 1968 Olympics, knocked the proposed boycott, berating, "Sports, has come closer to shoving the Great American Dilemma than any other endeavor. . . . We admit that it's not 'Peaches and Cream' in the United States. But telling the people of the world, about our problems, will not help one bit." Hall also argued: "For all the talk about being black Nation-alists, this is the only country we have ever known and our loyalty belongs here."[48] Lawrence Casey of the *Chicago Defender* asserted, "I can't see what good it'll do. I think black athletes such as Smith, Alcindor and others should continue to use the athletic arena to gain the better things in life such as education, position and subsequent wealth."[49]

But Sam Lacy sided with the young athletes, noting, "The action by Smith, Alcindor and the others is typical of the new colored man. They belong to the young. They belong to the young crusade. It was their type that made up the freedom riders, the sittiners, the marchers on Washing-ton. Both these youngsters and their youthful predecessors defied the world with their courage and determination. And here is one guy from a generation that was brainwashed into 'accepting without complaint' who is with them 100 percent."[50] And an editorial of support in the *Michigan Chronicle* asked, "What must become more important to black youth, a few moments of fleeting glory or a self-respect that will last him a life time. . . . The name of the game is self-respect. . . and how can a black youth call himself a champion, when he performs under circumstances that continue to rate him as second-class, regardless of how you look at him."[51] L. I. Brockenbury also showed solidarity: "It's purely a strategically maneuver, designed to throw worldwide attention on the cancerous racial discrimination that always has existed, and still exists in this country." He added, "Those who argue that the Negro athlete should be thankful for the opportunities afforded him in this country certainly miss the point that every step forward made by these athletes has NOT come through any widespread gentility on the part of those who control American sports." Pressure, he argued, was the only way athletes and activists made changes in sports and society. Brockenbury was right.[52]

In one of the biggest successes of the boycott movement, the OPHR, along with other civil rights organizations and leaders, like H. Rap Brown, organized a successful boycott of the NYAC's annual indoor track and field meet, to protest the club's refusal to allow blacks, Jews, and Puerto Ricans membership. The world's leading hurdler Russ Rogers explained his decision to stay away, simply by stating the obvious; "Why should we help them have a successful meet if they have no use for us before or after the meet?" Jackie Robinson, in his weekly column, praised the boycott, "I honor the black athletes who have mobilized to make a mighty try at smashing the disgraceful jim crow situation at The New York Athletic Club."

Of course, many naysayers asked, "why now" and why not the past? The NYAC had had its racist policies for nearly 100 years. Eddie Conwell, a leading sprinter in the late 1940s and early 1950s, explained to the *Philadelphia Tribune* that he always boycotted the meet as an individual, because of its policies, but most other athletes chose to go. Why did other athletes in Conwell's generation compete? The simple answer: no major movement existed and athletes did not have the backing of civil rights organizations and their schools. If a coach told an athlete he or she was going to an event, he or she was going. But in 1968, a number of schools like Morgan State and Maryland State pulled out of the event, giving their athletes cover.[53]

Also, to be clear, organizers of the boycott like Edwards and Brown used strong-arm tactics to keep potential athletes away. High jumper John Thomas, who had boycotted a meet in Houston in 1961, received threatening calls to stay away from the meet, and like many athletes who wavered, Edwards called Thomas an "Uncle Tom," an unfortunate and unfair characterization of black athletes who did not want to participate in the boycott. In the end, more than 100 of the top athletes stayed away from the meet and hundreds lined the streets and protested at Madison Square Garden on the day of the races. Of the big names that showed up, like long jumper Bob Beamon and his UTEP teammates, these athletes claimed they felt uncomfortable and competed only because they wanted a free trip back East to see their families. Hurdler Charlie Mays, one of the most vocal protesters, observed, "It's an insult to watch Negroes go inside while we stand up for our rights."[54] Besides the name-calling and the threats of violence, the event marked the first major success in the boycott movement, because it forced the United States Olympic Committee and IOC to pay attention to the black athletes. Changes would have to be made and, in some cases, immediately.

While black athletes prepared to boycott the NYAC in February, the IOC made another insensitive move to show its racist card; it voted to reinstate South Africa back into the Olympic Games. Five years prior, in 1963, the IOC banned South Africa from the games because its racist athletic policies prevented blacks and whites from competing against each other—to say nothing about its apartheid system. To get back in the games, however, its state-sponsored sports committee promised that all athletes would be allowed to compete for its Olympic team and that all athletes would live together at the Olympic village. In other words, it would temporarily lift discrimination in sports, but apartheid in society would remain. Despite that small concession to an unjust system, in a controversial vote, the IOC voted to reinstate South Africa into the games. On hearing this news, 33 African nations immediately voted to boycott the games, and other countries including Cuba and Malaysia agree to withdraw too. Harry Edwards said, "When they readmitted South Africa they, in effect, turned their backs on all Negro athletes."[55] In solidarity, the OPHR called on all athletes, white and black, to boycott the games. Fearing the withdrawal of so many African nations, and also a potential problem from black Americans, one IOC member said, "We did not want that chap from California [Harry Edwards] coming down to Mexico City and setting off riots."[56] Thus, a fearful IOC reversed its decision and once again banned South Africa. That move, more than likely, saved the Olympics. African nations withdrew their boycott, and it took steam out of the OPHR boycott movement.

In fact, despite South Africa's banishment and the successful boycott of the NYAC, most observers throughout the movement knew the athletes would not boycott the games. True, Lew Alcindor stayed away—he said the games conflicted with his education—but track athletes were not going to, and could not, give up their Olympic opportunities. Unlike basketball, track and field did not have a professional level. The games were their glory and their one shot to indirectly make money or earn fame. To maintain unity among the athletes, and to give everyone a fair shot to pursue their dream, in the summer of 1968, the athletes decided to end the potential boycott.

Instead of a boycott, they all encouraged everyone to protest in their own way. Some wore black socks and some wore black shoes, but nothing resonated more with onlookers' imagination and had a longer-lasting legacy than when after earning first and third place in the 200 meters, respectively, Tommie Smith and John Carlos walked up to the Olympic podium shoeless, wearing black socks, unzipped jackets, and black gloves, and raised their clinched fists in what was then known as a Black Power salute, during the national anthem. On the salute, Carlos contended, "We wanted all the black people in the world—the little grocer, the man with the shoe repair store—to know that when that medal hangs on my chest and Tommie's chest, it hangs on his also."[57] And at meeting with the press after the event, he added, "After the job is done, we are not supposed to think. We wanted to do something to signify black. We want people to know that we are not animals, not lower animals, not rats and roaches."[58] Wyomia Tyus, who defended her 100-meter Olympic title, proclaimed, "It was their moment. They had won the medals and they had a right to make a protest."[59] The two sprinters, Smith and Carlos, however, faced harsh consequences. Both men were unfairly kicked out of the Olympic Games, and when they returned home, the discrimination and difficulties they faced only heightened. Each brave man struggled to make a living in their chosen profession.

While most in the white press, like Brent Musburger, who said they looked like black-skinned storm troopers, castigated them, the black press's response varied. Sam Lacy, who had previously supported the boycott, complained that "their entire behavior was ill-advised" and that they should have stayed home and protested instead of embarrassing the country.[60] Jim Hall of the *Louisiana Weekly* denounced the protest too. He maintained, "Carlos and Smith had the right to protest the inequalities that black man suffers in the world," but asked, "What was accomplished by the black-glove fist act in Mexico by the twosome?" Hall suggested, "Carlos and Smith along with many others, have been protesting before the Olympics and will continue to do the same after the games, but where we are sitting perhaps Black power is fashionable now, but in the United States, Green power is the way of life."[61] Larry Austin of the *Sacramento Observer* rhetorically asked to those saying Smith and Carlos chose the wrong time and platform, "When is there a better time? Of the hundreds of Negro athletes down through the years, how many have gone on to better positions? How many do you hear on the radio? How many do you see on television? How many Negro coaches are there? How many Scouts are there?"[62] Fulton O. Bradley of the *Michigan Chronicle* argued the athletes who were kicked out of the games for their "untypical behavior" on the medal stand and retorted, "Untypical is much that America does to its own kind, who in their black-rage exception to treatment meted out, are saying to America that we have learned well how to be 'untypical.' Now it's America's chance to unlearn many of its 'untypical' bad behavior habits."[63] Roy Wilkins, head of the NAACP, told a black reporter, "Smith and Carlos didn't insult their country; they didn't spit on the American flag or tear the flag. They didn't say a thing."[64] Claude Harrison Jr. noted that most of the critics were white and did not understand what black people in general, and black athletes in specific, had to face and fight in the form of racism. For him, blacks "filed two centuries ago and the grievances committee has yet to act." Harrison, however, also cautioned blacks, "It is not enough to shout defiant words or to raise black-gloved fists. The battle must be carried to the ballot box, where this country's most vital races are won and lost."[65]

But to black youth of their generation, regardless of how the election went down, Smith and Carlos were heroes in their community. Blacks greeted each other with clinched fists in the air, hung the famous photo of Smith and Carlos on their wall, and invited them to campus to speak. Albert Cleage, of the Black Power church, the Shrine of the Black Madonna in Detroit, summed up black feelings best when he declared, "It does not bother us one bit that white folks did not like your gesture, because a protest is meaningless if it can be ignored by people who are guilty of the things which you protest."[66]

Moreover, the OPHR movement monetarily changed the sports scene. A month before the games, Herb Douglas, a graduate of the University of Pittsburgh and a bronze medalist in the long jump in 1948, said that he was glad that the athletes decided to participate in the games, because "having won a medal, many doors that may have remained closed, opened. It gave me an opportunity to sell myself for employment." But Douglas also had to admit the full scope of the problem. In reality, he admitted, his athletic success "didn't aid me in my quest for the job I really wanted. . . . I know I was refused because of being black and not because I didn't have the ability." When pushed on why he and his fellow athletes did not protest, Douglas gave a pointed answer that spoke to the change in society. "It's simple," he said. "The militant atmosphere did not exist at the time. Although every sane athlete I knew in college was fully aware of the unfairness and mentioned it, they were handicapped because there was no journalist in daily publications that would reveal such problems to the public."[67] Twenty years later, those days were done. The boycott movement produced a "militant atmosphere" that allowed students to protest their special grievances and forced a press to hear them out. Thus, the biggest impact the OPHR had on society is that it gave black student athletes a new platform from which to speak, a stage to challenge status quo, and an atmosphere to demand change.

The Revolt on Campus

As Herb Douglas noted, the black athlete knew that white coaches, professors, administrators, students, and business owners treated them unfairly, but athletes of the past did not have a movement to give them strength and give them cover when they revolted against the system. Now they did. Between 1967 and 1970, an estimated 37 schools witnessed black athletes' revolts on campus. Of course, this caught white writers, administrators, and coaches off guard, because they always believed they were doing right by the athletes by simply taking them out of the ghetto or the dilapidated farm, and giving them a so-called chance. As George McCarty, the athletic director of UTEP, told *Sports Illustrated*, "In general, the nigger athlete is a little hungrier, and we have been blessed with having some real outstanding ones. We think they've done a lot for us, and we think we've done a lot for them."[68] Whites wanted blacks to think that they were one false step from going back to the farm or the factory. But a new day had arrived.

The boycott, along with the growing Black Power movement across the nation, and the new black student movements that demanded black studies courses and the hiring of black faculty, emboldened the athletes. They could no longer sit on the sidelines if people in their community and campus were aggressively demanding change. "A few years go," Lee Evans said in 1968, "I didn't know what was happening. My white junior college coach used to tell colored boy jokes and I'd laugh. Now I'd kick his ass."[69]

Instead of fighting back physically, like Evans suggested he wanted to do, the black athlete fought back by using the one lever he had, his body. Black athletes on college campuses threatened to stop playing for their white schools. They knew that their schools needed to exploit black athletes to make money, and the coaches needed the black athletes to succeed to keep their jobs. The black athlete demanded a better education, fair treatment from coaches, the hiring of black coaches, more black students on campus, and better living conditions off campus. By May 1968, for example, black athletes at Berkeley, UTEP, Michigan State, Marquette, the University of Washington, Oklahoma, Arizona State, and Kansas rebelled. If the black athlete was going to give his body to the school, he wanted something in return, not just a varsity jacket.

One consistent complaint revolved around academic exploitation. By the late 1960s, with most schools looking to integrate their teams—some schools in the South, like Kentucky basketball and Alabama football, still had not integrated—these white institutions had an arms race, so to speak, to see who could get the most "tan talent." For the black athlete, however, this only meant that now there were more black athletes on campus to be exploited and then discarded. As Harry Edwards suggested, "Black Students aren't given athletic scholarships for the purpose of education. Blacks are brought in to perform. Any education they get is incidental to their main job, which is playing sports."[70]

In truth, because of systemic racism in America that saw overcrowded classrooms and under-education in America's ghetto and separate and unequal schools in the Jim Crow South, most black students were not fully prepared to attend the colleges that awarded them athletic scholarships. Colleges had created special admission policies to allow under-qualified students, usually student athletes, to enroll in school in the hopes that being away from their environment and in a place of higher education would improve their learning. But instead of trying to get athletes academic help—athletic academic advisors did not exist until the 1970s and were a result of the increase in the enrollment of black athletes—coaches had the athletes "major in eligibility." That is to say, they would put them in the right number of classes to keep them eligible to play the season, but when it came time to graduate, the athlete remained a significant amount of credits short. Once he lost athletic eligibility, the school discarded him with little education. Infamously, by the late 1960s, none of the five all-black starters from the famed Texas Western (UTEP) championship team finished school with a degree. They won the championship, built the school's reputation, which saw a major increase in admissions, but did not get their graduation papers in return. Instead, after they used up their eligibility, they got their walking papers. Dave Lattin, a star on that championship team, complained, "If you played basketball you spent more of your time in the gym, on and off season. You didn't get a chance to spend much time studying. So you'd drop behind your classmates. The only way you could stay in the ball game was to kind of lighten up on your courses."[71] As Don Smith, a star player from Iowa, said, "They don't care about the black athlete per se. They just want him to produce. Instead of trying to help us they want us to pass just enough to get by."[72]

Black athletes refused to take this exploitation. At Michigan State, in April 1968, black players boycotted practice, until their lists of grievances were met, including the suggestion, "Academic counseling for Blacks is designed to place them in courses where they will maintain eligibility. They are forced to take nonacademic courses rather than academic courses that will enable them to graduate in four years."[73] And when black athletes at San Francisco State threatened to withdraw from athletics if their demands were not met, they included a statement about academics, arguing the coach and college showed an "indifference to whether Black players ever finish their college education, interested only in whether or not Black athletes are eligible for competition, and flagrantly lying to Black athletes in order to get them to enroll here."[74] At Kansas, players demanded that the university hire a black professor to teach black history courses. At each institution, administrators said they would look into the academic problems, and eventually made changes. But, to be sure, the racial problems many institutions had remained. Any casual observer of big-time college sports knows that black athletes continue to be under-educated and exploited by these universities.

Along with better education opportunities, players demanded that coaches treat them equitably. Every black athlete, in fact, experienced some form of racism. These forms of racism ranged from the coaches telling "colored jokes" to coaches ordering black players not to date white women. In one instance, members of the UTEP's basketball team met with their athletic director (AD) for one minor request: stop pronouncing the word "Negro" as "nigra," but the AD, George McCarty, could not even give those players that simple courtesy, and he could not, in his words "break that habit." To make things worse, when he talked to white people, McCarty still referred to his athletes as "niggers," as if they had no humanity.[75]

Athletes quickly realized, however, that as individuals, if they challenged this discriminatory dilemma, they risked losing their scholarships. But if all players banded together, they held the power. At Cal Berkeley, in January 1968, after star basketball player Ron Presley, a Detroit native, was kicked off the team for supposed disciplinary reasons, black athletes at Cal, under the name, "Black Athletes of the University of California" united in a joint protest to address not only Presley's problems but also all related problems black athletes at Cal faced. Led by their spokesman Bobby Smith, a star football player, the players demanded they would not play sports for the school if their grievances were not addressed. Specifically, the football players asked the coaches end favoritism toward white players, allow black player Bernie Keeles to compete for the starting quarterback job, and urged, "We, the Black athletes, want a winning team. We want the best twenty-two players on the field. We want the best player in each position. THIS HAS NOT BEEN DONE. . . WE WILL NOT PLAY ON ANY TEAM THAT PERPETRATES THESE PRACTICES." The forcefulness of these athletes, and the reality that Cal would lose potential recruits if the protest continued, made serious changes to its athletic program. Most notably, the school, for the first time, hired black assistant coaches for basketball and football.[76]

To a man, black players throughout the nation listed the lack of black coaches as one of their primary concerns, and for athletic programs, this concern constituted one of their easiest fixes. Contrary to athletic directors' and coaches' past claims, there were plenty of qualified black coaches waiting for an opportunity to coach at a big-time university. At the University of Oklahoma, 15 black athletes who threatened to boycott met with the AD and voiced their complaints, pleading: "Why are there no Black counselors, coaches, trainers, secretaries and managers in the athletic department?" At San Francisco State, the black athletes urged, "In addition to our demands that Black athletes be chosen to fill some of the grad-coaching positions, we also demand that the department actively recruit and hire Black coaches, who can relate to and offer solutions to special problems of Black players." And at Michigan State, the players complained, "The college is not hiring enough Negro coaches." Facing a need, and a quick fix to temporarily placate the protests, at most of the institutions where black athletes demanded coaching changes, the university hired its first black assistant coaches. These actions signaled to the players that the schools would bargain in good faith, even though they continued to exploit the players. The move to hire black coaches also signaled to many players that after playing, they might actually have a chance to move on in a profession that until this moment was only open to them and black colleges and universities.[77]

But to be clear, hiring assistant coaches gave the school a quick fix to a specific problem. This did not attempt to break down the barrier of head coaching. While college men's basketball has had a better track record than other sports, to this day, most Division I college football teams have a white head coach. Very few black coaches get high-ranked coordinator jobs that would propel them to head coaching jobs, and very few universities have hired a black man to head their football team.

After 1968, the protests across campuses continued, including major uprisings at Syracuse and Wyoming, but by the early 1970s, most of the revolts ceased. Why? For one, athletes learned that there were serious consequences to revolting. Billy Smith from Cal, for example, went undrafted by the NFL even though he was a top prospect. At UTEP, after black track athletes refused to compete against Brigham Young University because the athletes rejected the Mormon faith's racist beliefs about black inferiority, the track and field coach kicked the athletes off of the team, including star long jumper and eventual world-record holder Bob Beamon.

But the most effective remedies to end the revolt of the college athlete came in the form of two National Collegiate Athletic Association rulings that gave coaches absolute power over their players. In 1969, the NCAA passed a resolution that allowed coaches to strip a player of his athletic scholarship if he quit the team. Prior to this ruling, athletic scholarships were considered four-year guaranteed scholarships; thus the player who revolted would be eligible to keep his scholarship regardless of whether he played or protested. Then, in 1973, the NCAA gave coaches even more power when the nonprofit regulatory agency said that scholarships could be one-year renewable agreements instead of guaranteed for four years. Under this setup, which still exists today, a player has to sign his scholarship every year, and a coach can kick his player off the team and get that scholarship back for any arbitrary reason. These one-year renewables, more than anything else, have eliminated the black athlete's willingness to risk his future in order to improve his playing conditions.

In fact, not until 2015, when football players at Oklahoma threatened to boycott spring practice to protest a racist fraternity incident, and when football players at Missouri threatened to boycott a game as part of a larger protest on campus against racial "micro-aggressions" and growing racial tensions, had black athletes collectively combined to revolt against the system. Today, however, as I am finishing this book, we have entered into a second revolt of the black athlete. Shut up and play is done.

Epilogue

During the 2016 NFL season, San Francisco quarterback Colin Kaepernick took a knee. Like Mudcat Grant 56 years before him, Kaepernick used the national anthem as his moment to protest injustice in America. Instead of standing up for the anthem, as is customary for fans and players to do before every game, Kaepernick—the first three games of the preseason he sat on the bench during the playing of the anthem—respectfully kneeled on one knee to protest what he saw as the continuous oppression of black Americans, particularly the threat of police brutality. His move sparked widespread debate across the nation and marked him as the leading athlete activist in a new day of an age of athlete activism.

Before he became an activist-athlete, however, Kaepernick had been apolitical and aloof about these situations. He, like most black athletes of his generation, had become the affable modern athlete, who with his riches—he once had a contract worth over 100 million dollars—lived a life of luxury and carefree worry that most black Americans could only dream of. Kaepernick had starred in a new era of "shut up and play" and had done exceedingly well. If the dual-threat quarterback remained silent about continued injustices African Americans faced, who would notice? Who would care? But then something clicked. The atrocities kept piling up, and videos of police killing unarmed black men and women kept streaming on the Internet and the news, yet the prejudiced justice system refused to indict officers despite video evidence that should have led to indictments. Kaepernick felt he had to get involved. He knew he could no longer ignore the continued oppression and brutality black people faced. Therefore, he took a knee to raise awareness. By the fall of 2016, with professional football players finally in the fight, it appeared that the second revolt of the black athlete was in full swing. But what took so long?

Kaepernick's protest represented a larger growing movement of black athletes shedding the "shut up and play" label and publicly using their platform to fight against injustices. Since the late 1960s, while there has been a continuous trickle of athletes using their public platforms to attack injustice, most notably when the Chicago Bulls visited the White House as part of the team's championship ceremony guard Craig Hodges wore a dashiki and handed President George H. W. Bush a protest letter in 1991 about his administration's treatment of minorities and the poor, an overwhelming majority of black athletes decided to avoid politics and the controversy, vitriol, and the potential loss of income, via their job or endorsements, that came with activism. They also learned valuable lessons from what happened to Hodges. Hodges never played in the NBA again after protesting to Bush, and also calling out teammates, including Michael Jordan, after the Los Angeles Riots in 1992, for being apolitical and afraid to use their platforms to fight for social justice. Afraid to rock the boat, most black athletes wanted to "be like Mike" and chose the safety of silence and the money of endorsements over resistance.

And big-time college athletes, who had been vocal in the past, had been silenced by the NCAA and their coaches when the NCAA passed legislation in 1973 making college scholarships one-year renewable options for the coaches. No longer protected by a four-year guarantee, if the player protested he would lose his scholarship. Most figured the potential loss of scholarship was not worth the protest. But in 2014, things changed.

In the wake of the police murders of Michael Brown, an unarmed teenager in Ferguson, Missouri, and the murder of Eric Garner, an unarmed man in New York selling "loosie" cigarettes (cigarettes sold individually), in which the officers in both cases avoided indictments, black athletes started to voice their opinions about the continued police brutality in their communities. After prosecutors failed to indict officer Darren Wilson for the murder of Mike Brown, five St. Louis Rams football players came out for their team's introduction before the game in a "hands-up-don't-shoot" pose, a motion many witnesses claimed Brown held before Wilson shot him multiple times. Less than a week later, Derrick Rose, the star point guard for the Chicago Bulls, inspired by mass Black Lives Matter protests he witnessed from his high-rise condo in Chicago, sported an "I Can't Breathe" t-shirt before his game—after the plea Garner repeatedly made to police while he was in their choke hold—an act that prompted a number of black NBA players, including LeBron James, to wear an "I Can't Breathe" shirt. A second wave of athlete activism was clearly on the horizon.

With professional players setting the standard, several college athletes, including men's and women's basketball players, joined in the movement and wore "I Can't Breathe Shirts." In March 2015, after a racist video featuring white University of Oklahoma students went viral, the university's football players boycotted spring football practices. Understanding that the school made millions of dollars off their free labor, the black football players refused to practice until the school properly handled the situation. With football players using their platform to publicly protest, the school promptly suspended the fraternity responsible for the racist video. Then came the events at the University of Missouri.

In November 2015, in one of the most memorable protests of the new athlete-activist movement, the school's black football players voted to boycott an upcoming game against Brigham Young University if the Board of Regents did not fire the school's president, Tim Wolfe, who had been accused of fostering a campus ripe with micro-aggressions—or acts of subtle, indirect racism—meant to harm minority students. The beauty about this potential boycott rested in the fact that the football players, understanding the power they held as athletes, joined activists on campus who had started the protest against micro-aggressions. In the end, facing a million-dollar loss if Missouri had to cancel the game, the Board of Regents fired the president. Afraid of more backlash, Missouri, and a number of other colleges across the country, hired more administrators to help their schools with diversity and inclusion.

The inspiration of Missouri football players' willingness to risk their athletic scholarships for a greater cause and the swelling Black Lives Matter movement—a nationwide protest movement that grew in popularity after the Michael Brown murder—prompted more athletes to get involved. With more cases of police brutality being captured on video, prompting more protests, black athletes knew they had to increase their commitment levels. In the summer of 2016, two months before Kaepernick kneeled, NBA superstars, and global icons, LeBron James, Dwyane Wade, Chris Paul, and Carmelo Anthony—the previous year Anthony had marched with protesters in Baltimore during an uprising protesting the police murder of Freddie Gray—took the stage during the nationally televised ESPN event, the ESPY Awards, to announce their commitment to social justice and implore other athletes to get involved. In their widely viewed speech, the athletic icons invoked athlete activists of the past, including Muhammad Ali, and Jim Brown. They knew that in dire and divided times, they needed to emulate brave athletes of the past who paved the way for athletic activism. Two months later, Kaepernick took that torch and has not looked back.

In the wake of his protest, Kaepernick spoke bravely and passionately about racial injustice. Like Jackie Robinson, Bill Russell, Muhammad Ali, and Kareem Abdul-Jabbar had done before him, he spoke truth to power. When asked why he kneeled, he boldly stated, "I am not going to stand to show pride in a flag for a country that oppresses Black people and people of color. . . . There are bodies in the street and people getting paid leave and getting away with murder." He also argued, "These aren't new situations. This isn't new ground. There are things that have gone on in this country for years and years and have never been addressed, and they need to be. There's a lot of things that need to change. One specifically? Police brutality."[1] Kaepernick was right.

African Americans had been protesting police brutality since emancipation, but they received no protection from the federal government. In the North and South, police terrorized the black population with no regard for human life. Finally, during Jackie Robinson's rookie year, the federal government, under President Truman's to "Secure These Rights" campaign, added police brutality as a fundamental problem that blocked progress and true civil rights for African Americans. Yet in 2016, as Kaepernick noted when he said "these aren't new situations," the federal government had not adequately addressed police brutality. Although Kaepernick was not the first athlete of his generation to protest police brutality, Kaepernick's protest garnered the most attention. Kneeling during the national anthem tugged at the moral fabric of a nation consumed with a self-congratulatory posture about becoming a post-racial society in the President Obama era.

Importantly, though facing much opprobrium from conservatives, he also garnered the support of protesters on the ground, because he refused to stand on a moral fence. In other words, he verbally attacked the problem rather than providing an answer that appeased everyone. He did not discuss so-called black-on-black crime, for example, when addressing police brutality, like others athletes had. For his actions and his words, however, he received considerable amount of flack, including hate mail and death threats. Some pundits even blamed the declining NFL viewership numbers on Kaepernick's protest. He never wavered.

Kaepernick's stance also touched athletes from all levels of play, from kids in Pop Warner football to high school to professional soccer where player Megan Rapinoe, white, was the first athlete to join Kaepernick in protest and linked her defiance to advocating for racial equality and LGBTQ rights. His fellow football players, however, did not show full support. Only a handful kneeled, and no white player showed solidarity with the protests during the anthem. To be sure, the whole Seattle

Seahawks team linked arms in a sign of racial solidarity, but as some critics pointed out, that move defused the real protest of police brutality. In a sign of solidarity with Kaepernick, and a symbol of sympathy for their black brothers and sisters in the struggle for justice, other black athletes chose to raise their black fists in the air, reminiscent of John Carlos and Tommie Smith at the 1968 Olympics. The few who chose to kneel included his teammate, safety Eric Reid. Reid is from Baton Rouge, Louisiana. The city had previously protested police brutality in the summer of 2016 after local police killed an unarmed black man, Alton Sterling. Sterling's slaying sparked nights of massive protests and became another catalyst for nationwide activism, eventually prompting Kaepernick to act.

With the reemergence of activist-athletes, I have been frequently asked to compare activist-athletes of the 1960s to those of today. In my response, I highlight a few similarities and differences to contextualize this new movement. For one, both movements were buoyed by a larger civil rights movement. Black athletes during the 1960s had a massive movement of activists willing to risk their lives for freedom even before a multitude of athletes got involved. Athletes knew they could no longer stay silent and let their play do the talking with 70,000 people involved in sit-in movements, hundreds of people being arrested during the Freedom Rides, or the tens of thousands of people in the Deep South marching and protesting for equality. Today, it is the Black Lives Matter movement that provides athletes cover while also pushing reluctant athletes to get involved. With thousands of black people mobilized across the nation, blocking bridges and streets, and disrupting businesses, black athletes saw an opportunity and a need to act. How could they stay silent while their brothers and sisters risked their lives while fighting for justice?

And like the black athletes of the 1960s, today the black sportswriters—including industry luminaries like Bill Rhoden, Michael Wilbon, Howard Bryant, Bomani Jones, Michael Smith, and Jemele Hill—prodded, pleaded, and pushed athletes to get involved. Compared to the black sportswriters of the past, these pundits today have a larger audience at their disposal to put further pressure on the athletes, while also providing athletes necessary cover from naysayers who would demand they shut up and play. As America makes its way through a new presidency in the Trump age—it is important to note the new revolt of the black athlete occurred during Barack Obama's presidency—black sportswriters remain an important voice in protecting athletes from vitriol, persuading athletes to be activists, and keeping their readers and viewers abreast on the interconnections between sports and civil rights politics.

The most glaring difference, however, between the movements of the past and those of today is the number of black women involved. One of the most important aspects of researching and writing this book, I felt, was working diligently to situate black women in the history of the civil rights movement and sports. This task became frustrating and difficult at times, because outside of major heroines like Althea Gibson and Wilma Rudolph, black women were largely ignored in the movement. This is not to say the black press did not cover their exploits—there is a surprising amount of coverage on bowling for example—but rather it is to suggest that the press and black male athletes did not give most black women athletes a platform to protest.

Today, black women athletes have the platform. And in many ways, they took the lead, especially in the summer of 2016. Athletes, including players from the Minnesota Lynx and the Washington Mystics, risked fines by wearing T-shirts during warm-ups with slogans and or names of victims including "Black Lives Matter," "Alton Sterling," and "#Dallas5," the latter in remembrance of the five Dallas police officers killed during a Black Lives Matter protest. Star forward, Tina Charles, who played for the New York Liberty in 2016 said, "My teammates and I spoke at length about how to pay tribute to the fallen lives in a way that would also contribute to the conversations around race and justice in our country." She also noted, "For me, this protest is personal. I believe I have an obligation to stand up, and it is not in my nature to shy away from using my voice." Charles, like a number of black Women's National Basketball Association players, grew up surrounded by police violence that impacted her life and her neighborhood in a myriad of ways.[2] Growing up, black WNBA players witnessed black women mistreated and families struggle under the weight of mass incarceration that took many black men from their neighborhoods. Thus, WNBA players knew they had a right and an obligation to speak.

And after the WNBA fined its activist-athletes in a misguided attempt to avoid negative publicity, the players bravely held what they called "black out" sessions and refused to answer any questions from the media unless the questions dealt with injustice in America, a brilliant and unprecedented display of solidarity. What became clear in 2016, and should have been clear all along, is that black women have always been doubly impacted because of their race and gender. They have an important voice that needs to be heard.

Following the WNBA's activism, iconic tennis great Serena Williams, who had been renowned for her activism as she and her sister, fellow tennis star Venus, have worked tirelessly during their careers to bring equal pay to women tennis players and also combat racism in tennis, spoke out against police brutality. In a message in September 2016, Williams, one of the greatest athletes of all time, wrote about a recent incident involving her 18-year-old nephew and the fear she had that the police might harm him simply because he is black. For Williams, this triggered an emotion that demanded she had to speak up against injustice, even if this meant losing fans, fame, and endorsements. In her protest, she quoted Martin Luther King Jr. and said, "There comes a time when silence comes as a betrayal. . . . I won't be silent anymore." With that Facebook post, right at the beginning of Kaepernick's stance against injustice, Williams joined the ranks of black athletes vowing to fight police brutality.

As we enter the dawn of the Donald Trump presidency, which seems openly hostile to protest movements involving marginalized folks, we must ask, what comes next for the activist-athlete? The activist-athlete, I believe, will be needed even more than before, because marginalized folks seem to feel as if they have less of a voice. While black athletes cannot speak for other activists, they can help beyond protesting, especially if they decenter themselves from the conversation. Kaepernick, for example, has committed his money to the fight for justice. Instead of centering himself in the movement, he has invested in grassroots organizations in their local communities that are working to bring elected officials to the table to create real change. In other words, Kaepernick is trusting the marginalized folks to create the serious changes that are needed. They know their neighborhood and know what works. His work, no doubt, will put him in the conversation with the list of all-time activist-athletes like Jackie Robinson, Bill Russell, Muhammad Ali, and Jim Brown who used their fame, power, and platform to radically change society.

Notes

Introduction

1. Sam Lacy, "A to Z," *Baltimore Afro American*, September 24, 1960.
2. L.I. Brockenbury, "Tying the Score," *Los Angeles Sentinel*, September 22, 1960.
3. Bob Hunter, "The Safari," *St. Louis Argus*, September 23, 1960.
4. James Boggs, *Pages from a Black Radicals Notebook: A James Boggs Reader* (Detroit: Wayne State University Press, 2011), 60.
5. Claude Harrison Jr., "Pro Grid Squads Discriminate against Tan QB's," *Philadelphia Tribune*, September 15, 1964.
6. Jim Hall, "Time Out," *Louisiana Weekly*, August 28, 1965.
7. "The Big Leagues Show How," *Ebony* (May 1948), 50.
8. Gordon Cobbledick, "Plain Dealings," *Cleveland Plain Dealer*, November 26, 1948.
9. "Gov. Lauds Tigers," *Michigan Chronicle*, May 5, 1962; Lawrence Casey, "Bill Billy's Bat Speaks Out," *Michigan Chronicle*, May 5, 1962.
10. Thomas G. Smith, *Showdown: JFK and the Integration of the Washington Redskins* (New York: Beacon Press, 2012), 113.
11. "Star Athletes Aid Rights Movement," *Sacramento Observer*, January 26,1967.
12. "Give Negro Try in Baseball Besides Playing," *Jet*, Vol. 26 (25) (September 24, 1964), 56.
13. "Joe Black," *Philadelphia Tribune*, July 16, 1968.
14. Sam Lacy, *Fighting for Fairness: The Life Story of Hall of Fame Sportswriter Sam Lacy* (Baltimore, Maryland: Tidewater Publishing, 1998), 49–50.
15. Dr. Martin Luther King Jr., "Hall of Famer," *New York Amsterdam News*, August 4, 1962.

Chapter 1 Democracy in Action: Sports and the American Dream

1. Al Sweeney, "As I See It," *Cleveland Call and Post*, January 3, 1942.
2. Margery Miller, *Joe Louis: American* (New York: Current Books, 1945), 180–181.

3. Rick Hurt, "Sports Train," *People's Voice*, June 23, 1946.

4. Doc Young, "Sportivanting," *Cleveland Call and Post*, October 25, 1947.

5. Edwin B. Henderson, "Henderson's Comet," *Cleveland Call and Post*, September 13, 1947.

6. David Halberstam, *Everything They Had: Sports Writing from David Halberstam* (New York: Hyperion, 2008), 124.

7. Jack Orr, "Jackie Robinson: Symbol of a Revolution," *Sport*, Vol. 29 (3) (March 1960), 59.

8. Bob Williams, "Sports Rambler," *Cleveland Call and Post*, April 15, 1944.

9. Joe Bostic, "Scoreboard," *People's Voice*, February 10, 1945.

10. Joe Bostic, "Players Must Act Now to Erase Baseball Ban," *People's Voice*, March 24, 1945.

11. Joe Bostic, "Scoreboard," *People's Voice*, April 14, 1945.

12. Joe Bostic, "Scoreboard," *People's Voice*, May 12, 1945.

13. Rick Hurt, "Sports Train," *People's Voice*, October 20, 1945.

14. Sydney R. Williams, "On the Whole," *Cleveland Call and Post*, November 3, 1945.

15. Adam Clayton Powell, "Comments," *People's Voice*, November 3, 1945.

16. "Ben Davis Lauds Victory," *People's Voice*, November 3, 1945.

17. "Good and Bad," *Sporting News*, November 1, 1945.

18. "Editorial," *Michigan Chronicle*, April 27, 1946.

19. Rick Hurt, "Sports Train," *People's Voice*, April 27, 1946.

20. "Editorial," *Cleveland Call and Post*, April 26, 1947.

21. "Editorial," *Kansas City Plain Dealer*, April 25, 1947.

22. "Enquiring Reporter," *Michigan Chronicle*, April 19, 1947.

23. "The Watchtower," *Los Angeles Sentinel*, April 17, 1947.

24. Cleveland Jackson, "Larry Doby Breaks into Lineup on First Day with Team," *Cleveland Call and Post*, July 12, 1947.

25. "Editorial," *Michigan Chronicle*, July 12, 1947.

26. Rick Hurt, "Sports Train," *People's Voice*, July 12, 1947.

27. "Editorial," *People's Voice*, October 4, 1947.

28. "Editorial," *Philadelphia Tribune*, October 11, 1947.

29. Alvin Moses, "Jackie Robinson Top 47' Athlete," *Philadelphia Tribune*, December 30, 1947.

30. "Bramham Scores 'Raid' Against Negro Loop," *The Sporting News*, November 1, 1945.

31. Ibid.

32. Jackie Robinson, *I Never Had It Made* (New York: Ecco Press, 1995), 49.

33. Ibid., 53.

34. Dixie Walker in *Baseball Has Done It*, by Jackie Robinson (New York: IG Publishing, 2005), 56–57.

35. Bobby Bragan in *Baseball Has Done It*, 58–59.

36. Robinson, *I Never Had It Made*, 60.

37. Jennifer Lansbury, *A Spectacular Leap: Black Women Athlete's in Twentieth Century America* (Fayetteville: University of Arkansas Press, 2014), 76–77.

38. Althea Gibson, "I Wanted to Be Somebody," *Saturday Evening Post*, August 23, 1958. This is a three-part series running throughout August and September.

39. Quoted in Lansbury, *A Spectacular Leap*, 89.

40. Doc Young, *Negro Firsts in Sports* (Chicago: Johnson Publishing Co., 1963), 193–194.

41. See Pamela Grundy, "Ora Washington: The First Black Female Athletic Star," in *Out of the Shadows*, ed. David K. Wiggins (Fayetteville: University of Arkansas Press, 2006), 79–92.

42. See Althea Gibson, "I Wanted to Be Somebody," *Saturday Evening Post*.

43. Mary Jo Festle, "Jackie Robinson without the Charm," in *Out of the Shadows*, Ed. David K. Wiggins (Fayetteville: University of Arkansas Press, 2006), 197.

44. "Detroiters to Send Ace Abroad," *Michigan Chronicle*, May 26, 1951.

45. Damion Thomas, *Globe Trotting: African American Athletes and Cold War Politics* (Urbana: University of Illinois Press, 2012).

46. See Festle, "Jackie Robinson without Charm."

47. "Editorial," *Michigan Chronicle*, July 13, 1957.

48. "Althea Gibson's Triumph," *Chicago Defender*, July 20, 1957.

49. "Reflect More Credit to the US," *Louisiana Weekly*, July 19, 1958.

50. Althea Gibson, "I Wanted to Be Somebody," *Saturday Evening Post*, Pt. 3, 78.

51. Frances Clayton Gray and Yanick Rice Lamb, *Born to Win: The Authorized Biography of Althea Gibson* (New York: John Wiley & Sons, Inc., 2004), 128–130; James L. Hicks, "Althea Gibson," *New York Amsterdam News*, July 18, 1959; James Trotman, "The Althea Column," *New York Amsterdam News*, October 10, 1959.

52. "Editorial," *Michigan Chronicle*, August 31, 1963.

53. Young, *Negro Firsts in Sports*, 7.

54. Doc Young, "How Sports Helped Break the Color Line," *Ebony* (September 1963), 114.

55. Ibid.

Chapter 2 White Allies

1. Margery Miller, "This Jackson," *Christian Science Monitor*, December 11, 1947.

2. George Trevor, "Levi's the Talk of Eli," *Sport* (November 1949), 52, 88.

3. Roscoe Simmons, "The Untold Story," *Chicago Defender*, December 12, 1948.

4. "Eli's Levi Jackson," *Life*, 4 December 1948.

5. Tom Cohane, "Levi Jackson at Yale," *Look*, Vol. 13 (October 25), 128.

6. Bill Corum, "Sports," *New York Journal American*, November 23, 1948.

7. Red Smith, "Levi Jackson," *New York Tribune Herald*, November 24,1948.

8. "Levi Jackson Rated as One of the Greatest," *Michigan Chronicle*, October 18, 1948.

9. George Trevor, "Levi's the Talk of Eli," *Sport*, 53.

10. Tom Cohane, "Levi Jackson at Yale," *Look*, 128.

11. Bill Chipman, "They Call Him Levi," *Varsity*, reprinted in *Negro Digest* (December 1949), 44.

12. "Editorial," *New York Age*, December 11, 1948.

13. Joseph Bibb, "Cheers for Yale," *Pittsburg Courier*, December 4, 1948.

14. Young, *Negro Firsts in Sports*, 190–191.

15. "Betty Hicks Asks for Equality in Bowling," *Michigan Chronicle*, February 7, 1948.

16. Al Sweeney, "As I See It," *Cleveland Call and Post*, October 25, 1941.

17. Quoted in Bob Williams "Sports Rambler," *Cleveland Call and Post*, December 15, 1945.

18. "Bowling Boom," *Ebony* (February 1947), 43–46.

19. Bill Matney, "Jumping the Gun," *Michigan Chronicle*, February 15, 1947; Bill Matney, "George Bennett Is Also Golfer, Family Man," *Michigan Chronicle*, February 22, 1947.

20. Bob Williams, "Clubs Opens Fight to End Ban against Negro Bowlers," *Cleveland Call and Post*, October 2, 1943.

21. "Reuther Warns ABC," *Michigan Chronicle*, April 28, 1948.

22. "Not in Buffalo," *People's Voice*, March 23, 1946.

23. "Sen. Mead Blasts ABC Bowling Rules," *Los Angeles Sentinel*, April 4, 1946.

24. Bob Williams, "Clubs Opens Fight to End Ban against Negro Bowlers," *Cleveland Call and Post*, October 2, 1943.

25. John C. Walter and Malina Lida, "The State of New York and the Legal Struggle to Desegregate the American Bowling Congress, 1944–1950," *Afro-Americans in New York Life and History*, Vol. 35 (1) (January 2011), 7–32.

26. "Warned by ABC After Agreement," *Michigan Chronicle*, March 27, 1948.

27. "ABC Votes to Retain Racial Ban," *Michigan Chronicle*, April 24, 1948.

28. Dan Parker, "How Democratic Is US Sport," *Sport*, reprinted in *Negro Digest* (January 1950), 58–59.

29. Ibid., 59.

30. "ABC Gives Up," *Los Angeles Sentinel*, May 25, 1950.

31. Ormund Curl, "Allen's Alley," *Michigan Chronicle*, February 9, 1963.

32. Lawrence Casey, "Bill Rodham: A Beacon for Young Bowlers," *Michigan Chronicle*, January 20, 1958.

33. Ormund Curl, "Allen's Alley," *Michigan Chronicle*, January 25, 1962.

34. Ormund Curl, "Allen's Alley," *Michigan Chronicle*, February 9, 1963.

35. "Knocking Down Things Way of Life for Sadie," *Philadelphia Tribune*, January 26, 1965.

36. Eddie Burbidge, "Laying It on the Line," *California Eagle*, November 1, 1945.

37. Tim Cohan, "A Branch Grows in Brooklyn," *Look*, March 19, 1946, 72.

38. Quoted in "Montreal Club First to Drop Color Bar," *Baltimore Afro-America*, November 3, 1945.

39. Jack Horner, "Bramham Scores 'Raid' Against Negro Loops," *Sporting News*, November 1, 1946.

40. Cohane, "A Branch Comes to Brooklyn," *Look*, March 19, 1946, 74.

41. Arnold Rampersad, *Jackie Robinson: A Biography* (New York: Random House, 1998), 122.

42. Ibid., 75.

43. Jules Tygiel, *Baseball's Great Experiment: Jackie Robinson and His Legacy* (New York: Oxford University Press, 2008), 75.

44. Ed Rumill, "Brooklyn Leads in Series Final," *Christian Science Monitor*, October 4, 1955.

45. "Montreal Club First to Drop Color Bar," *Baltimore Afro-America*, November 3 1945.

46. "Editorials," *Arkansas State Press*, November 9, 1945.

47. "Editorial," *Michigan Chronicle*, April 27, 1946.

48. "Between the Lines," *Kansas City Plain Dealer*, April 18, 1947.

49. "Editorial," *St. Louis Argus*, April 18, 1947.

50. "Editorial," *New York Age*, April 19, 1947.

51. David Bethe, "Brank Rickey," *Arkansas State Press*, May 2, 1947.

52. "Editorial," *Birmingham World*, January 27, 1956.

53. Marion E. Jackson, "Sports of the World," *Birmingham World*, January 24, 1956.

54. Jackie Robinson, "The Most Unforgettable Character I've Met," *Reader's Digest*, October 1961, 100.

55. Cleveland Jackson, "Headline Action," *Cleveland Call and Post*, April 26, 1947.

56. Ibid.

57. C.L. Peoples, "Even Bill Veeck Stoops to Snipe at Jackie Robinson," *Cleveland Call and Post*, May 24, 1947.

58. *The Call and Post* printed the signed letter on its front page, July 12, 1947.

59. "Coming Fair Employment Practice Ordinance Fight Seen in Council," *Cleveland Call and Post*, July 12, 1947.

60. "Editorial," *Cleveland Call and Post*, July 12, 1947.

61. "Speaks to Kids," *Cleveland Plain Dealer*, April 29, 1948.

62. Bill Matney, "Bill Veeck," *Michigan Chronicle*, June 28, 1952.

63. Gordon Cobbledick, "Plain Dealing," *Cleveland Plain Dealer*, May 13, 1948.

64. "Editorial," *St. Louis Argus*, August 1, 1952.

65. Bill Veeck, "The Way I See It," *Negro Digest*, Vol. 15 (10) (August 1966), 38–48.

66. Hy Turkin, "How Jim Crow Got the Gridiron Boot," *Negro Digest* (December 1948), 20.

67. Gordon Cobbledick, "Plain Dealing," *Cleveland Plain Dealer*, April 29, 1948.

68. William "Sheep" Jackson, "Cleve. Browns Democracy in Action," *Cleveland Call and Post*, August 11, 1956.

69. Al Dunmore, "Paul Brown Gave Tan Ace a Start," *Michigan Chronicle*, March 9, 1963.

70. Rick Hurt, "Sports Train," *People's Voice*, October 19, 1946.

71. William "Sheep" Jackson, "Cleve. Browns Democracy in Action," *Cleveland Call and Post*, August 11, 1956.

72. Al Dunmore, "Paul Brown Gave Tan Ace a Start," *Michigan Chronicle*, March 9, 1963.

73. "Editorial," *Cleveland Call and Post*, December 20, 1947.

74. Rick Hurt, "Sports Train," *People's Voice*, October 19, 1946.

75. Al Sweeney, "As I See It," *Cleveland Call and Post*, July 12, 1941.

76. "Kenny to Tryout with National League," *Los Angeles Tribune*, January 19, 1946.

77. A.O. Price, "Accent on Sports," *California Eagle*, August 21, 1947.

78. Joel Smith, "Surveying the Sports Front," *Atlanta Daily World*, January 7, 1947.

79. Charles H. Martin, *Benching Jim Crow: The Rise and Fall of the Color Line in Southern College Sports, 1890–1980* (Chicago: University of Illinois Press, 2010), 56.

80. Cleveland Jackson, "Highlight of Sports," *Cleveland Call and Post*, January 4, 1947.

81. "Editorials," *People's Voice*, January 11, 1947.

82. Cleveland Jackson, "Headline Action," *Cleveland Call and Post*, February 22, 1947.

83. Bill Matney, "Jumping the Gun," *Michigan Chronicle*, January 11, 947.

84. "Editorial," *St. Louis Argus*, January 10, 1947.

85. Quoted in Martin, *Benching Jim Crow*, 59.

86. "Miami Prof Quits Over Color Issues," *Pittsburgh Courier*, November 30, 1946.

87. "Jumping the Gun," *Michigan Chronicle*, November 30, 1946; "Jumping the Gun," *Michigan Chronicle*, December 7, 1946.

88. "Unique Non-Segregation Pact for Title Bout," *Michigan Chronicle*, January 28, 1961.

89. L.I. Brockenbury, quoted in *Louisiana Weekly*, March 25, 1961.

90. Jackie Robinson, "Its Changing Racial Attitude May Make Miami 'Your Ami' Too!" *Philadelphia Tribune*, March 9, 1965.

91. Bill Matney, "Jumping the Gun," *Michigan Chronicle*, November 16, 1946.

92. "Mississippians Will Not Play against Negro," *Michigan Chronicle*, October 4, 1947.

93. "Editorial," *Michigan Chronicle*, November 8, 1947.

94. "Editorial," *Michigan Chronicle*, October 18, 1947.

95. "MSC Appeasement Policy," *Michigan Chronicle*, October 25, 1947.

96. "Chronicle Cracks Bias on MSC Football 11," *Michigan Chronicle*, November 1, 1947.

97. "Hats Off to MSC," Michigan Chronicle, November 8, 1947.

98. "Walley Triplett's Score in Third Period," *Michigan Chronicle*, January 10, 948.

99. "Texans Like Negro Grid Stars," *Ebony* (November 1952), 23.

100. Ibid., 25.

101. Ibid., 23–28.

102. "Young Impressed with Dallas Fans," *Michigan Chronicle*, June 14, 1952.

103. "Texans Like Negro Grid Stars," *Ebony* (November 1952), 23.

104. "Young Impressed with Dallas Fans," *Michigan Chronicle*, June 14, 1952.

105. "Dave Hoskins: Texas League Pioneer," *Jet*, Vol. 7 (15) (August 7, 1952), 54–59.

106. Bruce Aldeson, *Brushing Back Jim Crow: The Integration of Minor-League Baseball in the American South* (Charlottesville: University of Virginia Press, 1999), 61.

107. Ibid., 58.

Chapter 3   The Press and the People: The Final Fight for Fairness

1. Arthur Kirk, "Breaking the Tape," *St. Louis Argus*, April 18, 1947.

2. Bob Williams, "Sports Rambler," *Cleveland Call and Post*, February 3,1946.

3. Arthur Kirk, "Breaking the Tape," *St. Louis Argus*, October 1, 1948.

4. Arthur Kirk, "Breaking the Tape," *St. Louis Argus*, May 30,1952.

5. L.I. Brockenbury, "Tying the Score," *Los Angeles Sentinel*, April 30, 1959.

6. Russ Cowans, "Major League Teams Beating Bush for Men," *Michigan Chronicle*, August 9, 1947.

7. Bill Matney, "Will Tigers Liberalize Their Policy," *Michigan Chronicle*, April 21, 1951.

8. Bill Lane, "Tigers Can Get Along without Colored Players," *Michigan Chronicle*, April 28, 1951.

9. Roy W. Stephens, "Straight from the Shoulders," *Michigan Chronicle*, April 28, 1951.

10. Bill Matney, "Will New Owners Changer Tiger Policy: Scuttle Veeck's Bid with Option Clause," *Michigan Chronicle*, July 21, 1956

11. The five-part series starts on May 26, 1956. Charles J. Wartman, "Baseball Fans Ask: Will Detroit Tigers Liberalize Policy," *Michigan Chronicle*, May 26, 1956; Charles J. Wartman, "Did Tigers Permit Top Negro Prospects to Miss Play Here?" *Michigan Chronicle*, June 2, 1956; Charles J. Wartman, "Tiger Policy Defies Liberal Sports Trend Here," *Michigan Chronicle*, June 9, 1956; Charles J. Wartman, "Tiger Policy Has Definite Impact on Relations Here," *Michigan Chronicle*, June 16, 1956; Charles J. Wartman, "Tigers Watch Other Teams Sign Big League Prospects," *Michigan Chronicle*, June 23, 1956.

12. Charles J. Wartman, "Tiger Policy Has Definite Impact on Relations Here," *Michigan Chronicle*, June 16, 1956.

13. William C. Matney, "Absence of Negro Players Is Cited," *Michigan Chronicle*, April 26, 1958.

14. Bill Matney, "Sports Community Deserves Credit," *Michigan Chronicle*, June 14, 1958.

15. Quoted in Howard Bryant, *Shut Out: A Story of Race and Baseball in Boston* (Boston: Beacon Press, 2003), 28 and 25.

16. Ibid.

17. "O'Connell Calls Team 'American,'" *Chicago Defender*, May 2, 1959; "Clear Red Sox of Race Bias," *New York Amsterdam News*, June 13, 1959.

18. "BoSox Recall Pumpsie Green from American Association," *Chicago Defender*, July 23, 1959.

19. Quoted in "Fights Ban on Negro Amateur Boxers in D.C.," *Cleveland Call and Post*, January 20, 1945.

20. Edwin B. Henderson, "Jim Crow Boxing in U.S. Capitol. Negroes Seek Fair Play in Sports," *Cleveland Call and Post*, February 3,1946.

21. Edwin B. Henderson, "Negro Boxer Ban Cancels Golden Gloves Tourney," *California Eagle*, January 16, 1947.

22. Edwin B. Henderson, "Henderson's Comment," *Baltimore Afro-American*, April 3, 1948.

23. "Pro Redskins under Fire in Washington for Jim Crow Policy," *Michigan Chronical*, January 12, 1957.

24. Doc Young, "Inside Sports," *Jet*, Vol. 13 (7) (19 December 1957), 57.

25. "Editorial," *Baltimore Afro-American*, January 12, 1957.

26. "Negroes Picket Giants-Redskin Games in D.C.," *Jet*, Vol. 12 (25) (25 October 1957), 56.

27. L.I. Brockenbury, "Time's Running Out on Skins & Jim Crow," *Los Angeles Sentinel*, August 10, 1961.

28. "NAACP Thanks Supporters," *Los Angeles Sentinel*, August 17, 1961; Brad Pye, "Prying," *Los Angeles Sentinel*, August 17, 1961.

29. "Pickets Redskins in San Francisco," *New York Amsterdam News*, September 16, 1961.

30. Quoted in Charles Livingston, "Raps Smugness of Stars," *Pittsburgh Courier*, July 23, 1963.

31. Pete McDaniel, *Uneven Lies: The Heroic Story of African-Americans in Golf* (Greenwich, Connecticut: The American Golfer, 2000), 77–78; For black women and golf, see M. Mikell Johnson, *The African American Woman Golfer: Her Legacy* (Westport, Connecticut: Praeger, 2008).

32. Mark Harris, "Foul Play on the Fairway," *Negro Digest*, Vol. 6 (12) (October 1948), 36–40.

33. "Negro Women Golfers Get County Links," *California Eagle*, July 14, 1955.

34. See "Women's Golf Club Seeks County Ban," *Los Angeles Sentinel*, May 17, 1956; "Golfers Back Publinx Prejudice," *Los Angeles Sentinel*, July 18, 1957; Maggie Hathaway, "Maggie Hathaway Relates W. Coast Golf Bias Fight," *Chicago Defender*, 1July 18, 1959; "Golfers Picket Long Beach PGA," *Los Angeles Sentinel*,

July 18, 1963; "Western Ave. Gets Negro Golf Pro," *Los Angeles Sentinel*, December 19, 1963.

35. Mark Harris, "Foul Play on the Fairway," *Negro Digest*, Vol. 6 (12) (October 1948), 38.

36. See Pete McDaniel, *Uneven Lies*; John H. Kennedy, *A Course of Their Own: A History of African American Golfers* (Lincoln: University of Nebraska Press, 2000).

37. "Golfers Want Separate Links in Louisville," *Chicago Defender*, April 26, 1952.

38. "Bias Fades on Golf Course," *Birmingham World*, February 16, 1954.

39. Maggie Hathaway, "Tee Time," *Los Angeles Sentinel*, July 9, 1964.

40. "Editorial," *California Eagle*, November 10, 1955.

41. "Editorial," *Atlanta Daily World*, December 24, 1955.

42. Pete McDaniel, *Uneven Lies*, 94–96.

43. "Charlie Sifford," *Michigan Chronicle*, April 15, 1963.

44. Kennedy, *A Course of Their Own*, 130–131.

45. For information on her golf career, see Frances Clayton Gray and Yanick Rice Lamb, *Born to Win: The Authorized Biography of Althea Gibson* (New York: John Wiley and Sons Inc., 2004), 137–161.

46. Ibid., 154.

47. Ibid., 149, 153.

48. "Golf's Unsung Hero," *Michigan Chronicle*, March 9, 1963.

49. Quoted in Pete McDaniel, *Uneven Lies*, 85.

50. Quoted in Kennedy, *A Course of Their Own*, 50–51.

51. Mark Harris, "Foul Play on the Fairway," *Negro Digest*, Vol. 6 (12) (October 1948), 36–40.

52. Ibid.; Kennedy, *A Course of Their Own*, 49–64.

53. John Fuster, "Fuster's Sport Talk," *Cleveland Call and Post*, January 19, 1952.

54. John Fuster, "Fuster's Sport Talk," *Cleveland Call and Post*, January 26, 1952.

55. "Abie's Corner," *California Eagle*, June 19, 1952.

56. Quoted in Kennedy, *A Course of Their Own*, 83.

57. L.I. Brockenbury, "Tying the Score," *Los Angeles Sentinel*, November 7, 1957.

58. L.I. Brockenbury, "Tying the Score," *Los Angeles Sentinel*, October 24, 1957.

59. L.I. Brockenbury, "Tying the Score," *Los Angeles Sentinel*, December 4, 1958.

60. "Jackie Robinson," *Chicago Defender*, February 29, 1960.

61. Kennedy, *A Course of Their Own*, 128.

62. Ibid., 134.

Chapter 4 Deep Down in Dixie: Segregated Sports in a Post-*Brown* Era

1. Andrew Mariniss, *Strong Inside: Perry Wallace and the Collison of Race and Sports in the South* (Nashville: Vanderbilt University Press, 2014), 102.

2. Ibid., 246.

3. Ibid., 252–263.

4. Furman Bisher, "What about the Negro Athlete in the South?" *Sport*, Vol. 21 (5) (June 1956), 89.

5. Emory O. Jackson, "B'ham Peels Off Jim Crow in Sports," *Birmingham World*, January 29, 1954.

6. "Segregated Law Repealed by City," *Birmingham Post Herald*, January 27, 1954.

7. Marion E. Jackson, "Sports of the World," *Birmingham World*, January 29, 1954; "Editorial," *Birmingham World*, January 29, 1954; "Editorial," *Birmingham World*, February 19, 1954.

8. Reprinted in Emory O. Jackson, "B'ham Peels Off Jim Crow in Sports," *Birmingham World*, January 29, 1954.

9. "Here's What New Sports Plan Provides," *Birmingham Post World*, March 23, 1954.

10. "City Is Hands-Off on Segregation Vote," *Birmingham Post Herald*, March 25, 1954; "Editorial," *Birmingham World*, March 26, 1954.

11. "5 Persons Seek Injunction," *Birmingham World*, May 11, 1954.

12. "Editorial," *Birmingham World*, June 1, 1954.

13. "Editorial," *Birmingham World*, June 4, 1954; "Editorial," *Birmingham World*, June 8, 1954.

14. "Segregation Voted for City Sports," *Birmingham Post-Herald*, June 2, 1954; "Editorial," *Birmingham Post-Herald*, June 3, 1954.

15. "Dixie Threatens Kids Baseball," *Baltimore Afro-American*, August 6, 1955.

16. Ibid.

17. Marcel Hopson, "Hits and Bits," *Birmingham World*, August 23, 1955.

18. "Fla. Little League Has Mixed Playoff," *Baltimore Afro-American*, August 20, 1955.

19. "OK Negro Little League Team for Florida Tourney," *Kansas City Plain Dealer*, August 18, 1955.

20. "Boston Scribe Hits Little League," *Baltimore Afro-American*, August 20, 1955.

21. "Dixie Threatens Kids Baseball," *Baltimore Afro-American*, August 6, 1955.

22. "Editorial," *Louisiana Weekly*, August 13, 1955.

23. "Editorial," *Pittsburgh Courier*, August 6, 1955.

24. "The Little Grown Ups," *Chicago Defender*, August 27, 1955.

25. Doc Young, "Inside Sports," *Jet*, Vol. 8 (14) (11 August 1955), 55.

26. Sam Lacy, "This Is Little League," *Baltimore Afro-American*, September 3, 1955.

27. For more on the 1956 Sugar Bowl game, see Lane Demas, *Integrating the Gridiron: Black Civil Rights and American College Football* (New Brunswick, New Jersey: Rutgers University Press, 2010), 72–101.

28. Marion E. Jackson, "The World of Sports," *Atlanta Daily World*, November 30, 1955.

29. "Tech Students Protest," *Atlanta Daily World*, December 4, 1955.

30. "Angry Students Burn Effigy of Georgia Govn'r," *California Eagle*, December 8, 1955.

31. Ibid.

32. "Editorial," *Michigan Chronicle*, 10 December 1955; "Editorial," *Baltimore Afro-American*, December 17, 1955.

33. Doc Young, "Inside Sports," *Jet*, Vol. 9 (7) (22 December 1955), 55.

34. "Editorial," *California Eagle*, December 8, 1955.

35. "Mississippi Faces Tough Interracial Foe Saturday," *California Eagle*, December 8, 1955.

36. Marion E. Jackson, "World of Sports," *Atlanta Daily World*, December 7, 1955; Marion E. Jackson, "World of Sports," *Atlanta Daily World*, January 2, 1955.

37. Jim Hall, "Time Out," *Louisiana Weekly*, December 10, 1955; Jim Hall, "Time Out," *Louisiana Weekly*, January 7, 1956.

38. Jim Hall, "Time Out," *Louisiana Weekly*, January 7, 1956.

39. "Editorial," *Louisiana Weekly*, December 31, 1955.

40. "N.O. Pelicans to Drop Five Tan Players," *Louisiana Weekly*, April 2, 1955.

41. "Pelicans Brass Irks Baseball Fans," *Louisiana Weekly*, April 9, 1955.

42. "Editorial," *Louisiana Weekly*, April 9, 1955.

43. Jim Hall, "Time Out," *Louisiana Weekly*, April 16, 1955.

44. Jim Hall, "Time Out," *Louisiana Weekly*, April 9,1955.

45. Jim Hall, "Time Out," *Louisiana Weekly*, June 25, 1955.

46. Jim Hall, "Time Out," *Louisiana Weekly*, June 11, 1955.

47. Jim Hall, "Time Out," *Louisiana Weekly*, May 7, 1955.

48. "Pelicans Brass Irks Baseball Fans," *Louisiana Weekly*, April 9, 1955.

49. Jim Hall, "Time Out," *Louisiana Weekly*, April 16, 1955.

50. Jim Hall, "Time Out," *Louisiana Weekly*, May 21, 1955.

51. Jim Hall, "Time Out," *Louisiana Weekly*, July 6, 1957.

52. Ibid.

53. "Governor Long OK's Ban on Mixed Athletics," *Louisiana Weekly*, July 21, 1956; For more editorial on the situation, see "Editorial," *Louisiana Weekly*, July 7, 1956; "Editorial," *Louisiana Weekly*, July 14, 1956.

54. "Editorial," Louisiana Weekly, August 4, 1956.

55. Jim Hall, "Time Out," *Louisiana Weekly*, July 28, 1956.

56. Jim Hall, "Time Out," *Louisiana Weekly*, July 28, 1956.

57. "Boycott Threatens Brown-Smith Bout," *Louisiana Weekly,* July 28, 1956.

58. "Jackie Raps Keefe Slur," *Louisiana Weekly*, August 4, 1956; "Keefe to Answer Robinson," *Louisiana Weekly*, August 11, 1956; "Keefe Answers Jackie's Letter," *Louisiana Weekly*, August 18, 1956.

59. "Sugar Bowl Crisis Looms," *Louisiana Weekly*, August 4, 1956.

60. Jim Hall, "Time Out," *Louisiana Weekly*, August 4, 1956.

61. "NBA Boxing," *Michigan Chronicle*, December 8, 1956.

62. "Joey Dorsey's Biggest Fight," *Jet*, Vol. 15 (9) (1 January 1959), 56–59.

63. "Joey Dorsey Files Amended Petition," *Louisiana Weekly*, May 25, 1957; "U.S. Court Voids Interracial Sports Ban," *Louisiana Weekly*, December 5, 1958.

64. "Joey Dorsey's Biggest Fight," *Jet*, Vol. 15 (9) (1 January 1959), 56–59.

65. Jim Hall, "Time Out," *Louisiana Weekly*, January 2, 1965.

66. Bobbie Barbie, "Throw Bias for a Loss," *Jet*, Vol. 27 (16) (28 January 1965), 52–57.

67. Ibid.

68. "21 Tan Players Quit La. Over Bias," *Philadelphia Tribune*, January 12, 1965.

69. "Editorial," *Louisiana Weekly*, January 23, 1965.

70. Jim Hall, "Time Out," *Louisiana Weekly*, January 23, 1965.

71. Quoted in Jim Hall, "Time Out," *Louisiana Weekly*, January 30, 1965.

72. "Editorial," *Philadelphia Tribune*, January 16, 1965.

73. "Letters," *Ebony*, Vol. 20 (5) (March 1965), 16.

74. "Editorial," *Houston Informer*, April 29, 1961.

75. "Athletes Vary on Boycott," *Houston Informer*, June 17, 1961; Lloyd C. Wells, "Texas Southern Track Stars Suspended," *Houston Informer*, June 17, 1961; Lloyd C. Wells, "Dateline Sports," *Houston Informer*, June 17, 1961.

76. "Editorial," *Houston Informer*, June 17, 1961.

77. "Athletes Vary on Boycott," *Houston Informer*, June 17, 1961.

78. "Eyes of the Nation Focused on Colts," *Houston Informer*, August 12, 1961; "Big Daddy Favors Tackling Bias," *Chicago Defender*, August 10, 1961; "Boycott Wins," *Pittsburgh Courier*, August 12, 1961.

79. Lloyd C. Wells, "Dateline Sports," *Houston Informer*, August 20, 1960.

80. Lloyd C. Wells, "Dateline Sports," *Houston Informer*, September 17, 1960.

81. Lloyd C. Wells, "Dateline Sports," *Houston Informer*, July 29, 1961.

82. Lloyd C. Wells, "Dateline Sports," *Houston Informer*, November 25, 1961.

83. Lloyd C. Wells, "Dateline Sports," *Houston Informer*, September 16, 1961.

84. Lloyd C. Wells, "Dateline Sports," *Houston Informer*, 25 November 1961.

85. Lloyd C. Wells, "Dateline Sports," *Houston Informer*, December 2, 1961.

86. Lloyd C. Wells, "Dateline Sports," *Houston Informer*, December 9, 1961.

87. Thomas R. Cole, *No Color Is My Kind: The Life of Eldrewey Stearns and the Integration of Houston* (Austin: University of Texas Press, 1997), 76–80.

88. "Warren McVae Goes Thisaway and Thataway," *Sports Illustrated*, Vol. 21 (19) (9 November 1964), 48–49.

89. Charles H. Martin, *Benching Jim Crow: The Rise and Fall of the Color Line in Southern College Sports, 1890–1980* (Chicago: University of Illinois Press, 2010), 90 and 90–92.

90. Bill Nunn Jr., "Change of Pace," *Pittsburgh Courier*, April 2, 1966; L.I. Brockenbury, "Tying the Score," *Los Angeles Sentinel*, April 28, 1966.

91. Frank Deford, "The Negro Athlete Is Invited Home," *Sports Illustrated*, Vol. 22 (24) (14 June 1965), 26–27.

Chapter 5   The Ban and the Banner: Black Olympians in a Jim Crow Society

1. "Eats From Cans, Sets AAU Record," *Baltimore Afro-American*, July 16, 1960.

2. "Connolly Airs Discrimination at AAU Meet," *Chicago Defender*, July 11, 1960.

3. "American Way," *Los Angeles Sentinel*, July 14, 1960.

4. Quoted in W.E.B. Du Bois, *Souls of Black Folk*, in *Three Negro Classics*, ed. John Hope Franklin (New York: Avon, 1999), 215.

5. Marion E. Jackson, "Sports of the World," *Atlanta Daily World*, December 27, 1955.

6. Rick Hurt, "Sports Train," *People's Voice*, January 12, 1946.

7. Quoted in "Sports Train," *People's Voice*, February 2, 1946.

8. Don Deleighbur, "Behind the Play," *Cleveland Call and Post*, February 3, 1946.

9. "Some Top AAU Stars Will Sell Out to Dixie Bias," *Pittsburgh Courier*, January 26, 1946.

10. Russ Cowans, "Sports Chatter," *Michigan Chronicle*, January 19, 1946.

11. "Some Top AAU Stars Will Sell Out to Dixie Bias," *Pittsburgh Courier*, January 26, 1946.

12. Rick Hurt, "Sports Train," *People's Voice*, January 19, 1946.

13. Rick Hurt, "Sports Train," *People's Voice*, February 9, 1946.

14. Rick Hurt, "Sports Train," *People's Voice*, July 13, 1946.

15. "Storm Over Our Olympic Track Coach," *Salute*, May 1948, 30–31.

16. A.O. Prince, "Accent on Sports," *California Eagle*, July 24, 1947.

17. A.O. Prince, "Accent on Sports," *California Eagle*, September 25, 1947.

18. Leslie Matthews, "Sports Chatter," *People's Voice*, August 9, 1947.

19. Arthur Kirk, "Breaking the Tape," *St. Louis Argus*, July 25, 1948.

20. Arthur Kirk, "Breaking the Tape," *St. Louis Argus*, August 6, 1948.

21. Dan Burley, "Conditionally Yours," *New York Amsterdam News*, August 7, 1948.

22. Arthur Kirk, "Breaking the Tape," *St. Louis Argus*, August 6, 1948.

23. Arthur Kirk, "Breaking the Tape," *St. Louis Argus*, August 13, 1948.

24. "Editorial," *Baltimore Afro-American*, August 7, 1948.

25. Ibid.

26. "Brave Effort," *Chicago Defender*, September 18, 1948.

27. Jenniffer H. Lansbury, *Spectacular Leap: Black Women Athletes in Twentieth-Century America* (Fayetteville: University of Arkansas Press, 2014), 57.

28. Russ Cowans, "No Color Line in the Olympics," *Chicago Defender*, August 7, 1948.

29. Sam Lacy, "Meeting Truman Coachman's Top Thrill," *Baltimore Afro-American*, January 15, 1949.

30. Edwin B. Henderson, "Tan Stars Shame USA in Eyes of the World," *Baltimore Afro-American*, August 14, 1948.

31. "British Press Raps U.S. for Its Race Problem," *Baltimore Afro-American*, August 28, 1948.

32. Edwin B. Henderson, "Olympics Over," *Baltimore Afro-American*, August 28, 1948.

33. "Through Ticket Serves to Kill Jim Crow Law," *Baltimore Afro-American*, September 17, 1949.

34. Damion L. Thomas, *Globetrotting: African American Athletes and Cold War Politics* (Chicago: University of Illinois Press, 2012), 83.

35. Jamie Schultz, *Qualifying Times: Points of Change in U.S. Women Sports* (Chicago: University of Illinois Press, 2014), 85.

36. Thomas, *Globetrotting*, 98.

37. "America's Track Hopes Placed with Negro Stars," *Jet*, Vol. 2 (12) (July 17), 56–57.

38. "One World After All," *Chicago Defender*, July 19, 1952.

39. "Mixed Athletics Aid Democracy," *Chicago Defender*, June 21, 1952.

40. Edwin B. Henderson, "The White Man's Burden in the Olympic Games," *The Negro History Bulletin*, Vol. 16 (1) (1 October 1952), 2.

41. "Raps Racism," *Baltimore Afro-America*, August 9, 1952.

42. "Dillard Stars Again," *Cleveland Call and Post*, August 30, 1952.

43. Bill Matney, "Jumping the Gun," *Michigan Chronicle*, February 11, 1956.

44. Arthur Kirk, "Breaking the Tape," *St. Louis Argus*, November 15, 1956.

45. "Editorial," *Louisiana Weekly*, December 8, 1956.

46. See Deborah Gray White, *Ar'n't I a Woman: Female Slaves in the Plantation South* (New York: Norton, 1999).

47. See Schultz, *Qualifying Times*, 81–84; Susan Cahn, *Coming on Strong: Gender and Sexuality in Twentieth Century Women's Sports* (Cambridge: Harvard University Press, 1994), 110–139.

48. Sam Lacy, "A to Z," *Baltimore Afro-American*, July 12, 1952.

49. Cahn, *Coming on Strong*, 117–118.

50. Edwin B. Henderson, "Henderson's Comment," *Cleveland Call and Post*, August 7, 1948.

51. "Natural Feminine Beauty," *Baltimore Afro-American*, July 12, 1952.

52. "Fastest Women in the World," *Ebony* (June 1955), 27–30.

53. "The Truth about Women Athletes," *Jet*, Vol. 6 (13) (5 August 1955), 56–59.

54. "Record Busting LA Housewife," *Jet*, Vol. 10 (13) (2 August 1956), 52–53.

55. Rita Liberti and Maureen Smith, *(Re)Presenting Wilma Rudolph* (Syracuse: Syracuse University Press, 2015), 42–70.

56. David Maraniss, *Rome 1960: The Olympics That Changed the World* (New York: Simon and Schuster, 2008), 146.

57. "Sport: To Do a Little Better," *Time*. Accessed September 2016. http://content.time.com/time/magazine/article/0,9171,939210,00.html.

58. "Olympic Star Gets Film and Contract," *Chicago Tribune*, November 15, 1960.

59. "Sport: To Do a Little Better," *Time*. Accessed September 2016. http://content.time.com/time/magazine/article/0,9171,939210,00.html.

60. Ibid.

61. "Rafer Johnson Carries U.S. Olympic Flag," *Pittsburgh Courier*, September 3, 1960.

62. Arthur Dailey, "Sports of the Times," *New York Times*, August 26, 1960.

63. Bob Hunter, "The Safari," *St. Louis Argus*, August 26, 1960.

64. "Off to a Good Start," *Los Angeles Sentinel*, August 25, 1960.

65. "A Fitting Tribute," *Baltimore Afro-American*, September 24, 1960.

66. "Editorial," *Michigan Chronicle*, 1September 10, 1960.

67. Sam Lacy, "How Come Uncle Sam Ignores His Nieces?" *Baltimore Afro-American*, August 9, 1960.

68. "Editorial," *Houston Informer*, January 7, 1961.

69. Liberti and Smith, *(Re)Presenting Wilma Rudolph*, 73.

70. Barbara Heilman, "Wilma and Ed," *Sports Illustrated*, Vol. 13 (20) (14 November 1960), 48.

71. "World Speed Queen: Wilma Glodean Rudolph," *New York Times*, September 9, 1960.

72. L.I. Brockenbury, "Tying the Score," *Los Angeles Sentinel*, September 15, 1960.

73. "NCAA Says Bias Shameful to Ralph Boston," *Chicago Defender*, September 17, 1960.

74. Sam Lacy, "A to Z," *Baltimore Afro-American*, September 17, 1960.

75. "Olympic Girl Champ Dreads Coming Home," *New York Amsterdam News*, September 10, 1960.

76. Liberti and Smith, *(Re)Presenting Wilma Rudolph*, 35.

77. Ibid., 95–96.

78. Mal Whitfield, *Better Than the Best: Black Athletes Speak, 1920–2007* (Seattle: University of Washington Press, 2010), 32.

79. Mal Whitfield, "Let's Boycott the Olympics," *Ebony* (March 1964), 95–100.

Chapter 6   African American Athletes and Activism: Everybody Has a Part to Play

1. "Negro Youth in Sports," *Ebony*, Vol. 22 (10) (August 1967), 131.

2. Ibid., 132.

3. Claude E. Harrison Jr., "Art Ashe Enjoys, Capitalizes on Being 'Branded,'" *Philadelphia Tribune*, February 15, 1966.

4. "First Negro Davis Cupper," *Ebony*, Vol. 18 (12) (October 1963), 154.

5. Claude Harrison Jr., "Arthur Ashe Plays for Self, Not for a Race," *Philadelphia Tribune*, July 28, 1964.

6. Quoted in Eric Allen Hall, *Arthur Ashe: Tennis and Justice in the Civil Rights Era* (Baltimore: Johns Hopkins University Press, 2016), 78.

7. Arthur Ashe, *Advantage Ashe* (New York: Coward-McCann, INC, 1967), 107.

8. Ibid., 108.

9. "Arthur—The New King of the Courts," *Life*, Vol. 65 (12) (20 September 1968), 34.

10. Ibid.

11. Quoted in Hall, *Arthur Ashe*, 82.

12. Ibid., 85.

13. Ibid., 84.

14. "Grid Star in College Protest," *Chicago Defender*, March 17, 965.

15. Charles Livingston, "Raps Athletes," *Pittsburgh Courier*, July 27, 1963.

16. Lloyd C. Wells, "Dateline Sports," *Houston Informer*, November 4, 1961.

17. James Baldwin, *Notes of a Native Son* (New York: Beacon, 1984), 64.

18. James Boggs, *Pages from a Black Radical's Notebook: A James Boggs Reader* (Detroit: Wayne State University Press, 2011), 43.

19. See A.S. Doc Young, "The Case of the Athletic Patsies," *Negro Digest* (July 1963), 28–33.

20. "Editorial," *People's Voice*, October 26, 1946.

21. "Editorial," *Cleveland Call and Post*, February 28, 1948.

22. Joe Louis, "My Toughest Fight," *Salute*, Vol. 2 (12) (December 1947), 16.

23. "Delegation to March to Washington to Seek Civil Rights," *New York Age*, May 29, 1948.

24. Charles W. Kellog, "Look Em' Over," *New Haven Register*, September 19, 1948. ,

25. Joe Louis, "Democracy Will Take a Stand," *New York Age*, October 30, 1948.

26. "Here's Sugar's Comment," *Chicago Defender*, October 27, 1951.

27. Ray Robinson, "How I Beat Jim Crow," *Negro Digest* (July 1946), 30.

28. "Jo Awaits Stork Apology," *New York Amsterdam News*, October 27, 1951.

29. Ray Robinson, "I'm Not a Heel," *Chicago Defender*, May 8, 1954.

30. "Sugar Ray Will Aid NAACP," *Chicago Defender*, December 24, 1955.

31. Charles Livingston, "Living with Sports," *Indianapolis Recorder*, August 15, 1964.

32. Michael G. Long, Ed. *First Class Citizenship: The Civil Rights Letters of Jackie Robinson* (New York: Times Books, 2007), 183.

33. "Text of Jackie Robinson's Statement to House Unit," *New York Times*, July 19, 1949.

34. "Some Negroes Critical of Humphries Stand," *Milwaukee Journal*, March 24, 1960.

35. "Jackie Robinson," *Chicago Defender*, April 13, 1960.

36. Jackie Robinson, "Kennedy Insults Negro Community," *Michigan Chronicle*, August 18, 1962.

37. Jackie Robinson, "Mr. Kennedy Is Doing Nothing for Civil Rights," *Michigan Chronicle*, March 2, 1963.

38. "Champ Lauds Those Who Fight for Rights in Dixie," *Chicago Defender*, February 27, 1962.

39. Gilbert Rogin, "We Are Grown Men Playing a Child's Game," *Sports Illustrated*, Vol. 19 (21) (18 November 1963), 80.

40. "Jesse Owens Hits Alabama Trip," *Chicago Defender*, May 16, 1963.

41. Jackie Robinson, "Jackie Says," *Michigan Chronicle*, June 1, 1963.

42. Charles Livingston, "Will Ball Players Let Jackie Down?" *Los Angeles Sentinel*, May 23, 1963.

43. Charles Livingston, "At the Ringside," *Kansas City Plain Dealer*, May 18, 1955.

44. Charles Livingston, "Stars Dodge 'Rights Issue,'" *Los Angeles Sentinel*, July 25 1963.

45. Charles Livingston, "Athletes Should Join Picket Lines Too!" *Los Angeles Sentinel*, May 18, 1963.

46. Edward Linn, "Trials of a Negro Idol," *Saturday Evening Post*, Vol. 23 (6) (2 June 1963), 70.

47. Bobbie Barbee, "Wouldn't Want Kin to Be Pro Athletes, Admits Mays," *Jet*, Vol. 27 (1) (8 October 1964), 54.

48. Edward Linn, "Trials of a Negro Idol," *Saturday Evening Post*, Vol. 23 (6) (2 June 1963), 70.

49. Quoted in Doc Young, "All Sports," *Michigan Chronicle*, March 2, 1968.

50. "Willie May's Answer," *Michigan Chronicle*, April 6, 1968.

51. Alex Poinsett, "Pro Football's Mightiest Player," *Ebony*, Vol. 19 (3) (January 1964), 38.

52. Doc Young, "All Sports," *Michigan Chronicle*, March 2, 1968.

53. Aram Goudsouzian, *King of the Court: Bill Russell and the Basketball Revolution* (Berkeley: University of California Press, 2010), 152.

54. Bill Russell, *Go Up for Glory* (Berkeley: Mass Market Books, 1966), 159–160.

55. Rogin, "We Are Grown Men Playing a Child's Game," 82.

56. Edwin Linn, "I Owe the Public Nothing," *Saturday Evening Post*, Vol. 237 (2) (18 January 1964), 61.

57. Ibid., 60.

58. Taylor Branch and Bill Russell, *Second Wind: The Opinions of an Opinionated Man* (New York: Ballantine Books, 1979), 210.

59. Edwin Linn, "I Owe the Public Nothing," *Saturday Evening Post*, Vol. 237 (2) (18 January 1964), 62.

60. Ibid.

61. Ibid.

62. "Russell Would Give Up Basketball for Rights," *Chicago Defender*, July 20, 1964.

63. See Goudsouzian, *King of Court*, 194–195.

64. "Mississippi Born Top Athletes," *Jet*, Vol. 26 (15) (23 July 1964), 57.

65. To be clear, Jim Brown was a controversial figure off the field, who was charged with statutory rape and also domestic violence. Not dealing with it in this manuscript is not absolving him of these charges. But unfortunately writers of his generation let him slide on these horrific acts.

66. Jim Brown, *Out of Bounds* (New York: Zebra Books, 1989), 57.

67. Myron Cope, "Jim Brown's Own Story," *Look*, Vol. 28 (20) (6 October 1964), 74.

68. Ibid., 76.

69. Ibid., 75–76.

70. Claude Harrison Jr., "Critics Don't Get under Jim Brown's Skin," *Philadelphia Tribune*, 6 October 1964.

71. Alex Poinsett, "The Controversial Jim Brown," *Ebony*, Vol. 20 (2) (December 1964), 72.

72. "Brown Calls It Quits," *Chicago Defender*, July 23, 1966.

73. "The Inside Story," *Los Angeles Sentinel*, December 29, 1966.

74. Doc Young, "Adam Had a Ball," *Los Angeles Sentinel*, January 25, 1968.

75. Charles Gillepsie, "Jim Brown Comes to Mississippi," *The Nation* (21 September 1970), 237.

Chapter 7 The Revolt of the Black Athlete

1. "Girl Track Star Refuses to Go to Russia," *Jet*, Vol. 14 (13) (31 July 1958), 54–56.

2. "Ex-Track Star Continues Jail Fast," *Chicago Defender*, February 3, 1960.

3. Ibid.

4. Harry Edwards, *The Revolt of the Black Athlete* (New York: The Free Press, 1970), 38.

5. Ibid., 38–39.

6. David Maraniss, *Rome 1960: The Olympics That Changed the World* (New York: Simon and Schuster, 2008), 77.

7. James L. Hicks, "The Uppity Negro," *New York Amsterdam News*, March 26, 1966.

8. Lawrence Casey, "Sports Ledger," *Michigan Chronicle*, November 24, 1962.

9. Alex Poinsett, "A Look at Cassius Clay," *Ebony* (March 1963), 36.

10. Michael Ezra, *Muhammad Ali: The Making of an Icon* (Philadelphia: Temple University Press, 2008), 54.

11. Randy Roberts and Johnny Smith, *Blood Brothers: The Fatal Friendship between Muhammad Ali and Malcolm X* (New York: Basic Books, 2016), 106; Brad Pye, "Prying Eye," *Los Angeles Sentinel*, April 4, 1963.

12. Roberts and Smith, *Blood Brothers*, 133.

13. Ibid., 135.

14. Ibid, 171.

15. Thomas Hauser, *Muhammad Ali: His Life and Times* (New York: Simon and Schuster, 1992), 102.

16. "Editorial," *Michigan Chronicle*, March 7, 1964.

17. "Editorial," *Cleveland Call and Post*, April 18, 1964.

18. Quoted in Jim Hall, "Time Out," *Louisiana Weekly*, March 21, 1964.

19. "Dr. Martin L. King Raps Cassius X," *Los Angeles Sentinel*, March 26, 1964.

20. Hauser, *Muhammad Ali*, 103.

21. Floyd Patterson, "Cassius Clay Must Be Beaten," *Sports Illustrated*, Vol. 23 (15) (11 October 1965), 80.

22. Hauser, *Muhammad Ali*, 140.

23. Eldridge Cleaver, *Soul on Ice* (New York: Delta, 1999), 115–121.

24. Hauser, *Muhammad Ali*, 154–155.

25. Ibid., 167.

26. Ibid., 169.

27. Cleaver, *Soul on Ice*, 149.

28. Quoted in Dave Zirin, *People's History of Sports in the United States: 250 Years of Politics, Protest, People and Play* (New York: New Press, 2009), 146.

29. "A Boo for a View," *Newsweek* (11 March 1968), 84.

30. Bill Russell, "I'm Not Worried about Ali," *Sports Illustrated*, Vol. 26 (24) (19 June 1967), 19.

31. Brad Pye, "Prying Pye," *Los Angeles Sentinel*, September 28, 1967.

32. L.I. Brockenbury, "Tying the Score," *Los Angeles Sentinel*, October 5, 1967.

33. Douglas Hartmann, *Race, Culture, and the Revolt of the Black Athlete: The 1968 Olympic Protests and Their Aftermath* (Chicago: University of Chicago Press, 2003), 70.

34. Edwards, *Revolt of the Black Athlete*, 53.

35. "A Step to an Olympic Boycott," *Sports Illustrated*, Vol. 27 (23) (4 December 1967), 30–31.

36. Ibid.

37. Ralph Boston, "Why They Should Not" Sport, quoted in *The Unlevel Playing Field: A Documentary History of the African American Experience in Sport*, ed. David K. Wiggins and Patrick B. Miller (Chicago: University of Illinois Press, 2003), 294.

38. Jack Scott, "The White Olympics," *Ramparts*, Vol. 6 (9, 10) (May 1968), 59.

39. Ibid.

40. "Where Are They Now," *Newsweek* (15 July 1968), 13; also see "The Angry Black Athlete," in the same edition.

41. "Norvell Lee, Ex-Olympian, Calls Boycott 'Senseless,'" *Baltimore Afro-American*, January 6, 1968.

42. "Where Are They Now," *Newsweek* (15 July 1968), 13.

43. "A Step to an Olympic Boycott," *Sports Illustrated*, Vol. 27 (23) (4 December 1967), 30–31; "Jesse Owens Raps Boycott," *Los Angeles Sentinel*, February 15, 1968.

44. "Wyomia Tyus," *Better Than the Best*, 145.

45. "Tigerbelle Talks about Boycott," *Michigan Chronicle*, February 24, 1968.

46. "Boycott of the Olympics by Negroes Hit," *Gettysburg Times*, November 30, 1967; Sam Lacy, "Dedication They Name Is," *Baltimore Afro-American*, February 20, 1968.

47. "Editorial," *Philadelphia Tribune*, 2 December 1967.

48. "Is the Boycott the Answer to Everything?" *Louisiana Weekly*, December 9, 1967; Jim Hall, "Medals Can't Buy Equality," *Louisiana Weekly*, December 9, 1967.

49. Lawrence Casey, "Boycott," *Chicago Defender*, March 4, 1968.

50. "Sports Editor Sam Lacy Backs Plan," *Baltimore Afro-American*, December 9, 1967.

51. "Editorial," *Michigan Chronicle*, March 2, 1968.

52. L.I. Brockenbury, "Tying the Score," *Los Angeles Sentinel*, November 30, 1967.

53. "New Day Coming for New York AC," *Philadelphia Tribune*, February 6, 1968; Jackie Robinson, "New York Athletic Club Heartily Deserves Boycott," *Philadelphia Tribune*, 1February 13, 1968; "Guess Who's Not Coming to Run in NYAC T&F Meet," *Philadelphia Tribune*, February 17, 1968.

54. Pete Axthelm, "Boycott Now—Boycott Later?" *Sports Illustrated*, Vol. 28 (80) (26 February 1968), 24–26.

55. "Edwards Says Plans for 'Open' Olympics," *Sacramento Observer*, March 14, 1968.

56. Tex Maule, "Switcheroo from Yes to Nyet," *Sports Illustrated*, Vol. 28 (17) (29 April 1968), 29; Scott, "The White Olympics," *Ramparts*, 60–61.

57. Hartman, *Race, Culture, and the Revolt of the Black Athlete*, 154.

58. "Carlos Airs Black Stars Protest," *Chicago Defender*, October 19, 1968.

59. "Olympic Star Wyomia Tyus to Take Job in Frisco," *Michigan Chronicle*, November 23, 1968.

60. Sam Lacy, "Lacy Hits Protest at Olympics," *Baltimore Afro-American*, October 19 1968.

61. Jim Hall, "Time Out," *Louisiana Weekly*, November 2, 1968.

62. Larry Austin, "Just Like It Is," *Sacramento Observer*, October 24, 1968.

63. Fulton O. Bradley, "Untypical Behavior on Part of Black Athletes," *Michigan Chronicle*, November 2, 1968.

64. "Olympic Committee Should Receive Gold Medal for Stupidity," *Michigan Chronicle*, October 26 1968.

65. Claude Harrison Jr., "Smith and Carlos Guilty or Not," *Philadelphia Tribune*, October 22, 1968.

66. "Athletes' Protest Lauded by Cleage," *Michigan Chronicle*, November 2, 1968.

67. "Ex-Olympians Proposes Self-Help Programs for Black Athletes," *Philadelphia Tribune*, September 22, 1968.

68. Jack Olson, "The Black Athlete: A Shameful Story, Pt. 1," *Sports Illustrated*, Vol. 29 (1) (1 July 1968), 15.

69. Quoted in Scott, "The White Olympics," *Ramparts*, 61.

70. Jack Olson, "The Black Athlete: A Shameful Story, Pt. 1," 16.

71. Jack Olson, "The Black Athlete: A Shameful Story, Pt. 3," 31.

72. Jack Olson, "The Black Athlete: A Shameful Story, Pt. 1," 19.

73. Edwards, *Revolt of the Black Athlete*, 148.

74. Ibid., 153.

75. Jack Olson, "The Black Athlete: A Shameful Story, Pt. 3," 30–41.

76. Edwards, *Revolt of the Black Athlete*, 143.

77. Ibid., 142–166. These pages in *The Revolt of the Black Athlete* provide a brief description of each protest.

Epilogue

1. Dave Zirin, "America Needs to Listen to What Colin Kaepernick is Actually trying to Say, " *The Nation*, August 30, 2016. https://www.thenation.com/article/america-needs-to-listen-to-what-colin-kaepernick-is-actually-trying-to-say/.

2. Tina Charles, "On International Stage with Team USA, Tina Charles Doesn't Plan to Hide Her Voice, " August 6, 2016. http://www.si.com/olympics/2016/08/07/tina-charles-activism-rio-olympics-team-usa-basketball.

Bibliography

Books

Abdul-Jabbar, Kareem, and Peter Knobler. *Giant Steps*. New York: Bantam Books, 1983.

Adelson, Bruce. *Brushing Back Jim Crow: The Integration of Minor-League Baseball in the American South*. Charlottesville: University of Virginia Press, 1999.

Bass, Amy. *Not the Triumph but the Struggle: The 1968 Olympics and the Making of the Black Athlete*. Minneapolis: University of Minnesota Press, 2002.

Boggs, James. *Pages from a Black Radical's Notebook: A James Boggs Reader*. Detroit: Wayne State University Press, 2011.

Branch, Taylor, and Bill Russell. *Second Wind: The Opinions of an Opinionated Man*. New York: Ballantine Books, 1979.

Brown, Jim. *Off My Chest. New York*. Double Day & Company, 1964.

Brown, Jim. *Out of Bounds*. New York: Zebra Books, 1989.

Bryant, Howard. *The Last Hero: A Life of Henry Aaron*. New York: Anchor Books, 2010.

Bryant, Howard. *Shut Out: A Story of Race and Baseball in Boston*. Boston: Beacon Press, 2002.

Cah, Susan K. *Coming on Strong: Gender and Sexuality in Twentieth-Century Women's Sport*. Cambridge: Harvard University Press, 1994.

Cleaver, Eldridge. *Soul on Ice*. New York: Delta, 1992.

Cole, Thomas R. *No Color Is My Kind: The Life of Eldrewey Stearns and the Integration of Houston*. Austin: University of Texas Press, 1997.

Demas, Lane. *Integrating the Gridiron: Black Civil Rights and American College Football*. New Brunswick, New Jersey: Rutgers University Press, 2010.

Edwards, Harry. *The Revolt of the Black Athlete*. New York: The Free Press, 1970.

Flood, Curt. *The Way It Was. New York*. Pocket Books, 1972.

Fussman, Cal. *After Jackie: Pride, Prejudice, and Baseball's Forgotten Heroes: An Oral History*. New York: ESPN Books, 2007.

Goudsouzian, Aram. *King of the Court: Bill Russell and the Basketball Revolution.* Berkeley: University of California Press, 2010.

Gray, Frances Clayton, and Yanick Rice Lamb. *Born to Win: The Authorized Biography of Althea Gibson.* New York: John Wiley and Sons Inc., 2004.

Halberstam, David. *Everything They Had: Sports Writing from David Halberstam.* New York: Hyperion, 2008.

Haley, Alex. *The Playboy Interviews.* New York: Ballantine Books, 1993.

Hartmann, Douglas. *Race, Culture, and the Revolt of the Black Athlete: The 1968 Olympics and Their Aftermath.* Chicago: University of Chicago Press, 2003.

Hauser, Thomas. *Muhammad Ali: His Life and Times.* New York: Simon and Schuster, 1991.

Johnson, M. Mikell. *The African American Woman Golfer.* Westport, Connecticut: Praeger, 2008.

Kahn, Roger. *Rickey and Robinson: The True, Untold Story of the Integration of Baseball.* New York: Rodale, 2014.

Kallis, Gregory J. *Men's College Athletics and the Politics of Racial Equality: Five Pioneer Stories of Black Manliness, White Citizenship and American Democracy.* Philadelphia: Temple University Press, 2012.

Kennedy, John H. *A Course of Their Own: A History of African Americans in Golf.* Lincoln: University of Nebraska Press, 2000.

Lacy, Sam. *Fighting for Fairness: The Life Story of Hall of Fame Sportswriter Sam Lacy.* Centreville, Maryland: Tidewater Publishers, 1998.

Lansbury, Jenniffer H. *Spectacular Leap: Black Women Athletes in Twentieth-Century America.* Fayetteville: University of Arkansas Press, 2014.

Liberti, Rita, and Maureen Smith. *(Re)Presenting Wilma Rudolph.* Syracuse: University of Syracuse Press, 2015.

Lomax, Michael, editor. *Sports and the Racial Divide: African American and Latino Experience in an Era of Change.* Oxford: University Press of Mississippi, 2011.

Long, Michael G., editor. *First Class Citizenship: The Civil Rights Letters of Jackie Robinson.* New York: Times Books, 2007.

Maraniss, Andrew. *Strong Inside: Perry Wallace and the Collision of Race and Sports in the South.* Nashville, Tennessee: Vanderbilt University Press, 2016.

Maraniss, David. *Rome 1960: The Olympics That Changed the World.* New York: Simon and Schuster, 2008.

Martin, Charles H. *Benching Jim Crow: The Rise and Fall of the Color Line in Southern College Sports, 1890–1980.* Chicago: University of Illinois Press, 2010.

McDaniel, Pete. *Uneven Lies: The Heroic Story of African Americans in Golf.* Greenwich, Connecticut: The American Golfer, 2000.

Miller, Margery. *Joe Louis: American.* New York: Current Books, 1945.

Miller, Patrick B., and David K. Wiggins. *The Unlevel Playing Field: A Documentary History of the African American Experience in Sport.* Chicago: University of Illinois Press, 2005.

Owens, Jesse. *Black Think: My Life as Black Man and White Man.* New York: William Morrow and Company, Inc., 1970.

Pepe, Phil. *Kareem Abdul-Jabbar.* New York: Tempo Books, 1970.

Rampersad, Arnold. *Jackie Robinson: A Biography.* New York: Ballantine Books, 1997.

Rhoden, William C. *Third and a Mile: The Trials and Triumphs of the Black Quarterback.* New York: ESPN Books, 2007.

Roberts, Randy. *Joe Louis: Hard Times Man.* New Haven, Connecticut: Yale University Press, 2010.

Roberts, Randy, and Johnny Smith. *Blood Brothers: The Fatal Friendship between Muhammad Ali and Malcolm X.* New York: Basic Books, 2016.

Robinson, Jackie. *Baseball Has Done It.* New York: IG Publishing, 2005.

Robinson, Jackie. *I Never Had It Made: The Autobiography of Jackie Robinson.* Hopewell, New Jersey: The Ecco Press, 1972.

Ross, Charles K. *Outside the Lines: African Americans and the Integration of Football.* New York: New York University Press, 1999.

Schultz, Jamie. *Qualifying Times: Points of Change in U.S. Women's Sport.* Chicago: University of Illinois Press, 2014.

Scott, Jack. *The Athletic Revolution.* New York: The Free Press, 1971.

Sifford, Charlie. *Just Let Me Play: The Charlie Sifford Story.* New York: British American Publishing, 1992.

Smith, Thomas G. *Showdown: JFK and the Integration of the Washington Redskins.* Boston: Beacon Press, 2011.

Snyder, Brad. *Beyond the Shadow of the Senators: The Untold Story of the Homestead Gray and the Integration of Baseball.* Chicago: Contemporary Books, 2003.

Thomas, Damion L. *Globetrotting: African American Athletes and Cold War Politics.* Chicago: University of Illinois Press, 2012.

Tida, Melina, and John C. Walters, editors. *Better Than the Best: Black Athletes Speak, 1920–2007.* Seattle: University of Washington Press, 2010.

Tygiel, Jules. *Baseball's Great Experiment: Jackie Robinson and His Legacy.* New York: Oxford University Press, 2008.

Wiggins, David K. *Glory Bound: Black Athletes in a White America.* Syracuse: Syracuse University Press, 1997.

Wiggins, David K., editor. *Out of the Shadows: A Biographical History of African American Athletes.* Fayetteville: University of Arkansas Press, 2006.

Wigginton, Russell T. *The Strange Career of the Black Athlete: African Americans and Sports.* Westport, Connecticut: Praeger, 2006.

Zirin, Dave. *People's History of Sport in the United States: 250 Years of Politics, Protest, People and Play.* New York: New Press, 2009.

Black Newspapers

Atlanta Daily World
Baltimore Afro-American
Birmingham World
California Eagle

Chicago Tribune
Cleveland Call and Post
Jackson Advocate
Los Angeles Sentinel
Louisiana Weekly
Michigan Chronicle
New York Age
New York Amsterdam News
People's Voice
Philadelphia Tribune
Sacramento Observer

Magazines

Ebony
Jet
Look
Negro Digest
Saturday Evening Post
Sport
Sports Illustrated

Index

Note: page numbers in italics indicate figures.

About the Author

Louis Moore is associate professor of history at Grand Valley State University, in Allendale, Michigan, where he teaches African American history, civil rights, sports, and U.S. history. His research and writing examine interconnections between race, gender, and sports. He is also the author of a forthcoming book, *I Fight for a Living*, from the University of Illinois Press. The book explores boxing, black manhood, and race in America from 1880 to 1915.